Assessment and Development Centres
Second Edition

Assessment and Development Centres

Second Edition

IAIN BALLANTYNE and NIGEL POVAH

GOWER

First edition published 1995

Published by
Gower Publishing Limited
Gower House
Croft Road
Aldershot
Hants GU11 3HR
England

Gower Publishing Company
Suite 420
101 Cherry Street
Burlington VT 05401–4405
USA

British Library Cataloguing in Publication Data
Ballantyne, Iain
    Assessment and development centres. – 2nd ed.
    1. Assessment centers (Personnel management procedure)
    I. Title II. Povah, Nigel
    658.3'124

ISBN 0 566 08599 2

Library of Congress Cataloging-in-Publication Data
Ballantyne, Iain.
    Assessment and development centers/Iain Ballantyne and
    Nigel Povah. -- 2nd ed.
        p.cm.
    Includes bibliographical references and index.
    ISBN 0-566-08599-2
    1. Assessment centers (Personnel management procedure)
    I. Povah, Nigel. II. Title.

    HF5549.5.A78B35 2004
    658.3'124--dc22

                                                          2003056905

Typeset in 9 point Stone Serif by IML Typographers, Birkenhead, Merseyside and printed in Great Britain by MPG Books Ltd. Bodmin

Contents

List of Figures

Preface to the Second Edition

Since the first edition of *Assessment and Development Centres* was published in 1995, there have been a number of changes in the world of assessment centres which warrant significant revision and overhaul of the content of the chapters. Without question, one of the most significant practical changes over the past eight years is the use of computer-based technology. In many respects the things that we predicted have come to life, particularly when it comes to computers easing the administrative burden in assessment and development centres. In common with most aspects of life, the 'feel' of a centre is becoming more computer-based than paper-based. In another significant development, we are seeing some leading organisations move away from separate exercises to whole day simulations. Thus we have made revisions to the chapters dealing with exercise design, centre administration and the evolution of assessment centres.

In addition to these technology-related changes, we examine two key developments in recent academic research which have arisen from the explosion of interest in assessment centres over recent years. The first point of focus is about the ability of assessors to distinguish between criteria, within an exercise, which is about 'discriminant' versus 'convergent' validity and relates to the thorny subject of construct validity. The second, which has lead to substantial revision of Chapter 6, is the exploration of different training strategies and understanding how different assessors contribute to the accuracy of assessments.

There has also been enormous growth in interest in, and the use of, development centres since we wrote the first edition and this is reflected in a new, expanded Chapter 10. Finally, Chapter 11 points to emerging issues and trends and how these might impact on the future of assessment and development centres. The massively increased use of assessment and development centres within the UK has also led the British Psychological Society to produce a set of Best Practice Guidelines. These are reproduced as an appendix to this book with the kind permission of the British Psychological Society.

In conclusion, we would like to acknowledge our debt to Sarah Cook who has been part of our team for the last three years and for acting as our research assistant while she completes her MSc course.

Iain Ballantyne and Nigel Povah
January 2004

Preface to the First Edition

This book was born on a journey to York in the autumn of 1992, when we were both on the way to run an assessor training programme for a client. Between us we thought we must have delivered what is effectively the contents of this book to dozens of different audiences over the previous ten years. As practitioners we were well aware of a growing demand for knowledge in this important area of human resource activity, but equally unaware of a plain-language reference source.

Most of what we had learned about assessment centres was originally academic study for the MSc in Occupational Psychology at Birkbeck College, London. Following different career paths, Nigel Povah acquired most of his practical knowledge through working with an offshoot of DDI whilst at ICL; Iain Ballantyne learned his with colleagues from Inbucon, whose background was dominated by Boyatzis. It was clear to both of us that there was a need for a text which would directly address the needs of the practitioner.

This book is aimed at the manager in the human resource function who wishes to research the area and may be charged with the implementation of assessment or development centres for the first time in his or her career. We therefore envisage our audience as very much like the one we meet in consultancy assignments, so we have written with four purposes in mind:

- To establish a thorough understanding of the concepts and best practice standards.
- To provide sufficient knowledge of the practical issues to enable the person with some experience to run at least part of their own events, and do so well.
- To provide the reader with sufficient knowledge to recognise where they may not have sufficient skills available to them and, therefore, need to call on specific expertise.
- To enable the reader who is seeking to engage consultants for the first time to ask some pertinent questions of their prospective supplier.

Much as we would like it to be otherwise, there are consultants whose knowledge in this area is weak. Part of our motive is to support potential clients to ensure that they find people with high professional standards.

The text should also be useful to people who are studying for professional qualifications in human resource management, or as part of a wider programme such as an MBA or postgraduate qualifications in psychology. Finally, we hope that this book will interest the many line managers who are keen to find out more, after they have been involved in job analysis research and training as an assessor.

While the primary audience is the human resource practitioner, we hope that the book does not offend our academic colleagues. We have tried to identify the concerns where they exist without weighing down the content with continuous references to substantial pieces of text in the academic style. Where something can be said in the first or second person using the active voice, it is.

The format of the book follows the flow of a typical assignment from the point of first meeting our prospective client to the end-point of validating the work.

Chapter 1 introduces the main concepts and background history, and places the competency-based approach at the centre of the human resource strategy, while Chapter 2 helps the practitioner with both selling the concept and settling it within HR policy. Chapter 3 presents both a rationale for, and some of the common techniques used in, conducting a job or competency analysis, which leads logically to designing appropriate exercises in Chapter 4. Chapter 5 describes the main planning tasks required in bringing all the resources together which, together with the assessor training identified in Chapter 6, completes the work that runs up to the event. Chapter 7 examines the logistics of the event itself. Chapters 8 and 9 look at life after the event. In the short term, this is mainly a matter of writing up reports and arranging feedback to participants. In the longer term the main focus is on validating the centre, which needs to be planned for as the event is born.

We would like to thank and acknowledge our debt to the many people who have been our mentors and also our clients who have taught us much of what we know today. While it is always invidious to produce a shortlist, Mike van Oudtshoorn and the sadly departed Russell Wicks stand out among the mentors. Among our clients we would like to thank Bianca Kübler at ICL, Nick Dalton and more recently Pippa Reid at Birds Eye Walls, John Gentry at Croda International, Terry Hodgetts at AT&T-NCR, Will Clarke and Regina Jackson of Clydesdale Bank, Jean Gentry, Denyse Corfield and Erica Town of Nestlé. This book would have been impossible to produce without the quiet and unassuming effectiveness of Della McGavin, our secretary.

Iain Ballantyne
Nigel Povah

1 *What is an Assessment Centre?*

What is assessment centre technology?

As almost every published paper will say, an assessment centre is an event not a location. The term was derived from the location which was used by AT&T in the United States to assess the management potential of hundreds of their staff.

We have used the term assessment centre technology because we believe it accurately reflects two key points. Firstly, the whole of the event is an integrated process of key components. Like many processes there are alternative routes to get to the same outcome, but there are also critical steps which if overlooked can lead to an unsatisfactory outcome.

Secondly, like most process technologies, there is a degree of flexibility over which tools you use to get the job done. This degree of flexibility can lead to two events having quite a different feel.

To start with, the events themselves may last anywhere from between a few hours to a few days. Sometimes assessment centres are known as development centres although this is usually because the information is gathered with the specific intent of supporting personal development. Most centres will use simulations of different kinds but this is not universally so. Indeed the original British model was really a series of interviews with some pencil and paper tests of ability. The simulations used were originally a relatively small part of a three-day procedure although their significance was quickly recognised. Some assessment centres may include some form of feedback from peers, some may include an element of self-assessment, some may include psychometric tests, where others do not include any of these features. Almost as confusing is the plethora of language that is used to describe the target of the assessment, variously known as attributes, competencies, performance dimensions or criteria.

Whatever the complexities are, any definition must encapsulate the essential or universal aspects of all these events. All assessment centres attempt to assess how competent a person is at present, either in their current role or, more usually, compared to the demands of some future job. All assessment centres focus on behaviour in two ways. Firstly, what is observed at an assessment centre is behaviour, since what someone says or does cannot be anything else. Secondly, behaviour is the start of the design process since what you are trying to do is assess the behaviours that are important to function well in the prospective job.

Defining assessment centre technology: the key features

The main feature of assessment centres as we now understand them is that they are a multiple assessment process. There are five main ways in which that is so. A *group* of participants takes part in a *variety* of exercises observed by a *team* of trained assessors who evaluate each participant against a *number* of predetermined, job related behaviours. Decisions are then made by pooling *shared data*.

MULTIPLE PARTICIPANTS

There are some events called assessment centres in which there is only one participant. These are usually for very senior appointments where the object is to give the participant a thorough final check before an appointment is negotiated between the parties. More often than not these are conducted by a search consultant or by psychologists attached to a search consultancy. However, as understood in general use, one of the features of an assessment centre (and all the variants) is that a number of participants will be brought together for the event. Although there are no absolute rules, the practical constraints of designing an assessment centre tend to demand multiples of four or six participants. At numbers of beyond 12 participants the logistics can get out of hand very easily.

COMBINATION OF METHODS

The focal point of most assessment centres is the use of work sample tests or simulations. The principle of their design is to replicate, so far as is possible, the kind of tasks that a participant would be required to do in the job for which they are being considered. To gain a full understanding of a person's range of capabilities, one simulation is not usually enough to develop anything like a complete picture. If, for example, we were interested in selecting future salespeople it is clear that a useful simulation would be to ask the participant to make a formal presentation. While this may suffice to assess some aspects of the job, it is also clear that effective salespeople are well organised and that a presentation would not of itself give adequate evidence of organising skills. To build the complete picture one needs to use other means of assessing the ability to organise, which could include another kind of simulation, possibly an interview or maybe a psychometric test. Without pre-empting the principle of design (see Chapter 4), we look for at least two sources of evidence of a particular skill, competency or capability, which in turn implies that no single method or instrument will fit the bill.

TEAM OF ASSESSORS

To escape the difficulties associated with the one-on-one interview, used either as a means of selection or in some aspects of performance measurement, it is important to use a team of assessors. There are endless debates about ratios in the literature; but the important points of principle are that each assessor should be able to observe each participant in one of the various situations in which participants are asked to perform. Ideally assessors should observe every participant, but not more than once. The reasoning behind these principles will be outlined in Chapter 6. The team of assessors should include a balance between experts – that is psychologists and human resource managers – and line managers, all of whom need appropriate training.

BEHAVIOURALLY BASED, FOUNDED ON JOB ANALYSIS

As with any other method of assessment, the start point has to be some analysis of the job to determine what it is that discriminates between the performance of successful job incumbents and those that perform less successfully in the same job. There are a wide variety of terms for the things that discriminate; among them are attributes, dimensions, criteria and most recently competencies.

Although it is quite clear in a wide range of management/professional jobs that specific knowledge is a component that has some importance, it is not usually a significant indicator of career success. To take a very obvious example, all doctors study medicine yet few become consultants. At the other end of the scale there are a few who should not be practising – so job knowledge in itself is not always sufficient to guarantee career success. Many lay people, particularly in management, will say that success is really a matter of personality but again no personality acts in a vacuum; it has to have a context.

Successful performance in any job is likely to be founded on a combination of factors, some of which may be to do with disposition, some to do with attitudes, some with particular skills that have been developed over time, some to do with energy levels, some to do with particular ways of thinking or problem-solving and some may be to do with knowing about particular things. The objective of a job analysis is to determine which of these things are most important. Russell (1985) identifies two groups of criteria for management jobs: problem-solving and aspects of the way managers relate to other people (more of this in Chapter 3).

In determining what to call the behaviours, we prefer to use the word 'criteria'. This is a neutral term meaning no more or less than the things against which performance is judged in an assessment centre and elsewhere. Although there will be exceptions, we will attempt to use 'criteria' throughout the rest of this book.

SHARED DATA

From the earliest days an essential feature of the design of assessment centres was that data about participants are shared between the assessors. In the case of a selection decision, no final decision is made until all the evidence is gathered from observations of participants in all the various situations and the assessors have conferred together to agree a final rating. This process of conferring together is variously known as the consensus meeting, the wash-up or assessor discussion and for the sake of consistency we will use the last term.

Whatever the title the objective is the same. A team of assessors meets to consider all the evidence at one time having had no previous discussions. In the case of a development centre, it is less likely that any kind of mark or score will be allocated as the objective of the data-sharing is to collect information together to feed back to participants on their comparative strengths and weaknesses.

Once again there are few absolute rules because a contemporary trend is to give more detailed feedback to participants even where the primary objective is to make a pass/fail decision. The most significant point is that, in a well-designed assessment centre, the individual assessor should not have all the data on any single participant until the assessor discussion has taken place.

Where did these centres come from?

It is a little known fact that assessment centres were invented in Europe not, as is commonly supposed, in America. Although it is probably true to say that most of what is available from consultants in the private sector is heavily influenced by America, there is a parallel European tradition that still exists to a large extent in the public sector. More of this later. For reasons connected with the subsequent careers of the researchers involved, it is probable that the best known precursor to what we now know as assessment centres is the Admiralty Interview

Board. The Board started in 1942 and followed similar developments that took place in other branches of the armed forces, particularly the War Office Selection Board (WOSB) in the army, itself preceded by a similar approach to officer selection in Germany.

The same period saw significant development take place in the field of psychometric testing. Both of these techniques were found to give significantly better results than the almost universal method of selection: the interview. The words 'significantly better' will be elaborated on in later chapters. For the moment we'll consider why these developments took place under the exigencies of war.

One of the ironies of war is that technology advances in leaps and bounds propelled, as it were, by the extreme and urgent need to overcome one's adversary by applying science. In the Second World War at least, the same was true for the application of the nascent science of psychology, to some extent because of the advances in other technologies.

When conscription started in earnest, all branches of the forces were faced with two key facts in relation to the ranks of serving men. The first was that while there was still a need for infantrymen and deck-hands, many more people would be involved in operating advanced equipment. Secondly, it was clearly too expensive and too time-consuming to wait until a course of training was over to find that someone could not successfully operate a radio transmitter. A way had to be found of identifying people who could at the very least benefit from a course of training and had the potential to develop their skills. Hence the rapid development of what we now know as aptitude tests.

In relation to the selection of officers, the situation was somewhat different. The prevailing culture relied on an assumption that a person's background was adequate preparation to lead other people. Although that background was often understood to be a matter of social class, it was also true that success in the ranks was a significant route to a commission. Although officers did receive some training, very little thought was given to understanding the capabilities that were required to lead other people in the prevailing conditions. In short, there was an embarrassingly high incidence of inexperienced officers being 'returned to unit' because of some perceived or actual failure in the field. The psychologist's contribution here was to develop a selection mechanism which considerably reduced that problem. There are two key features that mark this procedure as the forerunner of the modern assessment centre: the study of behaviour as an indicator of success and the use of multiple inputs of evidence to the selection decision.

Tracing the growth of assessment centres

Although the War Office Selection Boards were not universally accepted at first, they were able to demonstrate improvements in the selection of officer candidates for training versus the previously existing selection boards. The first significant validation study (Vernon and Parry, 1949) was able to comment that the 'Army was led to believe it was . . . getting the best possible officers'.

The next recognisable step takes us to the United States, again in a military context, where in 1944 the Office of Strategic Studies (OSS), the forerunner of the CIA, adopted the method for selection of intelligence agents. It is this event that is often thought to be the birth of modern assessment centres. Although this is not strictly true, later developments in methodology pioneered by the CIA provided the kind of simulations and content that are now commonly practised.

The difference between the British and American approaches still influences the style and content of assessment centres. To a considerable extent, assessment centres conducted in the public sector are identifiable as direct descendants of the WOSB or Civil Service Selection Board (CSSB) approach (described below). In the private sector the style is more like that developed by the OSS.

The 'British' approach would involve a number of interviews, carefully constructed to avoid overlap, unstructured discussions/debate on a topic, a piece of lengthy written work and a number of practical/physical exercises in which each candidate is assigned to lead the others solving a problem. By contrast, the 'American' approach does not assign leadership but discussions are prestructured and often require a candidate to take on an assigned role. This requires the candidate to bargain or negotiate resource in some way. American assessment centres are more likely to include one-on-one roleplays and use an in-basket rather than a lengthy written exercise.

On this side of the Atlantic Ocean the first civilian application was in the creation of the CSSB, which was used to assess the suitability of candidates for the fast-stream appointments in both the Home Civil Service and the Diplomatic Service. Initiated in 1945, the CSSB has operated continuously since that time. It was originally set up because the previous selection procedure relied heavily on educational attainment, clearly inappropriate for a generation of people who had been engaged in fighting the war rather than studying. Naturally there have been developments since then but the main components remain much the same. Exercises were designed to resemble the work of a senior civil servant, including sitting on a committee, writing an appreciation of a dossier, giving a short talk, handling a problem in committee. In addition candidates complete a battery of ability tests, are assessed by their peers, complete questionnaires and are interviewed by three different people.

The next noticeable development in civilian application was the use of assessment centres by the US telephone company, AT&T, which developed a longitudinal study of management progress. Starting in the early 1950s, the company's objective was to identify those people who would have the capability of progressing to a managerial career, regardless of educational attainment and previous background. This work has been heavily influential in two directions. Firstly, it has been a substantial source of data for validating the utility of the method. Amazingly, the data gathered at the time of the centre, in the form of a prediction of the grade the participant would ultimately achieve, were never released into the organisation. At periodic intervals comparisons were made between predicted grade and what was actually attained. Following publication of the results, other companies, notably in the US, started flocking to AT&T to find out what was going on and to adopt the method themselves.

The other development was that various people from AT&T decided to set up on their own to answer this demand and gave birth to the forerunner of DDI, a consultancy company that specialises in the identification and development of people's potential. As the commercial pioneer, initially in the US and soon after in Europe, DDI's influence is very much felt in the design approach taken by consultancies worldwide, particularly in the content and style of simulations, the criteria measured and the 5-point rating scale.

Throughout the 1960s and 1970s there was steady if unspectacular growth in the use of the methodology, mainly in America and in the main confined to subsidiaries of US multinationals in Europe. Dulewicz et al. (1983) pointed out that the main users of assessment centres at that time were subsidiaries of US multinationals such as IBM and Rank Xerox. However, the same competitor interest that affected growth in the US has been evident in the UK. As one example, Mars imported assessment centres for graduate selection to the UK in the early 1970s and for a while stood alone in the confectionery industry. By the end of the 1980s, both of the obvious competitors, Cadbury Schweppes and Rowntree Mackintosh, now part of Nestlé, were using assessment centres as their final selection mechanism in graduate recruitment.

Also, some market-leading European multinationals adopted the use of assessment centres from the middle of the 1970s. Among them were two Anglo-Dutch companies – Shell and Philips – and the German company Siemens.

Throughout this time the use of assessment centres grew in the UK public sector, perhaps the best-known example being the Home Office Assessment Unit. There was a further significant boost when in 1978, the Equal Opportunities Commission decided to adopt assessment centres as their method of recruiting administrative and some executive-officer grades into the commission. It should be no surprise to anyone that their main concern was to adopt a scrupulously fair mechanism for selection.

Various researchers have tried to estimate how widespread the usage of assessment centres is. Gaugler et al. (1987) published a study whose main objective was to analyse all the previously published data on validation, as we shall see later. As part of the context they tried to estimate the usage and found that at least 2000 American companies were using assessment centres. In 1989 a British researcher, Mabey, estimated that 37 per cent of companies employing more than 1000 people had used assessment centres within the past year, although their use was predominantly still in recruitment of managers.

Estimated current usage

A survey of usage published by Boyle et al. (1993) attempted to demonstrate the prevalence of assessment centres in the UK and conduct some further analysis. Broadly the conclusions were that assessment centre usage was more prevalent in larger companies and in the private sector. There are also substantial differences between sectors. Energy companies, banking and food, drink and tobacco companies use assessment centres extensively, whereas in education, the media and local government there were lower rates of use. Nearly half (49.9 per cent) of private sector organisations and 38.7 per cent of public sector organisations used assessment centres. While it is always difficult to verify these figures, the same is true for all the previous studies, so it seems fair to suggest that there is an accelerating rate of growth in the 1990s. There were some other interesting findings. The research examined different applications of the technology and identified four main uses:

- Selection at the point of entry, normally graduate recruitment.
- External recruitment at a more senior level.
- Identifying people for internal promotion opportunities.
- Career development.

Some organisations use the technology for all these applications and some events may have at least two purposes. The following differences were observed. Large private-sector organisations tend to use assessment centres for graduate recruitment, whereas the public sector, which do recruit graduates in large numbers, tend to use them for externally advertised senior positions. Large private-sector organisations are also much more likely than are public-sector organisations to use assessment centres for internal promotion. A survey by the Industrial Relations Services in 1997 indicated that assessment centre usage is increasing more rapidly than any other selection method in the UK, with over 65 per cent of organisations employing more than 1000 people using them.

In one respect, public and private sectors are very like one another. Today, career development appears to be the most frequent application of assessment centre techniques in both public and private sector organisations.

In 1999, the authors conducted research on behalf of the Association of Graduate Recruiters (AGR) to understand the extent to which the process had penetrated the graduate recruitment marketplace. Eighty-three per cent of the employers indicated that they used assessment centres at some stage of the recruitment process. Whereas the reseach of Boyle et al. (1993) showed differences in rates of usage between the public and private sectors, the AGR response noted no such difference; although AGR membership tends to represent central government, rather than the public sector as a whole. It was also clear, rather contrary to expectation, that assessment centres were being used by some (relatively) small organisations for graduate recruitment.

Where has the growth come from?

At least part of the growth outlined has been due to competitive pressure. It is quite surprising to hear comments from large companies that many are continuing to experience difficulty in recruiting 'good' graduates at a time when higher education is expanding fast. However real or unreal the perception is, many of our leading organisations still see themselves as competing annually for a relatively limited resource. The same is as true for legal practices or accountancy firms as it is for manufacturers. As in any other competitive situation, when one of the leading players in a particular market innovates in some way, their competitors respond, in this case by improving their own recruitment practices. We cited earlier the example of Mars, Rowntree Mackintosh and Cadbury Schweppes. In the energy business British Gas, BNFL, Powergen, BP and Shell all use assessment centres and all are competing for similar graduates.

Another significant contributor to the growth of this activity is the growth in consultancy by occupational psychologists and by people whose background may have been in personnel management or, more likely, training. Although professional qualifications may appear to be an important predictor of competence, it is not true that all occupational psychologists are well trained or even interested in the principles of assessment centre design. Equally, there are a number of ex-trainers who understand the principles well and construct very good and highly valid assessment centres. Regrettably, one of the functions of the growth of interest in assessment centres is the growth of poorly constructed assessment centres which are a disservice to their clients and, more seriously, can have a severely negative impact on the future of the people who undergo the experience. This issue is covered in the next chapter.

Perhaps the most significant contributor to the growth in use of assessment centres has been the rapid rate of change experienced by many organisations as we make the transition into the twenty-first century. Among other factors, there has been a decline in both manual and clerical semi-skilled work as computers have taken over much of the routine. In many organisations, the managerial role is changing from direct boss of bits of the hierarchy to contract manager of bought-in services. There is also a widespread recognition that skills acquired in one's twenties are no longer sufficient to span a working lifetime.

All of these circumstances are putting more pressure on more people to perform effectively and to adapt successfully to increasing rates of change. Organisations which wish to have a long-term future have simply had to become more professional in identifying and developing the talents they need. The growth in use of assessment centres reflects that increasing professionalism.

Costs and benefits

In the next chapter we examine in detail how to calculate the costs and benefits of using assessment centres. Suffice it to say that one of the main inhibitors to even more widespread use of these techniques has always been the cost. Costs come in two forms: the cost of development and the cost of providing a number of assessors for an event of anything up to a week's duration. Normally assessors are people of reasonable seniority who have other equally important calls on their time. Despite this, these very busy people become converts to the process and we have to ask why this should be so.

There is, of course, a substantial body of research evidence that testifies to the validity of assessment centres and this will often be used as part of the initial sales case and during the training of assessors. This is perfectly proper, since one can demonstrate that assessment centres have a predictive validity roughly three times better than interviewing (Gaugler et al., 1987). But that still does not account for the genuine commitment that assessors give to the process once they have been engaged in it.

What seems to happen is that people stop looking for rational evidence once they become involved emotionally, and with assessment centres people do become passionate advocates. Among the reasons for this are:

- The persuasive logic of the design. Important criteria are immediately visible and if they are not, this raises queries either about the design or about the participant in a way which is not evident in an interview.
- Both participants and assessors regard the process as intrinsically fairer than one person's judgement of another. Indeed there is evidence that graduates accept offers more willingly and stay longer with employers who use assessment centres.
- Both participants and assessors agree that the participant is getting a fair preview of what it is like working in this job or job level. Occasionally people will say that they have been turned away from their ambition to go into management. Whilst regrettable in the short term, this self-insight can be important for employer and employee alike.
- There can be no denying that the behaviour actually took place (provided it was accurately recorded). When it comes to giving feedback in a developmental context, that fact and the fact that many assessors have observed a person, makes it much more difficult for a participant to resist unpalatable information.
- As a place to start a developmental process, the development centre has obvious appeal. It is a high-impact, one-off event which the participant sees as low threat (provided it is advertised as such). Most people have more profound self-insight and are therefore more inclined to plan their own future success at a development centre than any number of career development discussions.

Spin-off benefits

Before closing this chapter, we should mention some spin-off benefits that are frequently observed although they are not central to making a case in favour of using assessment centres.

OVERLOOKING APPARENTLY POORLY QUALIFIED CANDIDATES

In recruitment regimes that narrow the basis of choice to academic qualifications and experience, good candidates are frequently overlooked. Ample evidence of this was found in the early WOSB studies where many soldiers, sailors and airmen were able to demonstrate real ability, despite educational disadvantage.

Asking for specific kinds of experience often indicates intellectual laziness, because it fails to raise the fundamental question of what an organisation expects someone to have learnt (to have developed skill in) as a result of having had that experience.

ASSESSORS GAIN IMPORTANT INSIGHT INTO HUMAN RESOURCE ISSUES

Without question, acting as an assessor involves the development of skills that transfer readily back into normal working circumstances. Primarily, their observations about people in general become more accurate and, as a consequence, they and those around them have increased confidence in their judgement of people-related issues. Many human resource professionals see the benefit in terms of being better able to share their concerns with their line manager colleagues.

Strategic use of assessment centre technology

The next chapter elaborates on the need to develop a policy statement, including the need to make public the reasons for adopting assessment centre technology. A point that is often not recognised initially, but does become apparent over time, is that this approach can be a central strategic plank of all human resource management issues. To be more precise, it is the understanding that human performance is based on behaviour and the ability to share a common behavioural language that become the cornerstones of a human resource strategy.

Strategic issues are often subtle and abstract. They are also often overlooked by managers at all levels and in all sorts of organisations who tend to be driven by more immediate concrete demands. At the risk of grossly oversimplifying things, *the* strategic human resource issue is how to achieve the optimum performance from people.

The expression of optimum performance depends on the values of the organisation. In manufacturing, optimum performance is usually concerned with productivity, whereas in a hospital the imperatives are to do with excellent medical care. These value systems are driven by the organisation's mission, that is its view of what it exists for. In turn, the mission is susceptible to change by ongoing interaction with the wider environment. This sequence of events is illustrated in Figure 1.1.

The most significant component in turning these visions and values into reality is having competent managers. The term 'manager' is applied loosely here. The head teacher of any school will use all of the talents that we recognise among people who have 'manager' in

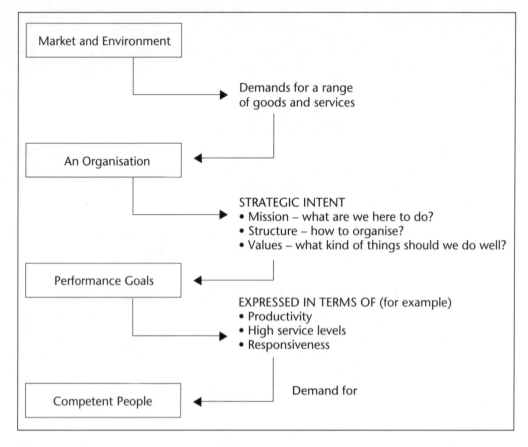

Figure 1.1   Organisational factors that affect human resource strategy

their job title. It is the recognition of what those talents are that provides the unifying force for a human resource strategy. In case anyone should think that this is an excessively managerial argument, we believe that the same strategic logic applies to non-managerial jobs.

Much day-by-day personnel work is involved in recruitment, training and writing policies and procedures, supervising appraisal schemes and so on. Figure 1.2 demonstrates how behaviour becomes the focal point that gives a unifying sense of purpose to those disparate activities.

Finally a brief comment about the use of the terms 'participant' and 'candidate'. In this chapter we have tended to use both depending on context. From now on, in the interest of consistency, we will use the term 'participant' unless it is inappropriate to do so.

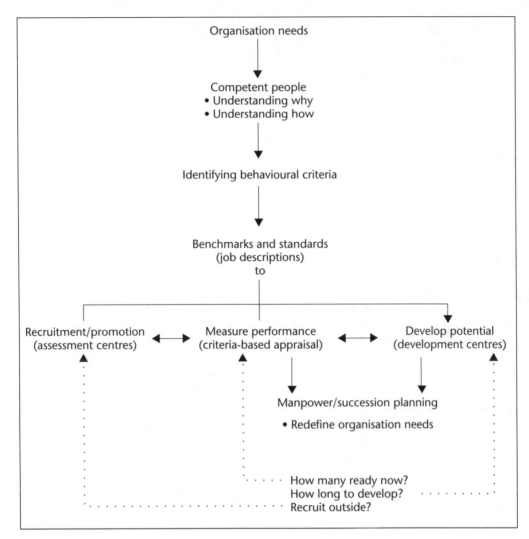

Figure 1.2   The role of behaviour in HR strategy

2 *Getting Started*

Assessment centres are complex events and as such require careful forethought and planning, particularly at the embryonic stage when the idea is first mooted. This chapter outlines the issues to be considered in moving from the concept on the drawing-board through to the completion of the first centre.

Why an assessment centre?

This obvious question is extremely important for assessment centres are purely a means to an end. If an organisation is attracted to the process out of curiosity, or because it seems the thing to do, then it is in danger of missing the point. All assessment centres must have a clearly defined purpose and that purpose should relate to the achievement of the organisation's objectives. Clarity of purpose is important because it will help shape the type of assessment centre and will have a significant influence on many design and procedural issues. In simple terms there are two types of assessment centre: there are those designed to determine simple hire/not hire or promote/don't promote decisions and those designed to diagnose strengths and areas for development. The former is unquestionably an assessment centre, whilst the latter is often referred to as a development centre. The distinction between the two is explained in greater detail in Chapter 10.

So let us assume that someone with sufficient knowledge and inclination has recognised that an assessment centre could meet an important organisational objective – how should they start?

Implementing an assessment centre

Given the size and complexity of an assessment centre, it is helpful to have a clear view of the stages that need to be undertaken to implement such a project. Figure 2.1 depicts those stages. A rough timeframe for the launch of an assessment centre would be about four months from the initial idea.

When it comes to gaining commitment to the principle of an assessment centre, two factors will frequently feature in the debate about whether to run a centre or not. They are to do with the validity of the process and the cost-benefit justification.

Validity of assessment centres

Much has been written about the validity of assessment centres, indeed it is one of the principal arguments for using them. In simple terms validity means the extent to which

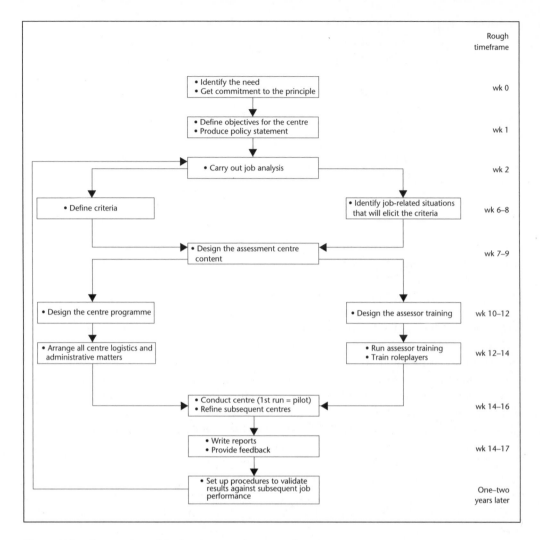

Figure 2.1   An overview of the implementation stages for an assessment centre

something does what it is meant to do. Since assessment centres are generally run with a view to predicting future potential, we are most interested in what is referred to as their 'predictive validity'. The predictive validity is calculated by correlating individuals' overall assessment ratings on an assessment centre with some form of performance criterion measure, such as appraisal ratings, promotion/salary increases, or independent ratings by managers.

Although there can be quite a variation in the published findings, the vast majority of predictive validities seem to strongly support the use of assessment centres. Researchers have been inclined to combine the results from different studies so as to establish a larger research base and provide a clearer comparison with other assessment methods. This process of combining the validities from different studies, is referred to as meta-analysis, and one such recent set of results based upon a review by Schmidt and Hunter (1998), is shown in Figure 2.2.

Work sample tests	0.54
Cognitive ability tests	0.51
Structured interviews	0.51
Personality tests	0.40
Assessment centres	0.37
Biodata	0.35
References	0.26
Unstructured interviews	0.20
Graphology	0.02

Figure 2.2   Predictive validity coefficients

This figure indicates that assessment centres, along with other respected selection methods such as cognitive ability tests, personality tests, structured interviews and biodata, all have good predictive validity. Furthermore, Schmidt and Hunter along with other researchers (Salgado, 1999) note that by combining two or more of these methods the predictive validity can be increased to as much as 0.65. This of course makes the topic of comparing different selection methods tricky, as a classic question arises as to what constitutes an assessment centre; some will include psychometrics (cognitive ability and personality tests) or structured interviews and others will not. Furthermore, even the researchers (Hermelin and Robertson, 2001) admit that their meta-analytic studies are not entirely reliable, due to not always being able to compare 'apples with apples'. However, what matters as a practitioner is that we know that the assessment centre will provide fairly accurate predictive data about an individual's ability to perform in a given job. Whilst some of the other selection methods have higher predictive validities, they can pose other problems.

Work sample tests have been around for a long time and there is much to commend them. They are based on the premise that in order to test someone's ability to do a job, you can't do much better than to test them by using an extract of the job. Indeed a driving test is a good example of a work sample test. However, the limitation with work sample tests is that whilst they are very effective for testing skill acquisition, for example, driving ability, typing ability or the ability to fly an aircraft as illustrated in a flight-simulator, it is much more difficult to test management tasks in the same way. The problem being that the candidate needs to have a meaningful contextual understanding of the job environment before their ability to do the job can be objectively tested. Indeed this explains why work sample tests are very rare in testing 'white collar' jobs and why assessment centres are so popular; they follow the same principle, but use work simulations as opposed to work samples as the test vehicle.

Cognitive ability tests have always enjoyed a high predictive validity and they undoubtedly have value, but there are two concerns with them. First, their focus is purely on cognitive (intellectual) ability and it has long been recognised that successful job performance is not predicated solely on intellectual ability. Indeed there has been a great deal of interest in the relatively new concept of emotional intelligence, or EI (Goleman, 1996), which describes a form of practical intelligence based upon how people perceive, understand and manage emotion. Whilst no predictive validity has yet been established between EI and effective job performance (Robertson and Smith, 2001), its appeal supports the popular view that you need more than just intellect to be a top performer. The second concern with cognitive ability tests is that they cause the greatest problems in the area of adverse impact, which is when members of one sub-group are selected disproportionately more or less often than members of another sub-group. This has been a major problem in relation to people from different ethnic minority groups in the US for some years and it has now started to become a significant concern in the UK and other European countries. Fortunately, assessment centres do not suffer from this difficulty to anything like the same extent and, if anything, can provide a degree of reassurance in this area (see Chapter 11 for further details).

Personality tests have a similar level of predictive validity to assessment centres and their popularity has been increasing over the last decade. However, their 'Achilles heel' is the risk of 'faking' and the level of reliance they place upon the individual to be frank and honest in their completion of what is a self-report instrument. Hough (1998) reports that applicants do distort their responses when personality questionnaires are used in a selection procedure, but the surprising view amongst researchers is that this has no detrimental impact on predictive validity. Whatever the case, it is strongly recommended that personality tests should not be used in isolation. To base selection decisions largely on a self-reported inventory would be a risky policy which has led some unwitting employers into industrial tribunals, resulting in them having to pay compensation.

Finally, there is the interview, which features in the selection process 99 per cent of the time, yet which has come in for a lot of criticism over the years, as it has been a much abused selection method. However, the good news is that the evidence shows that a structured interview can achieve a very respectable predictive validity, whilst the more widespread unstructured interview still rightly suffers from a poor reputation. The two main ways of structuring interviews are situational interviews and behavioural event interviews. The former is the more powerful, attaining predictive validity coefficients as high as 0.50, but it is reliant upon a significant degree of research to define appropriate questions and behaviourally-anchored responses against which the interviewer can rate the candidate's answers. Such an approach is time-consuming and costly to set up and it has limited value in that the approach has to be started afresh for each job being assessed, so it is of most use with large volume recruitment. Behavioural event interviewing, also known as competency based interviewing, achieves a less effective predictive validity of 0.39, which is still highly respectable. The technique is an off-shoot of the assessment centre method. It is based upon the principle of 'behavioural observation' of situations encountered by the candidate in the past and these examples are subjected to probing and analysis to align the data with targeted competencies. It is therefore not uncommon to see such interviews incorporated into the design of an assessment centre, or run as a separate stage pre or post the centre.

Despite these findings, a number of researchers (Dukes, 1996; Higgs, 1996; Hermelin and Robertson, 2001) suggest that we need to be guarded in our interpretation of such results. Their concerns relate to debates about the statistical limitations of correlational techniques, which is beyond the scope of this book, and the practical difficulties in obtaining accurate predictive data from a multitude of studies. Another concern is the ever-present 'criterion-problem': how to define an accurate and reliable measure of job performance against which to compare one's predictions.

This brief review of the most popular selection methods serves to indicate that the assessment centre can and does enjoy a central role in the selection process, for it has as much, if not more, to commend it as any of the other selection methods. Before we leave the concept of validity, we should mention that apart from predictive validity which is the most researched validity measure for assessment centres, there are of course other validity measures which are worth commenting on briefly.

FACE VALIDITY

Face validity is concerned with perception: does the assessment centre *appear* to measure what it should? Will participants view it as fair? On the whole this is one of the assessment centre's great strengths in that, if it has been designed properly, participants should feel that they have been exposed to the demands of the future job or circumstances for which they are being assessed. Thus face validity (often referred to as 'faith validity') for assessment centres is generally very high.

CONTENT VALIDITY

Content validity is concerned with ensuring that the exercise content reflects the demands of the target job as accurately as possible. It is therefore a matter of judgement as to whether the range of tasks is broad enough and deep enough to encapsulate the nature of the target job. Again content validity is generally regarded as a great benefit of assessment centres, and this contrasts with some psychometric tests for example, where the connection between test content and job content is sometimes tenuous.

CONSTRUCT VALIDITY

Are the constructs that make up the assessment centre appropriate and are they clearly defined? In other words, are the criteria/competencies being measured, discrete variables that relate to the target job? If effective job analysis has been carried out as indicated in the next chapter, then we can be confident that the assessment centre is attempting to measure the right variables. However, there has been a lot of debate in the literature as to how well assessor ratings actually discriminate between the competencies being measured and we will return to this important point in Chapter 11.

CONCURRENT VALIDITY

Do assessment centres produce consistent results in comparison with other valid measures? Researchers indicate this to be so and there is no reason to doubt their appropriateness.

Justifying the cost: utility analysis

Once the technical justification for an assessment centre has been established, the next stage is to be able to demonstrate its cost justification. It is true that assessment centres are resource-hungry and as such are generally viewed as quite costly. These costs need to be considered in relation to the financial benefits that can be achieved. Human resource professionals have been able to demonstrate a way of calculating the financial return on using some of the tools of their trade. This method is called utility analysis and is well described by Cascio (1982) and Smith (1988). The method can be quite complicated, so we have tried to describe it as simply as possible with an example.

Imagine an organisation wishing to hire 15 people from an anticipated group of 45 applicants, giving rise to a selection ratio (SR) of 1 in 3 or 33 per cent. It is normally reasonable to assume that for most jobs there will be a significant spread in capability from the high performer at one extreme to the low performer at the other extreme. If no such spread exists, you wouldn't need to use sophisticated selection methods. Now assuming for one moment that you used a random method of selecting your candidates, statistically you would be likely to achieve a 'normal distribution' with most of your candidates being around the average and the two extremes being in balance.

To achieve a *perfect* selection decision based on your SR of 33 per cent, you would need to select successfully the 15 applicants who would be the high performers. These 15 would appear at the top end of the normal distribution curve as shown in Figure 2.3.

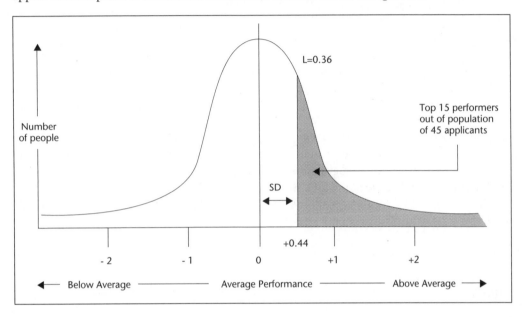

Figure 2.3   Normal distribution curve

In order to interpret this scenario we need to go through the following steps:

STEP 1

Statistical tables show that the top third of performers would appear 0.44 standard deviations (SDs) above the average for the whole group of applicants and the ordinate (L) at that point is 0.36. The ordinate (L) corresponds to the height of the curve at a particular point and indicates the proportion of successful candidates.

STEP 2

Now assuming we have picked the best 15 performers through perfect selection, how would *their* average performance compare with the whole group of applicants? This is calculated by dividing the ordinate of 0.36 by the selection ratio of 0.33, giving rise to the finding that the average performance of these top 15 would be 1.09 (0.36 ÷ 0.33) SDs above the average for the whole group.

STEP 3

At this point we need to adjust our calculations to reflect the fact that our assessment methods, whilst hopefully better than random, are certainly not perfect. To do this we multiply the previous calculation by the appropriate predictive validity coefficient for the assessment method we intend employing. So whilst perfect selection will enable us to realise an improvement of 1.09 SDs above the average in expected performance, this is adjusted to 0.4033 SDs for an assessment centre (1.09 × 0.37) or 0.218 SDs if unstructured interviews are used (1.09 × 0.20), where 0.37 and 0.20 are taken from Figure 2.2.

STEP 4

The next step is to translate these improvements in the SDs into cash terms. Thus we need to establish the value of a SD. Whilst this too can be complicated, we are indebted to research by Schmidt and Hunter (1983) which indicates that the value of one SD can conservatively be estimated at about 40 per cent of salary. So in our example, if we assume a salary of £20 000 p.a., one SD is worth £8000 (£20 000 × 40 per cent), and one applicant selected by an assessment centre is likely to generate £3226 (£8000 × 0.4033) more benefit for the business in that year than would an average performer. This is clearly not the complete story, since we need to apply this principle to the total number of applicants to be recruited.

For example, if we fill all 15 positions using an assessment centre the total benefits would be:

£3266 × 15 = £48 990.

STEP 5

Next we need to calculate their average length of service in the target job, since these benefits should be realised over a number of years. So assuming the average period of service in the job is 2.5 years we arrive at:

£48 990 × 2.5 = £122 475.

STEP 6

Finally, having calculated the financial benefits, we obviously need to subtract the selection costs. These will vary from one selection process to another and will be dependent on numerous factors, such as methods employed, number of applicants, cost of materials, and design and implementation costs. However, as many of these costs cannot be eliminated, it should quickly become apparent that the benefits of a process such as an assessment centre significantly outweigh the costs.

So in summary the benefits can be calculated by the following equation (Bedford, 1988):

Gross benefit = L/SR x r x SD x n x t

Where:

L =   ordinate of the normal distribution curve which corresponds to the proportion of successful candidates.

SR =   selection ratio (proportion of applicants declared successful).

r =   correlation of selection procedure outcome with criterion performance (usually the predictive validity).

SD =   standard deviation of the value of performance on the criterion in £s over a one-year period (annual salary × 40% is a good estimate).

n =   the number of successful candidates.

t =   the average length of subsequent in-job service in years.

Utility analysis calculations have shown considerable financial benefits are being achieved when assessment centres are used instead of other selection methods. Jones (1988) cites that for one type of officer recruited into the Royal Navy by assessment centre instead of just an interview, they 'saved some third of a million pounds in training costs over a four year period for one year's worth of candidates alone'. Bedford (1988) refers to the use of assessment centres to select senior police officers to attend a Senior Command course at the National Police College at Bramshill. Successful completion of the course invariably leads to advancement and effectively creates the pool from which most Chief Police Officers are drawn. Through utility analysis the net benefit of the assessment centre was, at the very least, £800 000 per year.

So having established the technical justification and the cost-benefit justification for assessment centres, we need to consider what else is involved in securing the commitment to proceed.

Selling the concept

As the champion of the assessment centre cause, one needs to sell the concept repeatedly to numerous people, from the Board right through to the actual participants. We look now at some of the arguments and issues that could be used to facilitate the sales process at different stages with different people.

THE BOARD

For most assessment centres to stand a chance of being launched and supported, it is quite often important to gain approval from the Board. It is at this level that one must ensure the link is clearly defined between the use of assessment centres and the resolution of an important organisational objective. If the assessment centre is to be used as a selection tool, as in graduate recruitment for example, or to enable important management appointments to be made, the purpose is clear. But why use an assessment centre to aid these processes? What is the organisational justification? More often than not, we have to focus on the cost-benefit arguments for moving to the greater sophistication of assessment centres and these have already been covered.

Another issue to recognise at this level is the political implications of such a process. It is not uncommon to encounter comments from senior personnel professionals who would like to implement assessment centres but feel their organisation isn't ready for it! Often such comments indicate that the culture would find it difficult to adjust to such an objective process. We have worked with clients who have admitted they are desperately keen to encourage the Board to move into the twenty-first century and who have been told they are happy being in the nineteenth century! Thus sometimes the challenge is to get the Board to recognise that objective assessment is beneficial to the organisation and the 'old school tie' syndrome is, as it implies, of the 'old school'!

ASSESSORS

As assessors will usually be senior managers at least one level above the participants, their influence on the success of the whole process will be quite significant. They will need to be convinced of the value of the assessment centre, usually achieved during their assessor training (see Chapter 6). Long before that event, their commitment and understanding needs to be secured. One of the biggest obstacles here is reluctance to commit the time required to be trained as assessors. This usually stems from a failure to appreciate the complexity of the process, in the misguided belief that 'they've done this sort of thing before'. Choosing and briefing assessors prior to the training is covered in Chapter 6, but it is worth noting that their earlier involvement is often achieved through the job analysis stage and/or the process of exercise design.

PARTICIPANTS' MANAGERS

Often ignored as far as an assessment centre is concerned, in that they don't always appear to have an obvious role, yet participants' managers can play an important part in ensuring the assessment centre is ably supported. It is quite likely they will be involved in the job analysis stage, possibly the exercise design stage and perhaps as assessors, although not for their own direct reports. A more fundamental and sometimes overlooked role is the possible influence they have on the participants before and after the event.

Before the event they may have a say in nominating people to attend and could well be involved in the briefing process for their own direct reports. This inevitably can have an impact on how a participant might approach an assessment centre and their expectations about the event. Thus they need to be clear about what they should and shouldn't say to the participants.

After the event, they will often need to be committed to assisting their direct reports in the execution of a personal development plan. This is particularly true for a development centre and is explained in more detail in Chapter 10.

PARTICIPANTS

It is probably true to say that initially most participants feel anxious or even threatened when they attend an assessment centre. No matter how good the earlier communication of the idea, or briefing about what to expect, participants are likely to experience some anxiety. Fortunately this usually passes quickly once they get into the event. To minimise their concerns, the most important points to address are 'Why is the event being run?' and 'How will the results be used?'

The answers to these questions and others should be made available to the participants and all interested parties well in advance of the events, in the form of a policy statement.

Writing and publicising the policy statement is a vital first step for any assessment centre, particularly if you are concerned that motives may be questioned or may be viewed as unclear.

The policy statement

It is very important to develop a policy statement at the outset when designing an assessment centre so as to ensure potentially ambiguous issues are avoided and everyone benefits from a clear understanding of the event. The policy should be written and made generally available and is likely to include the following:

1 The purpose/objective of the centre.
2 Who the event is targeted at and the procedure by which participants will be nominated. This should also include an indication of nomination criteria.
3 Who will act as assessors, how they will be selected and trained. Again this could include an indication of criteria for assessor selection.
4 How the assessment centre results will be used. This encapsulates the purpose for which the results are being collected – on many occasions a multiple purpose. For example, the primary purpose might be to facilitate a considered selection decision; it may also be intended to use the information gathered to assist with the on-the-job development of internal candidates who are unsuccessful in achieving the promotion for which they were being considered.
5 Who has access to the data from the centre and what form will they take? This relates to the important issue of ownership of the data. More often than not the data are collected in the form of a report and many centres acknowledge the individual's rights to have a copy of the report. Some go as far as to place the responsibility for generating the report in the hands of the participant!

   Others, however, allow the participant to see the report, but not keep a copy; this is more likely where there is a concern about potential misinterpretation of the data, or perhaps in the case of external recruitment where the organisation is reluctant to release the data for fear of revealing exercise content.

   Who else should be allowed to either see or possess a copy of the report also needs to be considered. Again concern about the ability to interpret the data correctly may influence the policy here.
6 What is the policy on feedback? Who will give it? When? Who else might be present at the feedback session? More often than not, feedback is given by assessors, on or as soon after the event as possible. An important question that needs to be considered, however, is how and when to involve the participants' managers in this process.
7 Where will the results (reports) of the assessment centre be stored? Will they be kept on personnel files and if so, for how long? It is often recommended to put a reference on the front of the report saying 'Not to be used after, say, 2 or 5 years after the date of the assessment centre.' This is because changes within the organisation, the nature of the target job, as well as the individual's circumstances, could well invalidate the relevance of the data within the report. It is difficult to be precise about the timeframe of the 'shelf-life' for such a report, since it will vary from one organisation to another and will depend on the type and level of the target job, but generally speaking between two and five years is advisable.

8 Depending on the nature and purpose of the assessment centre, it may be helpful to indicate who is responsible for ensuring that follow-up actions are implemented. This is clearly more applicable in the case of a development centre.

9 It may also be helpful to indicate any opportunities that may exist for reassessment and any constraints such as timeframe that may apply.

The above list indicates the sort of issues that need to be considered as early as possible, when the idea for an assessment centre begins to take shape. When the policy is drafted, it needs to be approved, perhaps at Board level. Once defined, it should be used as a set of practical guidelines which if necessary should be subject to redrafting and refinement, leading to further approval. The message here is to be careful about setting the policy statement in 'tablets of stone', for it should reflect the evolving needs of the organisation and its use of assessment centre technology for a specific purpose. Figure 2.4 shows a specific example of a policy statement for a Career Development Centre, which one of the authors was associated with at ICL. It is reproduced with ICL's kind permission.

ICL (UK) Ltd	Ref:	HQFIN/DO6UK
FINANCE DEVELOPMENT UNIT	Issue:	01
	Date:	SEP 1989
FINANCE CAREER DEVELOPMENT CENTRES	Section:	03
	Page:	1 of 3

FINANCE CAREER DEVELOPMENT CENTRE LEVEL 1 – POLICY STATEMENT

1   WHAT IS IT?

FCDC is a four day event which offers individuals the opportunity to assess their own potential, supported by objective methods such as aptitude tests, occupational questionnaires, written exercises, career advice and counselling. This process is a collaborative method of staff progression and requires the commitment and involvement of all concerned. It is not a pass or fail exercise, but is aimed directly at producing personal and career development plans, to cover a two/three year period.

2   WHAT IS THE OBJECTIVE?

The Centre will identify the individual's strengths and needs in relation to their career development. Attendance at a Centre does not result in a pass or fail; the analysis of the individual's performance will result in a personal development plan. This plan will cover skill enhancement, training, career development actions and personal actions together with target time scales for achievement. All agreed actions will be closely linked to the business requirements and opportunities available.

Figure 2.4   Example of a policy statement

3   WHY THIS APPROACH?

Due to the changing nature of the working environment in the finance function and the rapid growth of the business, there is a need to identify individual development and promotion potential as early as possible. This will ensure a pro-active resourcing approach to future business strategies and organisational requirements. Complementary to this is a requirement to provide career development and personal growth for all individuals in accordance with the Finance Career Structure.

This approach will ensure individuals are channelled correctly and given the opportunity to develop to their full potential.

4   WHO SHOULD ATTEND AND HOW ARE THEY SELECTED?

These events will be run for people on Level 3 of the Career Structure whose nomination by their line manager has been approved by the next level manager and agreed by Training and Development. Individuals will normally have a minimum PR rating of 3 and will have demonstrated a desire and the ability to progress to a role at Level 4 of the Career Structure.

5   WHAT DOES IT INVOLVE?

The finance career development centre consists of a number of individual and interactive exercises. These exercises are likely to be in the form of presentations, assigned and/or unassigned role plays, written exercises and pencil and paper tests. The event will include a significant degree of self analysis, including the completion of a learning styles questionnaire, an interest inventory and an occupational personality questionnaire. The criteria against which performance is measured are specified in Appendix 1.

6   WHO WILL ASSESS THE PARTICIPANTS?

Assessments will be carried out by a combination of managers, generally from the Finance function and direct reports to the Finance Director ICL (UK) or their direct reports, and the participants themselves; all of whom will be trained in the relevant assessment techniques. An individual will not be assessed by his/her own manager.

7   FEEDBACK

Management and peer feedback on specific exercises will occur on the event, where the individual will also receive feedback on the test results. The individual will start to formulate draft development plans at the Centre in readiness for discussion with their managers. Guidance and career counselling will be available on the final day of the event.

Figure 2.4   Example of a policy statement (continued)

8   PERSONAL DEVELOPMENT PLAN

This will always be discussed on a one to one basis between participants and their managers, no later than four weeks after the event. As a result, a formal training and career action plan will be agreed and established. The Finance Development Manager, in conjunction with the local Training & Development Manager/Consultant will, in all instances, monitor the implementation and progression of the plan. A part of this monitoring process will be continual review against organisational plans and job definitions to ensure that the plan remains relevant to the needs both of the organisation and the individual. Both vertical and horizontal progression (ie cross streaming) will be considered at all times.

A copy of the agreed plan should be sent to the Finance Development Manager no later than 6 weeks after the Centre.

9   ACCOUNTABILITY

Primary responsibility for driving the plan will rest with the individuals concerned and their managers.

Nominating Managers will continue to review the progress of the individual's development to ensure the completion of development plans. Evidence of such will be required prior to the individual being proposed for subsequent panel promotion.

10   OWNERSHIP OF RESULTS

By virtue of the dual purpose of the development centres ie to establish career development plans in the joint interest of the individual and the organisation, the data will be jointly owned. Individuals will have a clear view of their current development opportunities which will be consistent with the anticipated skill and experience requirements of the organisation. The Company will additionally gain statistical information for future development and training strategies.

All output from the event will be placed on the individual's Personnel file with an expiry date of 2 years after attendance at the event.

Figure 2.4   Example of a policy statement (concluded)

Using consultants

It goes without saying that it is difficult for us to comment upon the use of consultants without allowing a little bit of bias to creep in! Having worked on both sides of the fence – that is, previously in the capacity of Personnel and Training Managers and now as external consultants – we can point to the fact that in our experience, using assessment centres is one area where you are well advised to buy in the expertise when you are starting out.

Indeed this view is reinforced by the highly respected academics Clive Fletcher and Neil Anderson (1998) who reported that the explosion of interest in assessment centres has led to many which are superficial in nature. They cite a number of telltale signs, such as a lack of assessor training, no clear link between the exercises and criteria being assessed, and perfunctory consideration of the candidates during the assessor discussion. In short, these indicate a failure to appreciate the need to follow professional guidelines and this often means going to consultants, although this alone is no guarantee of getting things right, as they too can vary in quality!

How you might choose to use consultants will of course be determined by the desire and ability within your organisation to carry out the different stages that need to be undertaken. There is of course a benefit in involving consultants from the very beginning. Assuming they have the right expertise, they can guide the whole process and ensure a consistent and integrated approach. If you were to seek only a partial involvement from consultants, then you might consider them for one or more of the following major stages:

- Job analysis to define criteria/competencies.
- Designing exercises.
- Conducting assessor training.
- Designing the assessment/development centre.
- Acting as assessors.
- Managing the assessment centre.
- Chairing the assessor discussion.

We have been involved in centres where we have done all, some or just one of the above tasks.

The biggest issue when considering the use of consultants is how to be sure they have the necessary expertise in what is a complex area and where you as the client may only have limited knowledge. Clearly we hope this book will help, but the following checklist may be useful:

- How long have they been working with assessment centres?
- Who have they done work for? Who could you contact for references?
- Were these events assessment centres or development centres? How would they define the difference? (See Chapter 10 for an explanation.)
- Where were they trained in the use of assessment centres and by whom? (Look for some indication of professional standards.)
- Ask them to give you an overview of the stages involved in setting up an assessment centre. Their answer should be very similar to the model we have presented in Figure 2.1.
- Who would they suggest should act as assessors either for the centre you are contemplating or in general? What ratio of assessors to participants would they recommend? What level should the assessors come from? Which criteria should be considered when selecting assessors? (All these questions are covered in Chapter 6.)
- Which books would they recommend you read to help you develop an appreciation of assessment centres? This should give you some insight into their level of knowledge in the field, but beware of them being overly academic and well-read but with no hands-on practical experience of assessment centres.

Good books to which they might well refer would include:

- *Development and Assessment Centres* by Charles Woodruffe.
- *Tomorrow's Managers Today* by Andrew and Valerie Stewart.
- *Applying the Assessment Center Method* edited by Joseph Moses and William Byham.
- *Assessment Centers and Managerial Performance* by George Thornton III and William Byham
- and of course this one!

3 *Defining the Job Needs*

Job analysis

Job analysis is a generic term which covers a very wide range of activities, from direct observation of someone at work through to the completion of highly specific task or role inventories and checklists. In this generic sense it can mean any systematic procedure that is aimed at gaining detailed information about a job or role that is currently or will be performed.

The traditional role of job analysis within the area of personnel selection is to provide a clearly defined focus for all of the subsequent steps of the process. Needless to say, it is important to get it right and it is interesting to note therefore, that there has been curiously little new research into job analysis techniques, despite the fact that the world of work has been subject to some significant changes over the last decade or two. Most prevalent is the fact that jobs are no longer anywhere near as stable as they used to be, due to rapid changes in technology, organisations and work practices. Hough and Oswald (2000) note that these changes create difficulties for job analysis researchers, who as a result are tending to focus more on tasks and the cross-functional skills of workers, rather than the more traditional static aspects of jobs. They also note that this has led to some researchers using the US Department of Labor's database O*NET (online.onetcenter.org), which is a unique, powerful source for continually updated occupational information and labour market research, covering both work behaviours and worker attributes, with the latter including personality and cognitive variables.

In some respects job analysis can appear to be much the same as a time and motion study, particularly when the subject of the study is a production worker and the analyst is engaged in direct observation of that person. From the point of view of the person being observed, it really doesn't matter whether the objective of the study is to identify immediate efficiency gains or to develop a better training programme. For most people being observed is an uncomfortable process, almost certain to lead to some form of behavioural distortion. Tales of work-rate fixing are legion of course, but it is equally common for people to engage in all sorts of spurious activity to fill their day to please either themselves or the analyst. Either way the results may be open to question, especially if they are the only source of data. To summarise thus far:

- Job analysis is applied research.
- The first question any analyst needs to ask is *why* is this study being conducted?
- Using any single technique is likely to lead to inadequate understanding.

While there are many other applications of job analysis techniques (see Pearn and Kandola, 1988), the rest of this chapter deals with the typical job analysis approach for a managerial position assessment centre. The structure of this chapter follows the logical flow of the issues to be considered in a typical job analysis. As Spencer (1989) remarks, answering the question 'why' has a significant impact on the other components of the research strategy, the 'what', the 'how' and the 'who'. In this case the 'why' is straightforward. The 'what' identifies what information you need about a particular target job or job level. The 'how' relates to the particular method or methods used. The 'who' is about identifying a suitable study sample and also about who should conduct the work. The chapter closes with a consideration of some of the common questions we are asked about the value of the job analysis.

Why is the job analysis being conducted?

In the context of designing an assessment centre, the start point is a clear and accurate picture of what the centre is measuring. Getting this right is arguably the most important part of the design. If it is wrong, people are likely to be judged against inappropriate criteria, the exercises will be difficult to design and assessors will constantly complain that they are having difficulty in accurately classifying and evaluating behaviour. Eventually, this erodes line managers' faith in assessment centres.

Furthermore, the results of a job analysis frequently feed into other important areas of human resource management such as appraisal, training and development, as well as the general processes of recruitment. Once behavioural criteria become common language, it is not unusual to draft recruitment advertisements, design application forms and develop the mechanics of an appraisal system to reflect such criteria. The worst situation is, therefore, that an organisation continues to attract inappropriate people, selects badly, appraises performance poorly and helps its managers to develop irrelevant strengths. Naturally, no sensible organisation would allow this situation without making adjustments to their human resource practices. More positively, the fact that there are knock-on consequences strongly argues for putting resource and effort into this stage.

Creating a clear and accurate picture of what the centre is measuring also involves understanding the situations in which the behaviour is expressed. It is not enough to accept that planning and organising are important criteria. The way you see them being expressed is in the results or outcomes that people usually identify when they are talking about good performers. Managers will often cite as an example of creditworthy behaviour that Mr X always turns in reports on time. From our point of view this is an 'indicator' of ability in planning and organising. Understanding more about the circumstances helps you to understand why it is important (or trivial). If the reports are produced, for example, against tight deadlines or under circumstances where there are many other things happening concurrently, there is clear evidence that a skill is being used. It also is a good indication of the circumstances we would attempt to simulate in exercises. There are therefore three key objectives in doing a job analysis for an assessment centre:

- To identify the criteria for successful job performance.
- To identify the situations in which the criteria are typically expressed so that appropriate simulations can be designed.
- To identify task content so that simulations reflect the nature of work at the target job level.

IDENTIFYING CRITERIA

During the mid-1980s to mid-1990s, there was a resurgence of interest in trying to define some generic model of management behaviour, most notably in the UK through the Management Charter Initiative (MCI). The problem is that this model, like all generalised models, fails to answer the specific question: what is it that characterises successful managers of this type in that company? The characteristics of successful managers, or criteria, are all broadly related to the way they behave which is in some way different from their less successful colleagues.

Indeed it is worth noting that the MCI also contributed to the confusion that has arisen over the use of the terms competency(ies) and competence(s). At first, many viewed these terms as almost interchangeable, but the distinction has become much clearer over the last five years or so. Shevels (1998) helps to make the distinction by explaining that competency(ies) deal with underlying capabilities and the behaviours that people may need to do a particular job effectively. Whereas competence(s) are the task elements that give rise to the outputs required from a job role. Or to put it more succinctly, competencies describe the person domain, whilst competences describe the task domain and this distinction accounts for the traditional division of job analysis into task-oriented job analysis and worker-oriented job analysis (Sandberg, 2000). When designing selection processes and assessment centres in particular, our interest is more to do with competencies, although as we stated back in Chapter 1, we will continue to use the term criteria to minimise confusion.

These criteria can be anything concerned with behaviour: some may be related to attitudes, some to personality characteristics or traits, or skills acquired over time; others may be concerned with personal drives, motivation, the way a person reacts with others or particular approaches to problem-solving. The research paradigm is straightforward. See Figure 3.1.

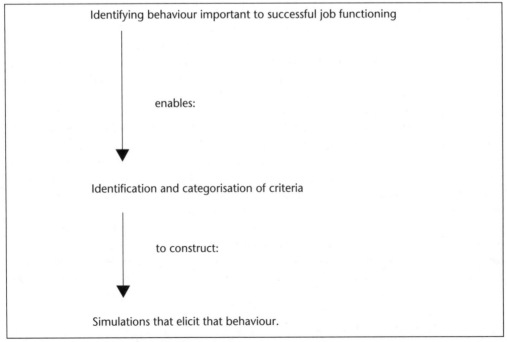

Figure 3.1   Research paradigm for job analysis

This simple model is quite difficult to put into practice. There are probably thousands of behaviours that contribute to successful or unsuccessful performance in a specific job role. Even the people who are seen as successful in an organisation are not wholly successful at everything they do or in all contexts. Quite often it turns out that the more successful are simply using certain particular behaviours more often than their less successful colleagues.

Much less frequently one finds that the more successful are using behaviours that the less successful do not use at all. Where this is so, one needs to be very careful to distinguish the extent to which this depends on the context the person is working in and the extent to which specific knowledge impacts on the situation.

At another level, much of what many managerial and professional people do could be classified as reading, writing, talking with or listening to other people. All of these aspects of communication are visibly tasks that are a significant part of the workload. If one were to take a strict behaviourist view (which says that the only evidence admissible in psychology is what can be directly observed), these communication skills might define many managers' jobs. A fairly light dose of common sense would tell anyone that what matters is the way the information is handled when, for example, a person reads an internal memo. Reading merely facilitates the process and is unlikely to be a significant criterion because nearly all the adult population can read.

The need is to identify criteria or examples of behaviour that are neither so general that they apply to most of the population, nor so specific that they only apply to the small detail of one person's job. To attain this goal, the solution is to cluster individual behaviours together in a way that has meaning to all the people likely to be involved. Therefore, a criterion has two aspects:

• It is a description under which behaviour can be reliably classified.
• It is what we want to know about a person relative to the job in question.

Reliability is critical in the context of assessment centres as it is in the design of psychometric instruments. The central point of concern is that a variety of different assessors, trained to the same standard, should be able to classify a sample of behaviour as the same thing. Repeatability is also essential. The same behaviour from different participants should likewise be consistently classified on a number of different occasions.

Criteria definitions are often taken to be the qualifications for success but some caution is needed. Some criteria have higher priority than others. It is rare to find participants who excel on all criteria. Possibly most important of all, some criteria predict success in only one direction (a good example of this is written communication). In most jobs, the absence of written communication skill would indicate failure but its presence rarely indicates success. Creativity, on the other hand, often indicates outstanding success in certain positions where the lack of it does not mean failure.

To facilitate the practical use of the criterion you need more than a name. To train people and establish common standards, any criterion needs a definition. Criterion definition statements are usually worded positively so that evaluations are scored higher when more is seen at an assessment centre. The other characteristics of a good definition are:

• Plain language, easy to understand.
• Short – one or two sentences at most.
• Not circular, that is do not use the criterion name in elaborating the definition.

- Where appropriate, tailored to the position or level.
- Do not give examples.

Definition statements are sometimes supplemented with further information, including examples, particularly where they are unique to the job. At the end of the job analysis, there will be a process to select which criteria are used for the assessment centre. That selection will be guided by a number of questions which need to be borne in mind at the outset of the research phase. They are:

- Do the criteria chosen differentiate between successful and unsuccessful performance?
- Can you defend their inclusion legally?
- Can the criteria be measured practically through simulations or other devices including interview or psychometric instruments?
- Is there overlap between criteria?
- Does the criterion differentiate between people before they come in to the target job or level?

The last question is particularly important when a selection decision is being made and even more important when internal and external participants are being compared. In first-line positions it is not uncommon to identify a criterion of 'hands-on problem-solving' or something similar. While it may be realistic to propose that this does indeed differentiate between the successful and the less successful, we also need to assess the extent to which this depends on specific knowledge of particular equipment, processes and procedures.

IDENTIFYING SITUATIONS IN WHICH CRITERIA ARE EXPRESSED

In many ways understanding the context in which a criterion is used is inseparable from discovering the criterion. None of the skills, attitudes and so forth operate in a vacuum and it is in the understanding of how the behaviour manifests itself that one begins to understand the relative importance of behavioural criteria. Gaining that understanding starts the process of identifying which type of simulations would be appropriate to use in an assessment centre and particularly identifying the level of the exercise content. (Exercise design is dealt with in the next chapter.)

Understanding the context of behaviour is normally easier than identifying the behaviour. To start with it is more easily amenable to direct observation. You can see a supervisor monitoring instruments whereas you cannot see the thought process that, for example, indicates that a correction is needed. It is also true for almost all jobs that there will be some elements of working alone, some aspects that involve working with others one-to-one, and some aspects that will involve working within a group. Different jobs tend to be characterised by differences of context. Salespeople work a great deal of their time one-to-one whereas, in contrast, a trainer works in groups for a significant part of their job.

Equally, while salespeople and a welfare officer may spend high proportions of their time working with people on a one-to-one basis, the content of their discussions may be quite different, as are their objectives. Both would be using a fair degree of interpersonal sensitivity, but the salesperson would predominantly be trying to persuade their customer, whereas the welfare officer would predominantly be listening. To an outside observer there would be significant differences in the talk/listen ratio, the degree of control exercised over the conversation, the time taken to reach the ultimate objective and so on.

In addition to the balance between working alone, working one-to-one, working in groups and the task characteristics, the analyst is interested in the level and the typical content of issues that a person might be dealing with. Almost everyone has to handle written information of some sort, but both the volume and the level of difficulty will impact on the amount of time the job incumbent spends dealing with it. In all probability, the more senior a person is the more likely it is that they will be dealing with more complex, more abstract issues that have some impact on large parts of the organisation.

Although this is a reasonable assumption, organisational cultures vary considerably. We have experienced situations where the CEO seems to be dealing with much routine correspondence and, equally, situations where people in lower level jobs are expected to produce discussion documents on matters that profoundly affect the future of the organisation. The objective of this part of the analysis is to understand the situation for a particular job holder.

IDENTIFYING THE APPROPRIATE JOB LEVEL

Taking a very broad overview of the work of managers, we can identify at least three different types of managerial role: the first-line manager, middle managers and executives.

First-line managers may have a wide variety of titles such as foreman, supervisor, team leader or chief clerk, but their work shares a number of characteristics. These characteristics define the nature of their work as different from the people that they supervise and also different from the people who supervise them.

In general their work orientation is towards the task that their part of the organisation is set up to do, whether that is to produce certain products in agreed volumes or to ensure that invoices go out on time. At this level technical knowledge is usually a very significant feature of the job. Problem-solving tends also to be related to the technical task and is fairly immediate in timeframe. Work-related relationships are likely to be confined to the subordinate group and immediate supervisor. The big difference for the first-line manager, who is often promoted from the work group, is that they then have to direct and organise the work of other people.

At middle-management level, the nature of the job demands are typically different. Their tasks are mainly directed at accomplishing specific objectives through the supervision of other people, sometimes quite separately from the task group. Work-based relationships are much more likely to spread across the organisation both between departments and up or down several layers. Decision-making is likely to occur after long timeframes and, with increasing seniority, becomes far less specifically technical. Although the shift from supervisor to manager is a significant change in job tasks, it is not normally as great a change as the shift from worker to supervisor.

The third level of management is broadly classified as executive. This level represents another significant change. Although the post-holder may be the head of a division, function or geographical location, they are now required to broaden their horizons and take into account the needs of the whole organisation. Decision-making is characterised by a focus on longer-term planning and policy formulation, often over years. Technical knowledge plays almost no part because the already known is of relatively little assistance. Most significantly, managers at this level are more likely to work on matters that are external to the company.

If we take it that all managerial work is concerned to some degree with decision-making, interpersonal skills, communication skills and managing processes, then all of these should be indicated in a job analysis of almost any management job. In general, it is the proportion of these criteria and their relative weight that are revealed in a job analysis.

Equally important, it is quite likely that some of the criteria that are identified will be seen as important at all organisational levels, but expressed in very different ways. To take one example, planning and organising is a criterion that is identified in virtually every theoretical model and every job analysis. At the first-line level, planning and organising means knowing what to do to assign people to tasks to meet today's production demand, and how to respond if someone fails to come to work or if there is a disruption to a routine. At the most senior levels the planning and organising is more concerned with the long-range objectives of the company. In both cases the skill would apply to minute-by-minute actions that are taken to use one's own and others' time and resources effectively.

Thus, a significant part of the job analysis is to identify the appropriate level at which the criterion is expressed. To a considerable extent, this is a matter of identifying the task content of the target job, so the simulations used reflect content that is appropriate to the level.

Having identified why the research is being undertaken and what information is required about the job, we will now move on to look at how a typical job analysis is conducted.

Structure of a typical job analysis

It should now be evident that the quality of the eventual assessment centre is significantly dependent on the quality of the research phase. It should also be evident that any one method is not likely to lead to a satisfactory result. The following describes the typical steps that we would take on the assumption that the target job already exists. Some of the techniques described can also be used in the comparatively rare circumstances where a job does not already exist. This point will be elaborated on later.

DIRECT OBSERVATION

An extremely useful opportunity is given by direct observation for the analyst to take an overview of the context in which a person works and the tasks that they do, at the start of a research programme. As the name suggests, direct observation means watching people work. There are varying levels of directness and precision, ranging from observing someone through a one-way mirror taking fairly precise notes and measurements of whole body movements, to sitting in with or going along with a manager as they go through their daily routine.

Even when studying a process worker on a bench, it is most unlikely that the analysis will be restricted entirely to observation. Sooner or later curiosity drives you to ask the person why, for example, they decided to do X at Y point of time. At a management level a large amount of what you want to know is hidden from direct observation – these issues include thinking, problem-solving approach or setting priorities. Thus the next step is to interview the job incumbent to find out why they do what they do.

INCUMBENT INTERVIEWS

The best way to understand what counts in a particular job is to go and ask the person who is currently doing the job. That said, it is important to be clear that what you are trying to understand at this stage is the demands of the job, rather than the skills of a particular individual. Understanding this will help to give shape and purpose to the interview, although there is a very wide range of potential interview styles. At one extreme there is the kind of interview in which the interviewer turns on a tape recorder and says 'Tell me about your job'; at the other, there is the detailed questionnaire. Both have problems and strengths. The totally unstructured interview can reveal very rich descriptive data, particularly about the 'hidden' aspects of the job. On the other hand, if you invite a person to ramble some will and the data analysis takes as long as the interview. Totally structured questionnaires have the great advantage that content analysis and data processing are standardised and quick to complete. The danger is that the analyst will miss significant input either because the structure doesn't allow it or because they have become bored with asking the same questions repeatedly. We prefer a semi-structured approach which has some fairly precise and detailed questions, particularly task-related questions, mixed with a number of open questions which may need discussion and further probing before a summary answer is recorded.

In many ways the structure we use is similar to the kind of interview one might conduct to establish a position description in a job evaluation. The difference is in the way the content is analysed. A typical interview schedule would encompass the following:

- A function statement (why people do what they do).
- Locating the position in the hierarchy.
- General description of responsibilities.
- Description of a typical day.
- What kind of activities take up most time.
- What kind of activities are seen as most important.
- Where are the biggest problems in the job.
- What do you think contributes to success/failure.

The task analysis might include a number of detailed questions, typically including:

- The nature of reports a person has to write.
- Attendance at meetings/purpose/role/frequency/formality.
- The reasons for having a one-to-one meeting with colleagues/their frequency/their difficulty.
- The number/nature/frequency of data on which the person has to act.
- The degree of analysis required/assistance available/from whom.

Each major question includes a need to clarify the level of contribution and the precise role that the incumbent fulfils. Some people are reluctant to sing their own praises, whereas others exaggerate their level of responsibility to a considerable extent. The best approach is to maintain a stance of complete naivety and to go on asking:

- Why did you do this/that?
- What was your exact role?
- Who else was involved?
- Did you consider alternatives?
- Why did you reject them?
- Why was that stressful/exciting/risky/boring?

In this way one can gather a large amount of data which is susceptible to analysis at a later stage, sometimes supplemented with an activity-based questionnaire. Most interviews will conclude with some questions related to performance, typically:

- What do you like/dislike most about the job?
- If someone did really well in this job, what types of thing would they do better than the acceptable individual?

Given reasonable length of service, most job incumbents can give answers to these questions. There are difficulties in relying on their opinions alone for qualitative information, particularly where this relates to understanding performance. We always conduct further interviews with managers of job incumbents for this reason.

MANAGER INTERVIEWS

Interviews with managers of job incumbents are conducted to unearth performance characteristics of the job, particularly to identify what makes people relatively successful or relatively unsuccessful in the job being studied. There are two likely approaches: most commonly, the critical incident interview and, less frequently, the repertory grid interview. Both are described below. As in the incumbent interview, the interest is in the demands of the job rather than any individuals.

Critical incident interviews

The first technique can be used either individually in an interview or collectively as a group discussion. We tend to interview a sample of managers individually, as a group discussion is often rather bland when the analyst is new to an organisation. Managers are asked to identify incidents that demonstrate both effective and ineffective job-related behaviour. A true critical incident is a mini case-study of a real incident that has occurred and is not some generalised description of critical performance areas. To qualify as a critical incident the situation has to be classifiable:

- The incident has to be observable; particularly there has to be a fairly specific outcome as a result of what someone said or did.
- The incident description has to be sufficiently detailed for inferences to be drawn from it about the person performing the act.
- It must be critical, that is it must occur in circumstances where the outcome, good or bad as the case may be, has significant impact on job performance.

The data obtained are in the form of anecdotes or stories about the way a number of individuals behaved on particular occasions. In a typical interview schedule, we would aim to collect at least three positive incidents and three demonstrating less successful behaviour from each person interviewed. Although there are drawbacks to this technique, the biggest single advantage is that they are generally very interesting for both interviewer and interviewee to do. The qualitative nature of the descriptions brings colour and life to a process that can otherwise be fairly dry and it is possible to analyse them quantitatively to get a good indication of the significance of various criteria.

Repertory grid interviews

The second technique was developed from the personal construct theory of George Kelly, who used it in the clinical context to help articulate the way in which people who are psychologically ill understand their world. The underlying concept is that we all use language to describe differences that we see between different things in life. These constructs are personal to the extent that the language labels we use are unique to every individual. They guide the way we behave and the way we see other people's behaviour.

In the context of job analysis a manager is asked to delineate those constructs that differentiate between the good performers and those who are less good. The interview typically follows these steps:

- The manager is asked to write the names or initials of the people they supervise on to separate cards.
- The interviewer then asks the manager to separate the cards into two piles, one of people who are good at their work, the other for those who are less good.
- The manager is then asked to pick two cards from the 'good' deck and one from the 'poor' deck. They are then asked to describe how the two good examples are similar to each other and how they are both different from the poor example.
- Working with the manager's initial description, the analyst probes further to get to some concrete description of the differences, usually by asking for examples.
- The interview continues along these lines until the interviewee either runs out of ideas or starts to repeat constructs that have already been identified.

As with the critical incident interview, the skill of the interviewer is to elicit a set of ideas that can be classified in such a way as to meet the requirements for good descriptive statements, without imposing their own constructs on the interviewee. This technique is particularly helpful when used well in revealing hidden criteria, such as decision-making approaches, the style of relationships with other people and so on. Like any other technique, it is foolhardy to rely solely on this approach to complete a job analysis. Its principal advantage is that an enormous amount of relevant data can be generated quickly even when only a few interviews have been conducted. The main disadvantage is that poorly trained interviewers generate vague and generalised concepts that in practice are very difficult to observe in an assessment centre with any precision.

CODING AND CLASSIFYING BEHAVIOURS

Up to this point the research has been exclusively concerned with gathering information on what incumbents do (task analysis) and how they behave when they perform well or less well (performance). Before going on to collect more quantified data, we need to go through the step of classifying the behaviour.

Inevitably this is a somewhat subjective process. On the one hand, you do not wish to miss identifying what may be truly unique about a particular job. On the other, many professional and managerial jobs can be reliably classified under a fairly limited set of criteria. The basic approach is to identify the behaviour, skill, competency, attitude or whatever that underpins the performance of a task. The example in Figure 3.2 will illustrate the process.

This kind of classification is rarely completely original. Most analysts will be working within a framework that they have acquired through study or training. The objective is to collect examples of how the criterion is exhibited in a particular job, which can be used later in composing a questionnaire.

Although it is possible to get some idea of the importance of the various criteria by doing a frequency count of the interview transcripts, it is generally not enough to refine the selection of the final criteria to go into an assessment centre. The next step in the analysis is to generate more quantitative data.

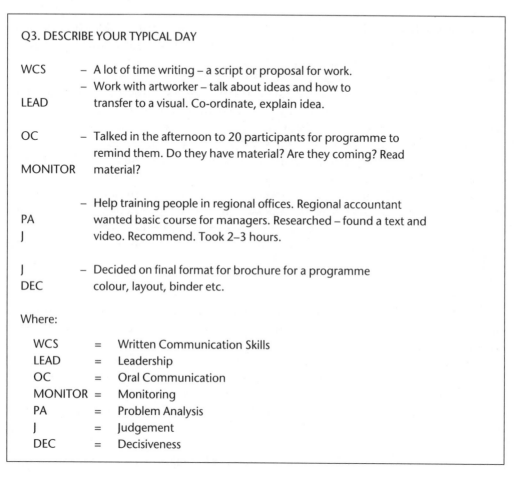

Q3. DESCRIBE YOUR TYPICAL DAY

WCS   – A lot of time writing – a script or proposal for work.
             – Work with artworker – talk about ideas and how to
LEAD   transfer to a visual. Co-ordinate, explain idea.

OC   – Talked in the afternoon to 20 participants for programme to
                remind them. Do they have material? Are they coming? Read
MONITOR   material?

             – Help training people in regional offices. Regional accountant
PA   wanted basic course for managers. Researched – found a text and
J   video. Recommend. Took 2–3 hours.

J   – Decided on final format for brochure for a programme
DEC   colour, layout, binder etc.

Where:

WCS	=	Written Communication Skills
LEAD	=	Leadership
OC	=	Oral Communication
MONITOR	=	Monitoring
PA	=	Problem Analysis
J	=	Judgement
DEC	=	Decisiveness

Figure 3.2   Example of an interview transcript

QUESTIONNAIRES

There are two types of questionnaire that can be developed to give further detail in a job analysis: a job activity questionnaire and a behavioural criteria questionnaire.

Job activity questionnaires

Job activity questionnaires are generally only used when you cannot interview enough incumbents to obtain a representative sample of their views. Frequently this will happen when a company employs similar kinds of staff doing much the same kind of work in widely dispersed geographical locations. The objective is not to gather new data but to expand, validate and quantify what you already have, although one should never overlook the possibility that the same job title may have significantly different job content. If that is found to be the case, a separate job analysis should be considered.

The questionnaires are constructed by listing all activities mentioned by at least two interviewees, then coding each statement by the criterion it appears to be related to and/or the exercise category that relates to it. If no such relationship can be established, the activity statement is discounted.

Respondents are then asked to rate these activities on a number of different scales. The most common scales are 'frequency of use' and 'importance'. Others that can be used, depending on the likely outcome, are the degree of difficulty experienced in performing the task or the degree of difficulty experienced in learning the task.

While it is rare to ask individuals to identify themselves, there is a need for a certain amount of biographical data so that spurious results can be avoided. For example, if the total population of, say, supervisors is responding to the questionnaire, one can code the respondents by length of service in the job and by previous skill group. Someone who has only a few weeks' experience and who doesn't understand the technical complexities may not understand how important an activity is and may therefore be discounted.

The outcome of the questionnaire is to identify those aspects of the job task that are both sufficiently frequent and sufficiently important to warrant inclusion in the assessment centre. Because all tasks are pre-coded to relate to exercise type and criteria you should also have a strong indication of the criteria that are most necessary for successful job performance and a good indication of the exercises needed.

Behavioural criteria questionnaires

Organisational constraints normally dictate that it will not be possible to interview all managers who are subject experts when critical incident or repertory grid interviews are being conducted. As already indicated, a relatively small number of such interviews can reveal very substantial and rich data. The objective of the behavioural criteria questionnaire is again to quantify what you already have, rather than search for new data. Nevertheless, one should not overlook the possibility that the interview sample could be skewed one way or the other.

The questionnaire construction is rather the opposite of the job activity questionnaire. The criteria that have been identified by classifying and coding interview transcripts are listed together with their definition. Often they are accompanied by a thumbnail sketch which illustrates the use of the criterion in a typical task application. For example:

Criterion title:	Independence
Criterion definition:	Taking actions based on own convictions rather than through a desire to please other people.
Criterion desriptive statement:	Each director is a functional specialist as well as having a general management role. Often, knowledge in this speciality may result in the generation of ideas for action which may be unique, possibly unpopular, and will have to be debated actively. How important is it to the effectiveness of a director that the incumbent press these ideas against the tide of prevailing opinion?

Respondents are then asked to rate their response on a scale of say 1 to 5. Alternatively the criteria are grouped together in some logical fashion and respondents are asked to rank order them in terms of importance for successful job functioning. More often than not we would ask respondents to identify the 8 to 12 criteria they consider to be most important – not necessarily in rank order.

DECIDING WHICH CRITERIA TO INCLUDE

The final part of doing a job analysis is to decide, on the basis of the available evidence, which criteria should be included at which part of a selection process and what simulations could be used in an assessment centre.

Many people overlook the opportunity to improve the total selection system by, for example, introducing criterion-based interviews into the 'milk round', re-designing application forms to highlight specific bio-data or using 'trade tests' for appropriate disciplines. With development centres in mind, much thought needs to be given to how people are selected to attend. In this case real job performance which is criterion-specific can be taken into account. Finally, the whole of a selection process should be integrated into one. Many graduate selection centres are guilty of repeating parts of the selection decision when perfectly competent data have already been gathered at an earlier stage of the process, for example, at a milk-round interview.

In deciding which criteria to include and which to exclude in an event, there are a number of complicated statistical rules that can be applied. In reality what we are trying to do is to have a manageable process in an assessment centre. Unless you have infinite time and resource, you are aiming to assess 8 to 12 of the most important criteria at least twice, preferably three times, in a variety of different situations over the course of one to two days.

Gaugler and Thornton (1989) demonstrated that the accuracy of rating or classifying declines when the number of categories is increased. They go on to recommend no more than six as the maximum number that assessors can actually make use of.

To reach that 8 to 12 most important criteria, a common-sense cut-off point is where at least half of the job content experts see the criterion as important for job success.

The next most important question is how observable the criterion is in an assessment centre context. One has to ask how easy it is to observe criteria like personal or subordinate development. Both of these criteria are more likely to be unearthed by skilled interviewing because they take more time than a one-hour simulation to demonstrate. Even so they may be quite important. Finally one needs to consider the degree to which a criterion is specifically developed on the job. If it can be developed on the job with relatively light training input it seems redundant to use the criterion in an assessment centre, particularly for selection or promotion. Oral communication and specifically oral presentation is a case in point. This criterion features in a large number of senior manager assessment centres, yet the techniques can be acquired in a one- or two-day course. You also need to ask whether this skill, body of knowledge or interest got Mr or Ms X to where they are today or whether it was working for a pharmaceutical company that gave them an interest in clinical pharmacology?

In short, deciding which criteria to finally select in an assessment centre is driven by practical considerations as much as by theoretical rules. The practical rules of thumb are:

- Include a criterion if at least half of the experts see it as important.
- Include a criterion if it is amenable to observation in a specific context or simulation, but not otherwise.
- Consider excluding criteria that can easily be learned.

Who to involve in the job analysis

Ideally you should include all job incumbents and all of their managers in the job analysis. Very few organisations are willing to make available significant parts of their managerial population, so the answer is to get a representative sample to interview and observe. Questionnaires are usually not a problem and the response rate is high.

- Representative means what it says. If the organisation is looking to recruit graduates into, say, 14 different functions then all 14 parts of the organisation need to be involved. Equally, to allow for different local cultures, samples should include all major regions or different manufacturing locations.
- Apart from any question of statistical validity, one must also bear in mind the opportunity for involvement of as many people at as many different levels as can practically be arranged. This pays dividends later when, among other things, you come to recruit assessors.
- Achieving a suitable sample size. When you arrive at the smallest reasonable organisational unit – that is, these people, in that discipline, at this location – the following is a good rule of thumb:

Size of population	Size of sample
1–10	80–100%
11–20	50–80%
21–50	30–50%
51–100	20–30%
100+	10–20%

Another important question is who should conduct the job analysis. Many readers may feel that they have sufficient experience of analytical techniques to go ahead and do it themselves. While we have a natural interest in arguing against this approach, we would strongly recommend the use of consultants in conducting the job analysis. The kind of techniques that are familiar to many human resource professionals are not relevant here. Consultants should bring with them experience of the techniques, broad knowledge of management competency and independence. If you are likely to hire consultants, you should establish that they have specific knowledge of job analysis techniques that apply to assessment centres.

Common queries about job analysis

The primary argument for using assessment centres is that they are one of the selection methods with the highest levels of predictive validity. However, this is only true if you can show that the criteria assessed are job-relevant and you simply cannot demonstrate this effectively unless a job analysis has been conducted in the first place. Nonetheless, there are a number of objections and queries that are often raised in relation to job analysis.

USING A GENERIC MODEL

It is argued that there are a large number of existing models of managerial behaviour. Among the better known are Boyatzis' Competent Manager (1982), the DDI Dimensions and the

MCI Competence Model (1987), which is now managed by the Management Standards Centre. If so much is already known about the competencies of managers, it is argued, why reinvent the wheel?

The answer is actually fairly straightforward. The MCI Competence Model, for example, has 13 dimensions clustered into four units. No one can deny that these aspects of personal behaviour are significant in most management jobs, but the question is which particular aspects of personal competence are the most significant to function well in a particular job. The answer will be very different for the target job of production manager at a chemical plant compared with that of a marketing manager in an Fast Moving Consumer Goods environment.

In short, we need a sense of priorities to understand which criteria are more or less relevant to success and we need to understand the context to construct appropriate selection methods, including simulations that reflect the nature of the task.

THE CROWN PRINCE SYNDROME

Some critics suggest that, by studying the current job incumbents, all you do is perpetuate the breed that you already have. While the concern about the 'crown prince syndrome' should be recognised and is worth further research, we would offer these observations. Any formal job analysis is better than none at all. While there is a danger of perpetuating the breed, you do at least know what the details of the pedigree are, and this should lead to better decisions. You should also attempt to assess the likely future demands of the job role as part of the study. As the general environment surrounding a business changes there will be corresponding changes in the demands of the job. This argues for a periodic review of a job analysis and careful validation studies to ensure that the criteria initially chosen are in fact valid.

WHAT IF THE JOB DOES NOT EXIST?

All we have said so far in this chapter rests on the assumption that the target job already exists. One cannot observe or interview current job incumbents when there aren't any. To be quite clear, this is not the situation where one might have a promotion board or development centre to assess a person's potential for a current or future vacancy. We are talking here of the situation where a new job is being created.

There are two main ways in which new jobs are being created: by devolving responsibility and hence the required competencies down through a hierarchy, or by expanding responsibilities from a known base. Often the political sensitivities preclude the logical approach which would be to conduct an analysis on the job above or below and later interview future job experts. In the case of a contracting workforce, it would be difficult to gain the trust and co-operation of people who suspect that their jobs may become redundant. In the case of expansion, there are often concerns about interviewing people whose abilities may already be in question.

Notwithstanding these sensitivities, a reasonable first step can be to interview job incumbents and their managers in job roles that are close to the prospective job, either functionally relevant or at a similar job level. The next stage is to interview the normally small number of people who are 'in the know' to establish how the nature of the job may change in future. The repertory grid technique is useful here, using the existing job and the future job as the elements rather than the good and less good incumbent. In this way, it is possible to identify the likely demands of the new job with an improved degree of precision. Although this may appear only to change guesswork into informed guesswork, you do at least have the basis for subsequent validation.

While there are difficulties associated with all job analysis techniques, we have no doubt that the time and effort invested in a good piece of research pays proportionate dividends. The better the job analysis the more valid the eventual assessment centre will be. It must also be remembered that the results of a job analysis particularly in identifying job-related criteria can become a central plank of a human resource strategy as outlined in Chapter 1. The consequences of a poorly conducted analysis go far wider than merely having an assessment centre that doesn't work too well, and for this reason we always recommend that an analysis is conducted.

4 Designing the Assessment Centre Content

The content of an assessment centre consists of a set of simulation exercises, possibly supplemented by various other ingredients such as interviews and psychometrics. The core elements are the assessment centre exercises for they are the means by which a participant has the opportunity of displaying behaviour relevant to the target job.

As we saw in the previous chapter, the job analysis process will have revealed the different types of situations that are encountered by people in the target job. This information, coupled with a clear understanding of the purpose of the assessment centre and the range of criteria to be measured, will determine the precise content of the event. The purpose of the assessment centre is important because if it is for selection, the event may well be shorter and have fewer exercises than would a development centre.

General issues

The following general issues need to be considered when selecting assessment centre exercises.

JOB-RELATED EXERCISES

An exercise must be able to elicit job-related criteria in a manner befitting the demands of the target job. This means that an exercise should not only enable a participant to display certain behaviours in relation to relevant criteria, but also relate to the way in which those behaviours would be shown for this level of job. For example, it is quite common to see a criterion such as 'leadership' measured on assessment centres by the use of group discussion exercises. Despite the fact that the definition of this criterion might be very similar on different assessment centres for first-line supervisors and senior managers, the types of group discussion situations they encounter will almost certainly differ. The exercise content needs to reflect this.

PARTICIPANTS' BACKGROUND

The likely educational and cultural backgrounds of participants must be considered. If the nature of the job is such that many present job holders come from a particular educational and/or cultural background, then it would clearly be unfair to choose exercises that would require a higher educational level or would disadvantage people from that cultural background. Once again, such problems can easily be avoided, by making sure that the exercises reflect the demands of the job in question.

NUMBER OF CRITERIA

One of the most important decisions to make when designing an assessment centre is the number of criteria that the centre should attempt to assess. As we mentioned in Chapter 3, it has been commonplace for most centres to assess between eight and twelve criteria. Clearly these criteria need to be selected on the basis of their relevance and importance to the target job. However, the concerns raised in relation to 'the exercise effect' (see pp. 46–7), have led to many researchers recommending that the number of criteria being assessed within each exercise and across the centre as a whole should be reduced, so that assessors do not suffer from 'cognitive overload'. So what constitutes a reasonable number of criteria?

Ahmed et al. (1997) reported on the exercise design principles followed by a group of experienced practitioners, who aimed to measure three dimensions (criteria) and certainly no more than five per exercise, in order to increase the likelihood of obtaining an accurate assessment of performance. Lievens (1998) in a review of factors that improve construct validity cited over 21 research studies dating between 1976 to 1997, four of which focused on the question of criteria. He observed that the research evidence concurred with Gaugler and Thornton (1989), who had recommended that the number of criteria to be evaluated should be limited to no more than six.

These are of course valid points, but it is evident that none of the research makes a critical distinction between the traditional use of assessment centres for selection and those used for development (development centres). A paper by Henderson et al. (1995), which reviewed ICL's graduate recruitment process, described how they reduced the number of criteria assessed from fourteen to five generic ones, plus one which was functionally specific, for example accountancy knowledge for the finance function. The five were considered as absolute 'must-haves', namely problem solving, interpersonal skills, communication, motivation and commercial awareness. However, each one contained quite large indicative skill-sets, for example interpersonal skills embraced creativity, initiative, judgement, negotiation, integrity, empathy, persuasiveness and assertiveness. Needless to say the underlying use of such a diverse range of sub-factors only disguises the fact that many traits are being assessed within the assessment centre. This problem is well illustrated when considering the situation from a developmental perspective. For example, the idea that a competency (criterion) such as communication includes both listening and presentational skills is not helpful. In general, where there is a problem, it is that good talkers aren't always attentive to others. Correspondingly, people who are good listeners frequently find it difficult to assert their point of view in a group, so it would be inappropriate, or at best imprecise, to say that both people have a communication problem. In development centres one frequently finds more criteria or competencies are being used, because the target is to help people develop in the round and to fully understand the nature of the issues to be addressed.

WEIGHTING CRITERIA

Another issue is ensuring that sufficient emphasis is given to those criteria which emerged as most important for success in the target job. An appropriate mix of exercises should be selected to give due weighting to the most important criteria. For example, if 'oral communication' is viewed as a much more important job requirement than say 'written communication', then there should be more exercises which would allow the participant to display the more important criterion.

ESTABLISHING THE RIGHT MIX OF EXERCISES

It is particularly important to establish the right mix of exercises in two different ways. Firstly, in order to be confident about a participant's ability to display behaviour relating to a particular criterion, you should usually aim to gather evidence on that criterion from three or more different exercises. Occasionally you may be able to use only one or two measures for a much less important criterion. Secondly, it isn't just how many different exercises measure a criterion, but the fact that people are usually expected to operate in a range of different situations. The content of the assessment centre needs to reflect those different scenarios. In simple terms we find ourselves working in three different contexts:

- In groups.
- One-to-one.
- Working on our own.

The balance of time and the nature of the tasks undertaken in these areas must be reflected in the exercise content of the assessment centre.

PRACTICAL CONSTRAINTS OF TIME AND RESOURCES

Clearly the number and type of exercises will have a significant impact on the duration of the assessment centre and the workload for all involved, particularly assessors. It is therefore important to select the minimum number of exercises required to provide an adequate amount of valid and reliable data. It is generally desirable to gather evidence on each criterion from at least three different exercises, so this will influence the choice of exercises. The duration of each exercise will need to be considered in relation to the total time available for assessment. As a result, it might be necessary to favour a number of shorter exercises instead of one long exercise.

The availability of resources will also influence your choice. For example, one-to-one exercises which require the use of roleplayers make additional heavy demands on assessment centres. Whilst the availability of such resources should be viewed as a secondary consideration when compared with the need to simulate the demands of the job, we have to take a practical view about what is feasible.

The criteria–exercise matrix

Once the job analysis has been carried out and the above issues recognised, the next step is to select a set of exercises that will adequately measure the criteria required for effective job performance. A useful document at this particular stage of the design process is one which shows the criteria that will apply to each exercise. This document is often referred to as a criteria–exercise matrix, an example of which is given in Figure 4.1.

As can be seen in this example, there are eight criteria being assessed across a range of five exercises and an interview. Each criterion is being assessed four times and each exercise is assessing between five and six of the criteria, with the interview covering four; this ensures a balanced spread of emphasis and would suggest that no single exercise is more significant than the others.

Criteria	Exercise					
	Co-operative Group Discussion	Competitive Group Discussion	Performance Interview Roleplay	Written Analysis Exercise	In-Basket	Interview
Planning and Organising		*	*	*	*	
Problem Analysis	*	*		*	*	
Judgement	*			*	*	*
Decisiveness		*	*	*	*	
Initiative	*	*	*			*
Leadership	*	*	*			*
Interpersonal Sensitivity	*		*	*	*	
Persuasive Oral Communication	*	*	*			*

Figure 4.1   Criteria–exercise matrix

The exercise effect

Before we review the type of exercises that often feature in assessment centres, it is worth examining what has been referred to as 'the exercise effect'. It is common practice on assessment centres to look at the performance of an individual on each criterion across a range of exercises, as depicted by a criteria–exercise matrix. This is based upon the expectation that the ratings on a given criterion should correlate across exercises more closely (convergent validity) than the ratings of different criteria within an exercise (discriminant validity). The research findings of Sackett and Dreher (1982) and Robertson et al. (1987) amongst others, however, demonstrate that within-exercise ratings of different criteria correlate more closely than across-exercise ratings for the same criterion. Further research throughout the 1990s (Schneider and Schmitt, 1992, Kleinmann et al., 1996, Russell and Domm, 1995, Lievens, 1998 and others) continues to support this view. Indeed, Robertson et al. (1987) point out that the 'halo effect' may be one explanation for why assessors give consistent ratings within exercises. They also point out that the assessor rating procedure might influence the results of such research studies. This is because the results from within an exercise would always be generated from a single assessor, whilst ratings across exercises are nearly always generated by a number of different assessors. Thus one possible explanation for the lower correlations across exercises could be low inter-rater reliability, which may in turn reflect on the quality of the assessor training.

Woodruffe (2000) offers another explanation for these findings, based on the fact that participants might differ in familiarity with the different exercise settings. We are inclined to go even further and suggest that there would seem to be no reason why participants should not display variable ability with a criterion across different exercise settings. After all, the demands for a criterion such as planning and organising can vary quite considerably in quality and quantity when comparing its application in an in-basket exercise with that in a group discussion exercise, and yet the underlying trait remains the same. Whatever the view on this matter, Woodruffe (2000) makes the important point that dispensing with criteria in favour of exercises alone is not really an option in assessment centre design. For without the ability to refer to specific criteria as the basis of management competence, it is difficult to provide constructive and meaningful feedback about individual performance.

In order to attempt to mitigate the possible impact of 'the exercise effect', and to improve the construct validity of assessment centres, Lievens (1998) has produced a practical list of recommendations that assessment centre designers would be advised to consider.

Criteria
- Use a small number of criteria, especially when assessment centres are conducted for hiring purposes.
- Choose criteria which are conceptually distinct (that is, which are relatively unrelated to each other).
- Define the criteria in a concrete and job-related way.

Assessors
- Psychologists should play a key role in assessor teams (for example, as a coach of line manager assessors).
- Focus on the quality of the training provided to assessors (instead of the length of the training).
- Give more emphasis to 'frame of reference' training (see Chapter 6) and ensure assessor familiarity with criteria, performance levels and consistent categorisation.

Situational exercises
- Try to develop exercises which generate a large amount of criterion-related participant behaviour and avoid exercises which elicit behaviours relevant to too many criteria.
- Train roleplayers to actively elicit criterion-related participant behaviour and try to standardise their performance in order to limit exercise variance.
- Reveal the criteria (and related behaviours) to participants, especially when running development centres.

Systematic observation, evaluation and integration procedures
- Provide assessors with an observational aid, such as a behavioural checklist, with 6–12 *key* behaviours for each criterion to be observed in each exercise; enhance assessor understanding by grouping behaviours in natural clusters.
- Use a rotation system to minimise rating bias. For example, try to ensure each assessor observes each participant only once. Seek the even mixing of participants within exercises and the pairing of assessors when required.

In any event, we must leave this debate in the hands of the academics, for although such findings have prompted Herriott (1986) to conclude that the rationale of rating by trait is unsound, as yet no definitive conclusion has been reached.

In order to interpret the criteria–exercise matrix in Figure 4.1 more readily, it is necessary to understand the types of exercise that are often included in an assessment centre.

Types of exercise

As already mentioned, the context of our working circumstances can be broken down to the three broad areas: working alone, with others one-to-one and working in groups. Traditionally, assessments have consisted of separate exercises that reflect these broad areas of management activity and those individual exercises are reviewed below. It is also worth restating that assessment centre exercises, when they are well designed, are specifically aimed at eliciting criterion-related behaviour, unlike say, the frequently but inappropriately used training activities such as 'Desert Survival'. We now review the specific exercises within these broad areas.

GROUP DISCUSSION EXERCISES

Group discussion exercises can take several forms but there are two main parameters by which they can be classified. Firstly, there is the purpose/type of meeting, which usually means choosing between a co-operative or competitive setting. Co-operative group discussion meetings usually have a problem-solving flavour about them, in that participants are required to analyse a set of information and to come up with recommendations within an allotted timeframe. Such exercises are often referred to as 'non-assigned roles' because participants are all given the same information and no one is assigned any particular role.

A competitive group discussion is the alternative type of meeting in which participants are required to persuade and negotiate in order to achieve the best deal they can. In this type of exercise, participants usually receive some common information as well as information that is exclusive to them. They then need to sell a particular viewpoint to the other team members with whom they are usually competing for limited resources. This competitive type of exercise is often referred to as an 'assigned role', since each participant has been tasked with an individual assignment.

An important aspect of this type of exercise is that the brief usually stipulates a twofold objective: to get the best deal they can, whilst *also* assisting the group to make the best decision. This provides an interesting challenge to most participants and allows them to display a wide range of possible behaviours. For example, some participants go out to win at all costs, whilst others tend to capitulate too early or concede to others' arguments.

The second parameter to consider when selecting group discussion exercises is whether or not to assign the role of leader. This decision is usually influenced by whether you are wishing to assess the quality of leadership or not. If you are, then you should arrange for each participant to be required to lead the group for part of the group discussion meeting. This might best be achieved by having the group tackle a number of smaller problems and each participant can be leader for one of the problems. The advantages of this approach are that each person is forced to act as leader so that their behaviour can be noted and it is less likely that any one person will dominate the group and prevent other participants from being observed.

Deciding whether to have a group discussion exercise, or choosing which type to have, is naturally going to be influenced by the nature and demands of the target job. Other factors may also influence the decision. For example, it is not uncommon for assessors to want an opportunity to see most, if not all, of the participants together at once. This, of course, is insufficient reason in itself for including a group discussion exercise. Another reason for including a group discussion exercise may be because the participants expect it. Again this is insufficient reason in itself, but if it contributes to the 'face-validity' of the event in the eyes of the participants, as well as providing meaningful data, then it adds to the justification.

Yet another factor to be considered with group discussion exercises is the size of the group. Clearly this will be affected by the number of participants but in general group sizes are best kept to between four and six. This allows each participant a reasonable amount of 'air time', that is, an average of about 10 to 15 minutes each, for a session of 45 to 60 minutes' duration. It also allows for the rotation of the leadership role as mentioned earlier.

If it is possible to include more than one group discussion exercise on the assessment centre, then it is worth considering a mix such as a six-person leaderless assigned-role exercise and a four-person non-assigned role with rotating leadership. This mix provides the opportunity to observe participants in different group discussion situations. Assessors can then form a view about participants' abilities in co-operative and competitive situations, when they are leading or not, and how they perform in groups of different sizes. An extract example of a brief for one of the participants in an assigned role group discussion is given in Figure 4.2.

Finally, it is interesting to note that the group discussion exercise is not only one of the most popular exercises to be included on an assessment centre, but is also seen as one of the most influential. One reason for this popularity is due to the fact that group discussion exercises tend to generate high inter-rater reliability scores of about .69 to .99 (Gatewood et al., 1990). This means that different assessors generally produce consistent ratings when observing the same participant in group discussion exercises. This enables assessors to develop confidence in the ability of their colleagues to comment on participants who they themselves have not observed.

ORAL PRESENTATION

An oral presentation might also be viewed as a form of group process, but one where the participant has a specific and highly visible role. It is of course also possible for the oral presentation to be run as a one-to-one session, although in this case it is likely to be less formal and might not even include the use of visual aids.

In an oral presentation exercise the participant is asked to prepare for and make a presentation. The level of formality and the nature of the presentation will be determined by the demands of the target job. It is not uncommon therefore to include such a presentation in assessment centres where participants are being assessed in relation to jobs in sales, marketing or training. The exercise can also elicit other important criteria, depending on the topic on which people are expected to present.

INTERVIEW SIMULATION EXERCISES

These exercises simulate one-to-one interactions between a roleplayer in the guise of a customer, colleague, boss or subordinate and the participant in the target job-role. It should be emphasised that, although the participant is asked to presume they are in the target job-role, they are *not* asked to roleplay. Indeed it is essential that the participant appreciates the

---

SELTEC MANAGEMENT MEETING

Introduction

This exercise involves each participant assuming one of six managerial roles. These are: Personnel Manager, Research and Development Manager, Production Manager, Sales and Marketing Manager, Information and Systems Manager and Finance Manager.

Exercise Duration

Once the participants have been assigned their roles they have 15 minutes to read through and make any relevant notes concerning the brief and the company profile. The group discussion will then commence and should continue for approximately one hour.

Brief for the Personnel Manager

You are the Personnel Manager within Seltec Limited, a small but highly innovative and successful electronics company. In fact the company has recently won a 'Leadership in Europe' award worth £15 000. This followed the news that Seltec has been acquired by Americorp, a major US multi-national.

As a sign of recognition for the award, Americorp has decided to match this figure with a further £15 000. This money is to be used at the discretion of Seltec's management, the only qualification being that the combined sum be spent on special projects and/or capital improvements.

A meeting has been arranged to consider how the combined figure of £30 000 is to be used. The meeting will be attended by Seltec's departmental managers and one hour has been scheduled for its completion. Each manager has his/her own uses for the money, but if a mutually agreed allocation cannot be reached by the end of the meeting then the money will be distributed at the discretion of the US organisation, in which case Seltec's allocation may be minimal.

You have had discussions with various members of your department, and have compiled a number of issues that you may wish to raise during the meeting. These are detailed below for you to consider. You do not have to raise all the issues outlined.

Use the time given to read through and make any notes on the issues concerning your department. The meeting will then commence.

Your task is to construct and present strong arguments in favour of the issues that you wish to raise, and to maximise the allocation for your department, while at the same time assisting with the best overall allocation of the available funds.

Your Brief

Within the Personnel department there is a general feeling that demographic changes will mean that it is increasingly important to retain and develop existing staff. The issues you can raise reflect concerns about turnover and utilisation of present human resources.

A You are particularly concerned about the rise in staff turnover that has been experienced over the past year or so. Although it is true to say that job mobility within the electronics industry generally has increased this is of little comfort when faced with ever higher recruitment costs (these are currently around £3000 for each position). In an attempt to identify where problems may exist a Job Satisfaction survey has been proposed. The intention is to be in a position to take action to improve the situation before it adversely affects turnover. Use of a consultancy to carry out such a survey for the whole organisation would cost approximately £5000.

Figure 4.2   Extract from an assigned role group discussion

need to be themselves and act as he or she would, if they were put in that role, otherwise assessors will not be able to observe their true behaviour. The only roleplaying in this type of exercise is that of the roleplayer who is usually either one of the assessors or an additional resource who has been trained specifically for this purpose (see Chapter 6).

The usual format for this type of exercise is to give the participant a detailed brief with general background information, a description of a particular situation and some notes about the person they are about to meet. They then have a period of time to digest the information and prepare for the meeting which is of a fixed duration.

The success of these exercises is highly dependent on the quality of the performance of the roleplayer(s), particularly as they need to be convincing, credible and most important of all, consistent in their approach. It is therefore essential that they are furnished with a well-written brief which describes their character's personality, personal history and the background to the scenario. As Boddy (2002) points out, failure to do this may lead the roleplayer to fill the vacuum with a character of their own creation, whose responses may deviate from what is required. The roleplayers' brief needs to include scripted guidelines to help them respond to key stages of the interaction, particularly when it comes to 'testing' participants' ability to handle specific challenges within the exercise. However, Boddy rightly points out that it is quite inappropriate to give roleplayers a rigid script, which they must adhere to, as this would provide too much of an artificial constraint. Our approach has always been to provide scripted guidelines, with the overriding instruction to the roleplayers that their behaviour must be guided by the behaviour presented to them by the participant.

The range of situations to which an interview simulation can be applied is quite varied. For example they can encompass a sales visit, a negotiation, a customer-service visit, a performance review meeting, a disciplinary review, a selection interview, a counselling session and so on. Indeed the interview simulation is a rich and powerful exercise, which is often viewed by assessors as providing a significant input to a participant's overall performance on an assessment centre.

FACT-FIND AND DECISION-MAKING EXERCISES

This is yet another type of one-to-one exercise. It is different to the interview simulation in that the emphasis is not so much on the behavioural interaction between the participant and roleplayer, but is more a test of the participant's analytical skills. In this type of exercise the roleplayer is often referred to as a resource-person, because they are in possession of a large amount of data and it is the participant's task to gather relevant information in order to make a decision and recommendation about a particular situation.

The format for this type of exercise might be as follows. The participant is given a very brief outline description about an incident and is told to prepare questions to put to the resource person. They are then allowed to question the resource person for a fixed period, at the end of which they must make a decision and appropriate recommendation. Once they have declared their decision, the resource person questions them to test the soundness of their arguments and their level of resolve. This provides an excellent opportunity to observe an individual's judgement, decisiveness and tenacity.

This type of exercise is very good at establishing how effectively a participant can 'think on his/her feet' and can reason with words and as such is particularly good at assessing skills in the areas of problem-solving and decision-making. An example of the instructions and a typical scenario for this type of exercise is given in Figure 4.3.

INSTRUCTIONS FOR THE PARTICIPANT

This exercise helps to determine your ability to research information, to make decisions and present those decisions. Following these instructions is a short description of a situation requiring investigation and recommendation. You are to take the role of a Director who has been asked to advise on this particular matter.

To enable you to reach your decision, a Resource Person will answer any questions you wish to ask about the situation. He/she has a considerable amount of information which you can obtain by asking specific questions. If you ask general questions you will be advised to make them more specific.

The Resource Person is an impartial outsider in this exercise and has no part in this situation. They represent no one in the organisation.

You will have 5 minutes to read 'The Situation' overleaf and to prepare questions. Then you will have 15 minutes to ask all the questions you wish, to consider the information, and to arrive at your decision. You will then be asked to make a formal presentation, stating your decision and giving in detail your reasons for it. The Resource Person will then question you on your decision.

Schedule

5 mins	Read the brief and prepare your questions.
15 mins	Interview the Resource Person to obtain information you require to enable you to make the decision. You may terminate the interview before the end of the 15 minutes if you so wish. Before the end of the time period, you should review the data you have collected, arrive at a decision, and prepare to present your decision and the reasoning behind it to the Resource Person.
5 mins	Present your decision and the reasons behind it.
10 mins	Resource Person questions you regarding your decision.

Do you have any questions?
Do not turn over until you are told to do so.

THE SITUATION

You are the newly appointed Production Director for Deltron Engineering and you have just been asked by David Palmer to make your first major decision, which is whether or not to close down the Nottingham plant.

Figure 4.3   An example of a fact-find exercise

IN-BASKET EXERCISES

The in-basket or in-tray exercise is perhaps the best known type of written exercise. The participant is asked to handle a typical pile of papers that simulate what would be encountered by someone in the target job. These papers might include letters, internal memos, reports, 'junk mail' and so on. The task for the participant is to sort through the items, determining priorities, deciding what can be delegated and to whom, and deciding how to action items – for example by writing letters, notes and planning meetings, phone calls and so on. In-basket exercises can vary in their length and duration. We have come across in-baskets that range from 10 to 40 items and last from one to three hours. As always the size and scope of this exercise should reflect the demands of the target job, for it is quite possible to have a large number of relatively simple items or a small number of more complex items. An example of the instructions is given in Figure 4.4.

OBJECTIVE

The exercise is designed to give participants an opportunity to develop skills in personal organisation and management. The media are a fictitious 'in-basket' and subsequent performance evaluation. Feedback is usually by a colleague/senior manager within the client organisation.

INSTRUCTIONS FOR THE PARTICIPANT

After an initial briefing you will work privately on the in-basket exercise.

THE SITUATION

For the next 1.5 hours you are to assume the role of Jay Barnard who has been made acting General Manager of Wholesome Foods Ltd. The appointment follows the shock announcement that Steve Dryden, the previous General Manager, has been taken seriously ill. Although his life is not in danger he is likely to be absent indefinitely, with early retirement a possibility.

Today is Sunday 1 June. Your appointment has coincided with the annual Corporate Strategy meeting that is to commence this evening in Edinburgh. Your attendance at this meeting is imperative, and it is due to take the whole of the coming week. You have gone into the office today to ensure that all runs smoothly during your absence. This is the first chance that you have had to take stock of the matters arising at Wholesome Foods Ltd.

It is now 1 p.m., you must leave the office by 2.30 p.m. in order to fly to Edinburgh in time for the Managing Director's opening address. While at the meeting there will not be any opportunity to contact your staff at Wholesome Foods.

THE COMPANY

Wholesome Foods Ltd is part of the Peterson-Adams Group which also includes The Sunrise Bakery and Bulmans Confectionery and Sweets. Wholesome Foods specialise in ready-made meals and was one of the first companies to enter this section of the food market. The products are primarily sold through retail outlets, although business through 'trade outlets' (for example, hotels, cafes, company canteens) is increasing.

The Company has three lines of ready-made meals: Classic Choice, Oriental Choice and Natural Choice. Each line has five or six varieties. The majority of the Company's retail outlets are small chains which also deal with Sunrise and Bulmans products.

THE IN-BASKET

The material in your in-basket is as left by Steve Dryden earlier in the week, with some additions from Marion Carlisle, the secretary.

Write action to be taken either on each item or clip a note (stationery provided) to the relevant item.

You can write notes, memos, letters, plan meetings, make decisions, request information and so on.

As you will not be back in the office until Monday 9 June and are not contactable in the interim, you must make sure that your instructions for each of the items are clear.

You should also ensure you leave the in-basket in the state you expect Marion to find it when she comes in to the office on Monday 2 June.

Figure 4.4   Extract from an in-basket exercise

One of the attractions of the in-basket as an exercise is that it nicely depicts the classic management challenge of multi-tasking. In other words the sheer variation of issues within the in-basket simulates the often-stated fact that managers usually spend an average of nine minutes on each task during the course of a working day (Mintzberg, 1973). Typically, therefore, in-baskets cover issues as diverse as customer complaints, sales opportunities, internal conflicts, requests for leave, recruitment issues, production levels, financial performance and so on.

The main skill areas measured by an in-basket are planning and organising, prioritising, decision-making and delegating. It is of course also possible to measure written communication skills as well as the level of interpersonal sensitivity employed. This is particularly important in jobs that necessitate handling difficult matters in writing.

Traditional in-basket exercises are normally set as open-ended tasks for the participant to deal with the issues in any manner they see fit. In that way it is a 'pure' assessment of the ability to juggle with competing priorities, make links between items that are relevant to a common point and put actions in place. In an effort to standardise the marking task for the assessor, a number of publishers structure some elements of the task for the participant, so that the exercise falls into distinct phases. The first phase usually asks the participant to rank order the items in priority, using some sort of guideline. This task then enables the assessor to compare their response with a model answer that has been worked out in advance, count the number of correct and incorrect responses and derive a score accordingly. The second phase might state a link between two or three items, which the participant has to write a summary of, and the third might state that a specific item requires an immediate action in a short timeframe. There are many arguments for and against such structured experiences. Those for the structure tend to argue from psychometric principles (fo example, Hennessy et al., 1998). Those against tend to argue that you don't get a structure given to you in real life (except what you develop) and that observing authentic participant behaviour is a key principle of design (for example, Schneider and Schmitt, 1992).

In addition to the classic paper-based in-basket exercise, we have seen attempts to develop the electronic equivalent, using the medium of e-mail. Given that most contemporary office work includes the use of e-mail, it is fitting that the traditional paper-based in-tray or in-basket exercise within an assessment centre should start to be superseded by e-mail versions which are now commercially available. The use of such versions affords several benefits:

- Firstly, participants are assessed in a manner that is consistent with the environment in which they will operate, using the technology that is commonplace in most organisations. This heightens face validity while at the same time avoiding the impression that the organisation is stuck in the Dickensian era.
- Secondly, the use of such technology ensures very consistent administration and therefore contributes to the fairness of the exercise. In common with modern psychometric instruments, all the information is generated on-screen, instructions are completely standardised and once you have started, the timing is controlled by the clock in the PC. Designers of these systems go to some lengths to eliminate potential difficulties like users being more or less familiar with different e-mail platforms, but some concerns remain. As with any new technology, the challenges change with the introduction of new processes.
- Thirdly, the use of such technology inevitably makes the marking quicker and simpler through a degree of automation. For example, because computers can easily record large

amounts of fine detail, it is possible to generate a record of how often a person visits any particular item, whether they change the response later on and see how they may visit a sequence of items, from which it can be inferred that they have established a link.

• It is also possible to semi-automate the process by which outputs can be created, commenting on the participant's performance on the exercise. This can be used during the assessor discussion and for subsequent feedback. However, it is important to appreciate that as things stand, the assessor (some would say 'thankfully') still has to exercise a substantial degree of judgement over the assessment, so the 'Holy Grail' of totally automated scoring is still some way off.

ANALYSIS EXERCISES

Analysis exercises require the participant to review a certain amount of information which may be presented in a verbal and/or numerical form and to reach logical conclusions. Once again the content and duration of the exercise should reflect the likely demands of the target job. Participants may receive two to three pages of text, possibly accompanied by tables and/or graphs (depending on the type of job) and could be allowed one to two hours to assimilate the information and write a report with recommendations.

Such exercises reveal a participant's analytical skills, namely problem-solving and decision-making. They also act as a good indicator of written communication skill and the ability to organise and structure their work. It is possible to link an analysis exercise to a group discussion exercise and/or an oral presentation if it is felt useful to do so. The idea of whether to link exercises or not is discussed in further detail in the next section.

SCHEDULING EXERCISES

Scheduling exercises require the participant to plan the effective utilisation of activities and resources. For example, a foreman might be asked to schedule the work for a series of operators on a shift. Given a set of constraints, including the requirement to meet some form of deadline, there are usually only a few viable solutions and it is customary to compare a participant's recommended solution with a 'model answer'. The main purpose of such exercises is to be able to assess a participant's analysis, decision-making, and planning and organising abilities. A particular example of this type of exercise was mentioned by Bedford (1987) who described how the Ontario Provincial Police Academy simulate a high-speed car chase and require participants to make a series of quick decisions, each of which is recorded and marked.

Variations in exercise design

Assessment centres usually comprise a series of unrelated exercises, notwithstanding the fact that they should all have job relevance. This does raise the question of context: should the content of any or all of the exercises be actual extracts from the target job and the organisation? Whilst it is usually recognised as desirable to simulate the job demands as accurately as possible, the exercise content must give all participants an equal opportunity of performing to the best of their ability. In particular, job or organisational knowledge, such as in-house jargon, should not be allowed to influence the participant's ability to perform against the relevant criteria. Adams (1987) suggests that scenarios should be chosen which will be equally familiar or unfamiliar to all participants. She proposes that this can be achieved by a rule of thumb, which is to set the context within the organisation for external participants and outside the organisation for internal participants. This is why many assessment centres exercises are set in the context of a fictional organisation, similar, but not identical, to the organisation in question. In this manner participants are not disadvantaged for any lack of knowledge, nor are they so likely to make unsubstantiated assumptions about the organisation's practices and procedures.

Returning to the question of whether the exercises should be linked together, there are advantages and disadvantages. The advantages of linked exercises are that the expanded nature of the exercise provides a level of continuity that may achieve a greater realism when comparing the situation with the real demands of the job. McCrimmon (1993) claims that this has the effect of enhancing a participant's level of emotional commitment to their recommendations, thus impacting more powerfully on their performance in interactive situations. For example, greater emotional engagement can be achieved by linking an in-basket with an interview simulation, as McCrimmon explains: 'If the candidate has already "encountered" the subordinate in the in-tray, whose performance is later to be reviewed, there is created a greater feeling that this is "my subordinate".' As for the disadvantages, these are most apparent if a participant believes he or she has done badly on the first part of a linked exercise, in which case it may have a negative impact on how they perform in the part(s) that follow. As assessors would still be observing valid behaviour, we tend to take the view that the disadvantages are not sufficient to warrant avoiding this type of arrangement.

Indeed one of the most interesting developments of the last ten years, which is mainly due to the increasing power and availability of technical equipment, has been the development of the whole day assessment known as 'A day in the life of . . .'. To give a flavour of the event, the participant is briefed in the morning that they will have to make a presentation at the end of the day on a subject that has been developing for some while. They are told that some preliminary work has been done on the topic, which they will find in their file drawer, but that much recent correspondence on this issue is in e-mail form on the office PC. With not much more information, they are sat at a computer screen in an office that has all the normal fittings and equipment that you would expect.

During the day, various things happen in what is actually quite a standardised way. For example, an actor walks in and simply asks the participant for five minutes to discuss a concern (which has already been flagged in the e-mail traffic), the group is brought together for a business discussion on a topic that they all have peripheral information on, the phone rings, various people interrupt, e-mail traffic continues through the day and other things happen. Everything is observed and recorded in the traditional way, except that it is done through one-way mirrors. Because the observers are not physically present, the end result is something that feels like a normal day at work to the participant, during which they actually complete a number of exercises of the type that were described earlier on in this chapter.

Another variation on a theme is to use a business game simulation, often run for competing teams. These simulations usually entail running a business operation through a series of trading periods, which necessitate making various management decisions such as whether to expand, or invest, how to use resources and so on. This type of team approach is generally more valid for a development centre, since it may prove difficult to be certain of assessing each participant in a fair and equal manner as their responses during the exercise may well be affected by the performances of their team colleagues.

Developing the exercises

Given that the exercises represent the core of the assessment centre, we need to ensure they have been carefully developed and are appropriately focused on the target job. This suggests that the ideal approach is to develop bespoke exercises for each assessment centre. (There is an alternative in going for 'off-the-shelf' exercises, which we will discuss in further detail later in this chapter.)

Ahmed et al. (1997) point out that there has been surprisingly little research into the most effective ways of designing assessment centre exercises, but a review of the literature produced the following guidelines regarding exercise content:

- Tasks should reflect the most important/significant activities of the job.
- The format used to present information in exercises should be the same as that experienced in the job (for example, written/written; spoken/spoken).
- The way participants are asked to respond to exercises should match the way they would be expected to respond on the job (for example, written or spoken).
- The overall design of the centre is coherent (for example, exercises are linked).
- The tasks within each exercise are matched to the level of difficulty and complexity required in the job.
- The form which the exercises take should encourage appropriate behaviours, for example an interactive exercise to measure interpersonal sensitivity.
- The exercises should reflect the organisation's practices and culture.

The following stages represent an effective process for developing bespoke exercises.

STAGE 1: ESTABLISHING A DESIGN TEAM

External consultants or an in-house HR specialist will probably lead the design team for it is important that the process is driven by someone with appropriate expertise. Unfortunately, there are many well-intentioned individuals who think that the design of assessment centre exercises is little different to designing a training exercise or writing a case study. Whilst there is certainly some similarity, issues of equity and fairness to all likely participants and the ability of the exercise to elicit the criteria to be assessed require that the designers have a good understanding of assessment centre principles.

The design team should include line managers with good knowledge of the target job, so as to ensure that the content and nature of the exercises represent a good fit. It may be appropriate to subdivide the team and have different subgroups develop different exercises. One obvious advantage of having line managers involved in the design of exercises, is that the exercises are more likely to be accepted as relevant to the target job when their input has been sought. This in turn should ensure that both participants and assessors see the exercises as legitimate measures of potential for the target job.

STAGE 2: PRODUCE FIRST DRAFT

The design team(s) produce their first draft(s), usually in consultation with the team leader who might provide examples of typical exercises of a particular type to assist them with ideas for content and format. It is important that the design team(s) are clear about the behavioural criteria to be elicited by their exercise(s), so as to provide them with a focus during their design effort.

Further factors highlighted by Ahmed et al. (1997) that ought to be considered when evaluating ideas for exercises include:

- Importance to the job – how does it relate to the key responsibilities and outputs of the job?
- Job or criterion related – ideally there should be a balance between the two, with behaviours related to the criteria being elicited from a scenario that relates to the job.
- Practical constraints – sometimes ideas are rejected because they cannot be practically incorporated into the exercise design due to time or technical constraints.
- Levels of accomplishment – it is important that exercises can reasonably elicit different levels of performance, to allow for meaningful differentiation between participants of differing levels of ability.
- Fairness – exercises must not favour any particular individual due to their background, experience or any other factor which is not job related.
- Politically acceptable – sometimes it is necessary to ensure that the scenario is 'politically neutral', to avoid any undesirable implications or consequences.

The design team should also give careful consideration to the wording of the instructions. It is very important that the instructions are clear and unambiguous, for they can play a significant part in encouraging participants to display behaviour that is relevant to the criteria being assessed. For example, in a group discussion exercise where you wish to assess leadership, failure to instruct each participant to act as leader for part of the exercise may result in a participant saying little or nothing during the exercise. This lack of tangible evidence does not necessarily mean the individual lacks the ability to lead. Their non-participation may be due to a number of possibilities, for example difficulty in understanding the problem being discussed. The surest way of evaluating their leadership ability is to require them to act as leader so that their ability can be judged. This is just one example of how the instructions can play an important part in creating the opportunity for a participant to display behaviour indicative of their capability.

It is also worth noting that instructions need to be prepared for the person(s) responsible for administering the exercises as well.

STAGE 3: TRIAL THE EXERCISE(S)

Once the first draft of an exercise is believed to be in a suitable form, then it is time for a trial run. The trialling of exercises is an important and useful opportunity:

- To check that instructions are clear and appropriate.
- To gauge whether the exercise is set at the right level of difficulty.
- To establish whether the exercise elicits behaviour relevant to the criteria being assessed.
- To determine whether the exercise enables participants to display varying levels of ability.
- To establish a possible benchmark standard.
- To check the timing of the exercise.

Ideally the exercises should be trialled on a group of people at the same level in the organisation as the target job-holders. Indeed, it may be possible to use a group of current incumbents. For example, one of our clients, a leading food manufacturer, trialled a particular analysis exercise on some of their recent graduates. The exercise was due to be used as part of their assessment centre for graduate recruitment and, as a result of the trial, they were able to fine-tune the exercise and establish some indication of standards. One issue that needs to be considered when trialling exercises in this manner is to ensure that the confidentiality and security of the exercises are maintained.

If trialling at this level is difficult, then an alternative, but less attractive option, is to have the assessors trial the exercises. This acts as a supplement to their assessor training and ensures they have a thorough understanding of the exercises. The obvious problem with this, however, is that they are likely to perform at a different level from the intended participants and this needs to be taken into account when considering any suggested revisions to the exercises.

It is also useful to have members of the design team present during the trialling stage, to enable them to appreciate the need for any necessary revisions. Indeed, if roleplayers are required, then design-team members could well be suitable candidates, given their thorough knowledge of the exercises. It also makes sense to video the interactive exercises, so that these can be used during assessor training.

STAGE 4: REVISE THE EXERCISE(S)

It is nearly always necessary to amend the exercise(s) in some way or another for it is very rare to get it absolutely right first time. Apart from checking those issues mentioned in the previous stage, it is at this point that you should seek to ensure that your exercises are presented in a consistent and professional style. This is not an argument for extensive artwork since we would expect the participant to write comments, use highlighters and make preparatory notes on the participant's brief during the event. However, there should be a consistent house style including such issues as typeface, layout and page numbering to aid clarity.

STAGE 5: DEVELOPING GUIDES FOR ASSESSORS

This is one of the most important stages in exercise design for it is of little use having a well-written exercise if your assessors don't know how to go about marking it. Guides for assessors – which go under various names such as marking guides, crib-sheets and model answers – can vary in their level of detail. We believe that at their bare minimum they should list the criteria that can be observed within an exercise and should expand upon the interpretation of each criterion definition by providing suitable behavioural examples. This is often achieved by listing typical positive and negative examples of behaviour for each criterion. Woodruffe (2000), however, points to the possible danger that some assessors lapse into using these as 'tick sheets' and this involves a risk of any unanticipated behaviours being unnoticed. Although we agree that there is this risk, particularly with less experienced assessors, it can be minimised in two ways. One is by training people not to use their guides as a substitute for good judgement, the other by ensuring that the centre manager monitors the assessors' work carefully. Our view remains that it is better to give clear guidance on the more common, therefore more predictable, behaviours than not.

If an exercise involves any numerical calculations or definitive judgements, then the guide for assessors should provide the correct answer to save assessors having to work it out for themselves. Similarly with written exercises, it is quite often helpful to provide a so-called 'model answer' as a supplement to the guide for assessors. This enables the assessors to see how a written report, for example, should be marked and helps them to gauge the quality of a participant's work.

A further refinement in the production of guides for assessors is to provide behaviourally anchored rating scales (BARS). These take the concept of providing behavioural indicators for each criterion to its extreme. They entail anchoring the behavioural indicators on each criterion to a chosen rating scale as shown in the example in Figure 4.5.

Whilst there are certain attractions in trying to be more precise and scientific, we would agree with Woodruffe (2000) that there is a danger in becoming a 'hostage to fortune' because one can never anticipate all the possible responses to an exercise.

STAGE 6: WRITE ADMINISTRATION INSTRUCTIONS

There is commentary on the administration of exercises in Chapter 7, which discusses running the centre. However, having designed everything else, it is important to commit key points about the administration of the exercise to paper if that has not already been done. The style of this document is similar to the instructions you find on any reputable psychometric test. It will tell the person who is running an exercise about setting the scene, providing and checking equipment, any special points about the layout of a room, what to say (usually verbatim), when to stop, how to handle completed documentation and possibly hints on frequently asked questions.

This procedure may sound pedantic, but there are several reasons why this should be done. The main one is that participants in a selection centre may feel that they have not been fairly treated if they perceive that other candidates (at the same centre) were advantaged because, for example, the others had more frequent time warnings. A second good reason is that the person giving instructions in a large volume recruitment event could be quite junior and may have little or no appreciation of the difficulty facing participants or the reasons that an exercise runs the way it does. Thirdly, if people lose their way in any kind of exercise, the administrator has a source document to help resolve the problem.

Inconsistent administration can also contribute to lower reliability, especially in a group discussion, because the person giving the instructions without such a script can (accidentally) give a false impression of, for example, the output required or the level of complexity required. Finally, consistent administration makes a contribution to fairness, both perceived and actual.

Bespoke versus off-the-shelf exercises

As already mentioned the bespoke approach is generally considered the best, but there are occasions when it is worth considering the use of off-the-shelf exercises. For example, if an organisation is experimenting with its first foray into assessment centres, it may be difficult to secure the budget approval and gain the necessary time commitment from line managers to support a bespoke approach. Alternatively timescales may not allow for a bespoke design. Indeed we were recently asked to tender for an important assignment for a client who is a leading exponent in the use of assessment centres and where their timescales demanded the use of suitable off-the-shelf materials!

Leadership

Utilisation of appropriate interpersonal styles and methods in guiding individuals or groups toward task accomplishment.

5 = Very high level of ability.

- Provides initial organisation and gets group started by deciding how long each person has to present and establishes the running order.
- Always acts as a mediator if disagreements arise.
- Keeps group focused on the task and keeps them operating on time.
- Other group members always look to for reaction and approval.
- Ensures quieter group members have their say and are heard.
- Seeks inputs from others on a regular basis.
- Always listened to when making a contribution.
- Summarises group decisions at various stages.

4 = High level of ability.

- Organises the group for much of the time.
- Mediates on occasions if necessary.
- Other group members often look to for reaction and approval.
- Occasionally seeks input from others.
- Very often listened to when making a contribution.
- Summarises final group decision.

3 = Acceptable level of ability.

- Displays some success at organising and directing the group.
- Sometimes acts as a mediator if disagreements arise.
- Other group members sometimes look to for reaction and approval.
- May summarise at some stage.
- Usually listened to when making a contribution.
- Might seek input from others.

2 = Less than acceptable level of ability.

- Attempts to organise the group are ineffective.
- Although not aggressive, tends to disrupt group consensus.
- Attempts to keep the group focused are ineffective due to misdirection or being ignored.
- Occasionally overtalks and interrupts others.
- Other group members rarely look to for reaction and approval.

1 = Unacceptable level of ability.

- Makes no or totally inappropriate contribution to group organisation (process).
- Tends to be aggressive and/or disrupt group consensus.
- Makes no effort to keep group focused, may even be major cause of straying.
- Often overtalks and interrupts others.
- Shows no interest in time management of the task, or totally mismanages.

Figure 4.5   An example of a behaviourally anchored rating scale

The process of using off-the-shelf exercises involves going through a catalogue and selecting exercises which are:

- At the right job level for your target job.
- Able to measure your criteria rather than those given by the exercise publisher.
- Consistent with the nature and content of your target job.

This may seem a 'tall order' at first sight, but may not be as difficult as it seems given that there are functional similarities across many organisations. Thus an exercise which has been developed with a particular organisation in mind can often be applicable to others. Likewise, although different criteria or competency definitions may be used, it is not too difficult to translate from one 'behavioural language' to another, assuming the language used by the exercise publisher is well-defined and consistent. As for the nature and content of your target job, it may be necessary to change some of the terminology within the exercise to make it suit your own organisation. This raises the issue of tailoring off-the-shelf exercises and the implications for copyright.

Firstly, it should be noted that some form of tailoring is always necessary, namely the Guide for Assessors which must relate to the criteria being measured on your centre. When it comes to tailoring the original exercise brief, the situation becomes more complicated, particularly with regard to copyright. Owen (1988) suggests that if adaptations are to be made to existing published exercises by the end-user for in-house use, they should contact the original publisher for permission to do so. It may be advisable to have the publisher assist you in making the changes; after all they should know their own exercise and the likely impact of any changes, as well as having experience in exercise design.

One disadvantage of off-the-shelf exercises is that they are not exclusive to your assessment centre and, if your purpose is for external recruitment, then it is possible that your participants may have encountered the exercise before. We have heard of cases in graduate recruitment where an organisation used a particular exercise only to discover that one of its competitors had used the same exercise weeks before and had even had some of the same applicants at their assessment centre. Although in our experience this only happens rarely, it is nonetheless a problem when it does, for you are almost forced to ignore those participants' efforts on the exercise in question. Adams (1987) suggests that one way of guarding against this danger is to develop parallel exercises, best undertaken at the original design stage when the material is first being drafted.

In summary, the bespoke approach is generally best, but there are occasions when an off-the-shelf approach has its attractions.

Additional assessment methods

In addition to exercise simulations, many assessment centres include the use of some other form of assessment method. The main reason for including them is to obtain further information in relation to the criteria being assessed. This information should facilitate the assessors' discussion, enabling them to reach clearer conclusions. It may also help the feedback process, particularly when it comes to providing the participant with recommendations for career development and action planning. A further reason for including such methods is to aid the scheduling of the centre, for it is often helpful to be able to give the participants a test of some sort, so as to relieve the pressure on assessors. This reason alone would not justify the inclusion of such material, but scheduling issues do need to be considered and are discussed in greater detail in Chapter 5. The additional assessment methods that can be used include the following.

INTERVIEWS

It is quite common to include one or more interviews within an assessment centre. Indeed the pioneering work at the WOSB made much use of the interview, to the extent that the process became known as an Extended Interview. This practice still exists today: for example the Post Office uses two assessors called the Operational Assessor (OA) and the Personnel Assessor (PA), both of whom carry out interviews, but each targeted at different criteria. The OA is responsible for those criteria that relate to the operational demands of the job, whilst the PA focuses on the individual characteristics that are deemed to be important for effective job performance.

In fact this approach highlights the important principle by which the interview can be seen as a valid component of the assessment centre: it must be directed at gathering evidence in relation to some of the criteria being assessed on the centre. This type of interview is often referred to as a 'Criteria Based Interview' (CBI) and it entails preparing specific questions before the interview which will elicit behavioural evidence of the criteria in question. If the principle behind assessment centres is that behaviour observed today in the present is a valid predictor of what a person might be able to do in the future, then the CBI uses the premise that past behaviour should also be a valid predictor of future behaviour. Once behavioural evidence has been collected, it is recorded and evaluated systematically, using the same rating scale that is applied to the simulation exercises.

Sometimes the interview is one of the best sources of evidence in relation to a particular criterion. For example, if the job demands suggest that the individual needs to have a high level of integrity and be sociable, then these characteristics are most easily explored within an interview, rather than through one of the exercises.

Further reasons for using one or more interviews include the opportunity to see a participant face to face and to explore their experience and qualifications in traditional interview fashion. This is particularly important in the case of external recruitment so that line managers, to whom the successful candidate will report, have a chance to interact with the candidate and to 'sell' the job and their organisation. Furthermore, as candidates usually expect to be interviewed, it is useful to include it on the grounds of 'face-validity', thus enhancing the candidate's feeling that the process was fair and reasonable.

PSYCHOMETRIC TESTS

The purpose of the assessment centre should as always influence the decision about whether to include psychometric tests or not. If the event is more of a development centre, then various psychometric tests might be included to facilitate the feedback process, enabling the participant to gain as comprehensive a picture as possible. If the event is more of a traditional assessment centre with a selection purpose, then we need to establish the value of including such tests in enabling the assessors to reach a valid decision.

Generally speaking aptitude tests of verbal and numerical reasoning are most popular and valid as predictors of potential (see Chapter 2 for reference to predictive validities). The key issue remains about how the results of such tests relate to performance in the target job and more precisely the criteria being assessed. This link should be established if you wish to use such tests with confidence. Crawley et al. (1990) found that correlations between aptitude test scores and criteria such as problem investigation and problem solving were as high as 0.44. They also found interestingly that the aptitude test scores had significant but lower correlations with other criteria such as planning and organising, and written and oral communication.

Whilst a theoretical link might exist between a criterion such as problem analysis and verbal reasoning test scores, it is dangerous to blindly assume that the highest test scores automatically suggest the highest capability within the criterion on your assessment centre. Furthermore, without some form of in-house statistical research, you cannot be sure what would constitute an appropriate cut-off point below which you might wish to question a candidate's ability. In other words, reference to the publisher's norm groups, whilst providing a general view, does not enable you to determine with absolute certainty whether you would be correct in rejecting a candidate with a lower score. Nor does it guarantee that a higher score will give you a better job performer. Thus, just as we have argued for job analysis to be carried out to define job-related criteria, then so should some form of dedicated research be conducted to define the relevance of test scores to the target job.

The relationship between behavioural criteria and personality traits as measured in instruments such as the Sixteen Personality Factor Questionnaire (16PF), Occupational Personality Questionnaire, Myers-Briggs and Firo-B and so on, is even more tenuous. Crawley et al. (1990) found the overall level of correlations between personality attributes and criteria was low. So whilst links between the traits and the criteria being assessed can often be established, it is important to remember that personality instruments such as these are not intended as measures of ability, but are indicators of an inclination to behave in a certain manner. Thus the scores you identify through the simulation exercises for a criterion such as planning and organising may not be consistent with a score for forward planning on the OPQ. This is because the former represents a measure of ability whilst the latter measures an inclination or preference to behave in that way, and our abilities and inclinations are not always consistent with one another.

Despite these observations, however, we would not rule out the use of psychometric tests within an assessment centre, be it for selection or development. When they are included in an assessment centre and are used as an input to the final assessor discussion, it is important that the test data is withheld until assessors have reached consensus based solely on the observed behaviour. This is advisable because assessors could otherwise be strongly influenced by the seemingly definitive results of the tests.

Finally, the key factor when using tests is to be absolutely clear about how they fit into the whole process and to be aware of their limitations. If used sensibly and with a degree of caution, we believe they can play a useful part in many assessment centres.

OTHER ASSESSMENT METHODS

There is a variety of instruments, forms, questionnaires and so on, which can be completed by the participant, peers on the event, boss and/or colleagues before the event and so on. As most of these serve to provide more data, much of which may be viewed as subjective, the use of such information is generally reserved for developmental purposes and we will discuss these in more detail when considering development centres in Chapter 10. In addition to those we consider some recent new ingredients in assessment centres in Chapter 11.

5 *Planning for the Assessment Centre*

Many first-time users of assessment centres find the logistics of running the centre daunting. There are many practical aspects to consider before, during, and after an assessment centre, some of which have already been described in Chapter 2. A summary of all the planning issues appears at the end of this chapter (see Figure 5.7). In terms of activities that occur during an assessment centre, the elements that need to be combined are: participants, exercises, assessors, equipment, rooms and, according to needs, roleplayers and resource people. All of the people concerned will need to know at any one time where they are supposed to be, what they are meant to be doing, with whom and, in the case of assessors, who they are observing.

It should be clear at this stage that the whole event cannot be managed on the hoof; there is simply too much detail to handle. Even where the event is well planned in advance, we advocate that there should be a dedicated centre manager. We will elaborate on this role later. The point to stress at this stage is that this person should ideally not be doing anything else, such as acting as an assessor, for the duration of the centre. Frequently this role is undertaken by the consultant on the first centre. The planning issues to consider are:

- The variety of people to be brought together.
- The number of people involved.
- Scheduling exercises.
- The master schedule.
- Room allocation.
- Equipment needs.
- Services at the facility.
- Briefing procedures.
- Checklists.

The variety of people to be brought together

One of the complex features of assessment centres is the need to co-ordinate a number of people fulfilling a variety of different roles. Well in advance of the assessment centre you will need to identify people who will fulfil the roles of centre manager, assessor, roleplayer if you are using one-to-one interview simulations, and resource persons if you are running a fact-find exercise. All assessment centres are attended by participants and co-ordinated by a centre manager. Most although not all are staffed by assessors, and many require the presence of roleplayers or resource persons. We will examine the planning issues for each of these groups of people in turn.

PARTICIPANTS

Where the purpose of the assessment centre is to make a selection decision at the point of entry, typically for undergraduates, it is normal to find that the participants will arrive at the centre having already passed through a number of screening decisions. At a more senior level the choice is likely to be more complicated. Whether external participants are being considered or not, it is highly likely that internal applicants will be looking at a promotion opportunity. If that is the case, there will nearly always be some element of preselection to consider before participants actually get to the centre. Good employee relations practice determines that a preselection method should be fair and transparent. In the case of development centres the rules of preselection probably need even more care.

In all cases, the choice of participants falls somewhere along a continuum between totally open access and very careful predefinition. The pioneering work done by AT&T was primarily motivated by the need to identify managerial talent in the total working population and was designed as an open access system. Even here, it was necessary to have attained a job at a predetermined level in the organisation. From a purely developmental perspective there is an argument for identifying managerial potential early and to say that the insights gained will benefit any individual. The counter-argument is that totally free access can lead to frustration through unrealised expectations. Free access can also lead to demotivation of individuals who are patently unready for more responsibility because feedback inevitably lowers their self-esteem.

Geographical dispersion is also a criterion for selecting participants. The effect is less important in recruitment where the decision is effectively hire/not hire. If there is any intention to give feedback, the maximum benefit is likely to come from a meeting soon after the event. For everyone's convenience it helps if participant and assessor are in the same locality.

The extent to which you invite anybody from anywhere in the organisation reflects an organisation's culture as much as anything else. There are no absolute right answers but most organisations who have thought it through, elect for managerial nomination of some sort. In these circumstances it is imperative that nominators have good quality guidelines so that the standards are clear. ICL's gatekeeping guidelines for one of their development centres are shown in Figure 5.1 (see pp. 68–9).

ASSESSORS

Identifying suitable people to act as assessors is dealt with in the next chapter, as is the debate about the correct ratio of assessors to participants. The critical point at the planning stage is to plan for the training of enough assessors to take you through the first cycle of events. Ideally this should be double the number you think you need after you have worked out the appropriate ratio, allowing for adequate line manager representation across all the disciplines or departments that are to be involved in the events. To give some idea of the scale, we trained 48 assessors for a series of graduate recruitment centres involving a maximum of six assessors at any one event, across what were effectively six disciplines and yet were short of at least one assessor on a number of occasions.

CENTRE MANAGERS

We would argue that there should be a separate centre manager at every assessment centre. Apart from the straightforward management of the process, which is quite demanding, the centre manager plays two important roles: chairing the wash-up and quality control during the event. Since both of these aspects require a person with in-depth knowledge of the criteria, the exercises and appropriate standards of evaluation, the centre manager should be an experienced assessor. They also need to be sufficiently senior and self-confident to control the wash-up process, essentially by insisting that people justify their evaluations on the basis of evidence. There is no point in going through this elaborate process if, ultimately, selection or development decisions are enforced by the most senior line manager present. Initially this role may be undertaken by a consultant and usually falls to a senior human resource manager thereafter.

ROLEPLAYERS

Certain exercises require people to roleplay – for example, in an interview simulation as a poor performing employee or in a presentation exercise as an actual or prospective client. While it may be perfectly appropriate to use assessors in these roles, this can make for complexity in the logistics. Effectively two assessors are required per participant: one to roleplay and one to observe for each interview or presentation. It is generally good practice to maximise the time available to assessors for them to consolidate the data they have gathered, so this is another argument for dedicated roleplayers who need only be available for specific periods.

In considering who to use, it is best to identify self-assured people of the relevant age group and job profile. If the roleplay involves interviewing a younger person, then pick some younger colleagues and train them for the specific role. Likewise if a presentation is to be made to a board some members of that board who are purely roleplaying could be drawn from a company's senior management.

Once their role is over, roleplayers can be released back to their normal work. As we will see later, there is also a technological solution to this problem.

Given the demands of this task, there is much to commend the use of professional actors as roleplayers and this has been an increasing tendency over the last decade. Indeed we have regularly used actors supplied by agencies, who specialise in the provision of roleplayers and we have had frequent feedback from both participants and assessors that they made the whole exercise seem totally real, to the extent that some have even forgotten that it was an exercise! Although this approach adds to the cost of the assessment centre, we believe that it is fully justified, as it significantly increases the quality of interview simulation exercises. This assumes of course that the exercises are well written (see Chapter 4) and the roleplayers have been thoroughly trained for their task, which we will cover in Chapter 6.

RESOURCE PEOPLE

In fact-find exercises, the resource person acts as a resource to the participant by providing requested data and subsequently challenging the participant's decision. Again assessors can be used in this situation satisfactorily, but it does imply the need to double-up assessors as the fact-find progresses. One acts as the resource person while the other observes the participant's questioning and response. It is possible, but much less satisfactory, for the assessor to act as a resource person and simultaneously observe and record the participant.

ICL (UK) Ltd   Ref: HQFIN/D06UK
FINANCE DEVELOPMENT UNIT   Issue: 01
                                                Date: SEP 1989
                                                Section: 05
FINANCE CAREER DEVELOPMENT CENTRES Page: 1 of 2

SECTION 5 – NOMINATION PROCESS

1   Having satisfied himself/herself that that individual is ready for
     attendance at a FCDC, the Manager will complete the nomination form
     (see attached). This, together with a current CV, any existing
     development plan for the individual, and any other pertinent
     information eg preferred timing, should be sent to the Finance
     Development Manager ICL (UK).

2   The Finance Development Manager will review the nomination, and be
     satisfied that it is relevant, before confirming a booking on the
     appropriate FCDC.

3   The individual will be sent full joining instructions once the
      booking has been confirmed.

4   Approximately six weeks prior to the FCDC any other pertinent
     information will be sent direct to the individual.

NOTE: The Manager is responsible for informing the Finance
         Development Manager of any relevant changes to the individual's
         profile, which take place after the initial nomination and before
         event attendance.

Figure 5.1   Nomination procedure

ICL (UK) Ltd
FINANCE DEVELOPMENT UNIT

Ref: HQFIN/D06UK
Issue: 01
Date: SEP 1989
Section: 05

FINANCE CAREER DEVELOPMENT CENTRES Page: 2 of 2

TO: Finance Development Manager   FROM:
          STE 04

<u>Staff Restricted</u>

FINANCE CAREER DEVELOPMENT CENTRE – NOMINATION FORM

NAME OF NOMINEE:
BUSINESS/HQ UNIT:
BUILDING CODE: CHARGE CODE:
NOMINEE CURRENT POSITION:
CURRENT CAREER STRUCTURE LEVEL: (GSS   )
LAST PERFORMANCE RATING:
NEXT MOVES CURRENTLY FORESEEN FOR NOMINEE
(STATE LEVEL/TIMING):

JUSTIFICATION FOR ATTENDANCE AT FCDC:

SPECIFIC ISSUES TO NOTE:

RECOMMENDED BY: .... (Immediate Manager)
APPROVED BY: .... (One up Manager)
AGREED BY: .... (Training Manager)

Figure 5.1   Nomination procedure (concluded)

We therefore always recommend that additional people are identified and trained in the role of resource person, because their presence is only normally required for a few hours.

The number of people involved

Although there are exceptions, most assessment centres will involve participants, assessors and a centre manager. The number of assessors required is a function of the number of participants, which of itself is a function of the exercises used. Although the precise shape of an assessment centre is not known until after the job analysis is completed, it is very rare for there to be no group discussion, and this usually indicates an absolute minimum of six participants. In practice, groups of less than four tend to be rather sterile and they often miss the insights that develop when a range of talents is assembled. More importantly, it only takes one person to be swayed to make a majority. At the other extreme, while groups of more than six can lead to some very lively discussions they can lead to a paucity of data on particular individuals. Observation becomes more difficult as conversations become entwined and some quieter people may simply become overwhelmed and say very little.

Even with six participants there will be no opportunity to observe participants within different group sizes or with different types of individuals. Doubling the size to 12 allows a number of options for switching participants so that they can work in groups of four or six. Figure 5.2 shows some possible combinations for arranging a series of group discussions so that no participant interacts more than twice with any other participant.

This is a rather idealised picture. Assessment centres that feature as many as four group discussions are rare and the most common format for a group of 12 is to run two parallel groups of six. This is because of the need to avoid excessive demands on the facility, minimise idle time for participants, create an appropriate balance of exercises and so on. With a group of 12 participants you also have a number of options for arranging the assessors' workload, as given below.

Participant groups	Management problem	Analysis problem	Assigned role group	Business game
A	4, 6, 10, 12	7, 5, 1, 11	2, 3, 4, 5, 6, 7	5, 6, 8, 10
B	8, 9, 7, 11	2, 6, 8, 12	1, 8, 9, 10, 11, 12	2, 4, 11, 12
C	2, 3, 1, 5	9, 10, 3, 4		1, 9, 7, 3

No participant interacts more than twice with any other participant in a group exercise.

Figure 5.2   Allocation of participants to group exercises

ALL SIX ASSESSORS DISCUSS ALL 12 PARTICIPANTS

Without doubt, all assessors discussing all participants is by far the most frequently used format because it complies with the fundamental design criterion of multiple assessment.

HALF THE ASSESSORS DISCUSS HALF THE PARTICIPANTS EACH

The time needed to conduct the assessor discussion is cut down in this option which is more likely to be appropriate for a selection centre than a development centre. This arrangement does require high levels of trust between assessors and would therefore normally only occur in organisations that have well established inter-rater standards. The primary disadvantage of this approach is that it can require two centre managers to run the assessor discussions.

BENCHMARKING ON TWO PARTICIPANTS

In this option, all assessors must observe the same two participants in all of the exercises. All assessors participate in the assessor discussion for those two participants to establish consistent standards. After the review of the two shared participants, assessors split into two teams where one discusses odd-numbered participants and the other evens. This approach can be very useful in the early days of setting up assessment centres or when introducing new assessors to the team.

LARGER NUMBERS

Occasionally we encounter assessment centres that attempt to bring 18 participants together with nine assessors. More often than not this occurs in smaller companies who are making their final graduate selection once a year. Although the economic appeal is obvious, it is a gross waste of time to have nine assessors discuss 18 participants. With nine people involved, the discussion on each participant, even for a selection decision, can take 30 to 45 minutes.

The only practical resolution is to divide the group into six participant/three assessor subgroups. Under normal circumstances involving between 8 to 12 criteria with six to eight exercises we find that a 12 participant/6 assessor configuration is the best. This allows all assessors to observe each participant at least once and therefore enables them to participate fully in discussion on every participant. A typical configuration of assessor-participant assignments is shown in Figure 5.3.

Assessors	Written presentation	In-basket	Fact-finding	Interview simulation	Analysis problem	Assigned discussion	Non-assigned discussion	Management game
A	1/2	3/4	5/6	7/8	9/10	11/7	12/2	5/7
B	3/4	5/6	7/8	9/10	11/12	1/2	6/10	1/3
C	5/6	7/8	9/10	11/12	1/2	3/12	4/9	6/8
D	7/8	9/10	11/12	1/2	3/4	5/6	8/11	10/12
E	9/10	11/12	1/2	3/4	5/6	4/8	7/3	9/11
F	11/12	1/2	3/4	5/6	7/8	9/10	5/1	2/4

Six assessors observe and discuss all twelve participants.

Figure 5.3   Typical assessor–participant assignment matrix

Scheduling the exercises

The final element to consider before constructing a master timetable is the schedule of the exercises. The criteria–exercise matrix (see page 46) merely confirms that the centre will fulfil one of the key design considerations – that each criterion is measured on a number of occasions. Now it is necessary to decide how the centre will run and in what order to schedule the exercises. There has been relatively little research into the effect of exercise order on assessment centre performance, but common sense tells us that we should be sensitive to the possibility. Assessment centres, like most assessment methods, benefit from as much standardisation as possible and there are a number of ways in which non-standardisation can possibly lead to unfairness (Cohen, 1978). One such issue is differences in the order that participants experience the exercises and variations in the length and nature of the breaks between the exercises. It is self-evident that this could have an impact, when you consider that participating in an assessment centre causes anxiety for most participants, and Fletcher and Kerslake (1993) have shown that anxiety levels correlate negatively with overall assessment centre performance. Thus some participants may benefit from a calming familiarity effect if they were to experience a sequence of similar exercises, whilst others were faced with a sequence of different exercises.

A recent study by Bycio and Zoogah (2002) sought to explore the impact of exercise order on assessment centre performance in more detail. They looked at ten different variations in exercise order across a range of nine assessment centre activities (five simulations and four questionnaires). Although they found little evidence of the different orders resulting in serious unfairness to participants, they did note that performance on the roleplay was stronger in the morning when compared with late afternoon and suggested that assessment centre designers should be sensitive to early versus late-day performance differences.

So bearing the above points in mind, the following elements should be considered when scheduling a centre:

- Start with a group exercise, frequently with a non-assigned role group discussion or a business problem discussion. This enables both participants and assessors to get going and to become familiar with the surroundings and the type of task that they have to do. Participants see the exercise as much less threatening than, say, a written analysis.
- Avoid putting exercises of the same type together. The schedule should provide a balance between individual, one-to-one and group exercises in each day, so avoid having group discussions sequentially or having an interview simulation followed by an actual interview.
- Allow some flexibility in timings. Even in the best-administered assessment centre there will be times when a group discussion overruns or a briefing takes longer than expected. Use breaks to lay out rooms for briefings, for example.
- If interviews are to be scheduled, it is possible to arrange them during, say, a three-hour period in which the participants complete a complex written exercise, such as an in-basket and/or some preparatory work for a later exercise.
- Try to avoid excessive hours. There are some company cultures that demand long hours of work and consequently build that into their assessment centre. As a result participants may be asked to continue with exercises which in fact contribute very little to understanding their competence. Participants who are tired cannot give their best. Just as important, assessors find it difficult to keep up with the workload and end up evaluating performance on exercises that were completed hours previously.
- Assessor write-up time is probably the most significant overall constraint. As suggested above, evaluating an exercise several hours after it has occurred puts unnecessary strain on assessors' ability to recall, even where they have detailed observation notes. The ideal situation, which is rarely attainable in practice, is that assessors go straight from observation to classifying and evaluating their observations, while participants do a piece

of written work or a test. What is frequently achieved by assessors marking work overnight, during meal breaks and while participants are otherwise engaged, is that they only have one exercise to complete after the participants depart. Figure 5.4 shows an example of how exercises could be scheduled for a one-day assessment centre. The use of assessor time is shown on the right-hand side.

Time	Participants (1–6)		Participants (7–12)		Assessors	
08.00	Welcome – Aims and Objectives					
08.15	Business game Group discussion Self-report form	(45)* (15)	Analysis exercise Self-report form	(90) (10)	Observe Business game	 (45)
09.15	Analysis excercise Self-report form	(90) (10)			Mark Business game	 (40)
09.55			Business game Group discussion Self-report form	(45) (15)	Observe Business game 2	 (45)
					Mark Business game 2	 (30)
10.55	Coffee					
11.10	Interview	(45)	Personality profile	(45)	Observe Interview 1	 (45)
11.55	Personality profile	(45)	Interview	(45)	Observe Interview 2	 (45)
12.40	Lunch				Mark 2 Analyses	(90)
13.40	Prepare a presentation			(30)		
14.10	Presentation Self-report form	(25) (5)	Ability test	(30)	Observe Presentation	 (30)
14.40	Ability test	(30)	Presentation Self-report form	(25) (5)	Observe Presentation	 (30)
15.10	Tea				Mark 2 Interviews	 (20)
15.25	Prepare for assigned-role group discussion			(20)	1 Presentation	(10)
15.45	Assigned-role group discussion Self-report form			(45) (15)	Observe 2 Participants	
					Mark 1 Presentation	 (10)
16.45	Participants depart				2 x group discussion	 (80)
18.00					Assessor discussion starts	

*Figures in ( ) refer to time in minutes.

Figure 5.4   Example of an exercise schedule

At this stage we have identified anything that involves an assessor being present in the room as 'observing', anything else as 'marking'. Neither of these descriptions is adequate, as will be seen in the next chapter.

The master schedule

Once the number of assessors, participants and others are identified and the exercises have been sequenced, many centre managers find it convenient to combine these into a master schedule. From this, one can complete the final element of the advanced planning, which is to identify the facility requirements. It also enables the centre manager to keep control of events in the actual assessment centre and would be used in the final preparation as a source to brief assessors and participants individually at the beginning of the centre. Individual timetables are worked out when all the people are finally identified, often only one or two days in advance. The principles themselves need to be worked out well in advance. This is not difficult, and simply requires a little time to think through the various combinations that should ideally be brought together. Compromise is nearly always necessary to achieve the end result, but one thing is a certainty – there is no hope of sorting out these issues in real time! Even where participants or assessors fail to materialise, last-minute adjustments are manageable when you have a good plan.

Figure 5.5 shows an example of a master schedule. It shows how a group of twelve are often split into subgroups of three, four and six, how groups are recombined to avoid the building of alliances, and how assessors are rotated to observe each participant at least once. Readers may notice the absence of one-to-one exercises. This particular example was taken from a development centre where it was thought politically inappropriate because many of the participants were known to assessors, at least by reputation, and sometimes had direct reporting relationships.

Room allocation

The most obvious need is to ensure that there are an adequate number of rooms. Although it is possible, for example, to interview in the corner of a large conference room, it is hardly conducive to putting the participant at ease. At a pinch, hotel bedrooms can be commandeered to act as small interview rooms, but this is less than satisfactory. Assuming that the centre is a twelve-participant/six-assessor event, the minimum requirements for a satisfactory event are as follows:

- One large room which can take everyone in comfort. Participants need sufficient individual space to spread out their work without interfering or colluding with one another. Horseshoe is ideal. In addition every assessor should be able to station themselves in a comfortable chair and the centre manager needs a top table.
- Two smaller meeting rooms. Although it is possible to manage with one, this means constantly rearranging the master room – yet another complicating factor which is best avoided. Both rooms need to take six participants and be able to accommodate three observers at a distance. An ideal room layout is shown in Figure 5.6.

ASSESSOR
1.   .
2.   .   A.   PARTICIPANT
3.   .   B.   E.   J.
4.   .   C.   F.   K.
5.   .   D.   G.   L.
6.   .   H.   M.

EXERCISE & TIME	ASSESSOR / PARTICIPANT	LOCATION — MAIN ROOM						ANNEX 1			ANNEX 2	
Tuesday												
08.30 GMA-A		ALL										
09.10 Watson Glaser		ALL										
09.55 Flatacraft & Break	ASSESSOR	1			5			3	6		2	4
	PARTICIPANT	BH			FM			DK	GA		CJ	EL
11.55 Critical Incident		ALL										
12.40 Lunch												
13.40 Top Problems	ASSESSOR	2			6			1	4		3	5
	PARTICIPANT	KL			BJ			CD	MA		EF	GH
14.55 Where There's a Will	ASSESSOR	1			6			2	3		4	5
	PARTICIPANT	EM			CK			DF	HL		BG	AJ
16.00 Break												
16.15 Spraymix	ASSESSOR	1	2	35	46							
	PARTICIPANT	AEH	DJF	GLC	BKM							
18.00 Apportioning the Pool	ASSESSOR	4		5		6		1	2	3		
	PARTICIPANT	AC		BD		EF		GJ	HL	KM		
19.00 ISQ		ALL										
19.55 ISQ Lecture		ALL										
Wednesday												
08.30 16PF		ALL										
09.35 Manufacturing Exercise and Break	ASSESSOR	1	2	3	4	5	6					
	PARTICIPANT	FK	AM	GH	HJ	BC	DE					
10.45 In-Basket	ASSESSOR	2			4			1	5		3	6
	PARTICIPANT	AG			HL			BK	FM		DJ	CE
12.00 Obituary		ALL										
12.30 Lunch												
13.30 Teamwork Challenge	ASSESSOR	2	5	4	6	1	3					
	PARTICIPANT	EG	DK	CF	HL	JM	AB					
15.05 Roundup and Review		ALL										

Figure 5.5   Master schedule

- If individual fact-find, interviews, presentations or interview simulations are indicated, four additional rooms will be necessary, equipped with a minimum of an occasional table and three chairs.
- An assessors' room. This should be big enough to store all the equipment needed, including the paperwork which is likely to cover one or two normal desks. This room should also allow assessors to work, preferably at an individual desk.

- Room equipment. The main room and meeting rooms should all have flipcharts on properly mounted stands with pens to facilitate group discussions and to make announcements.

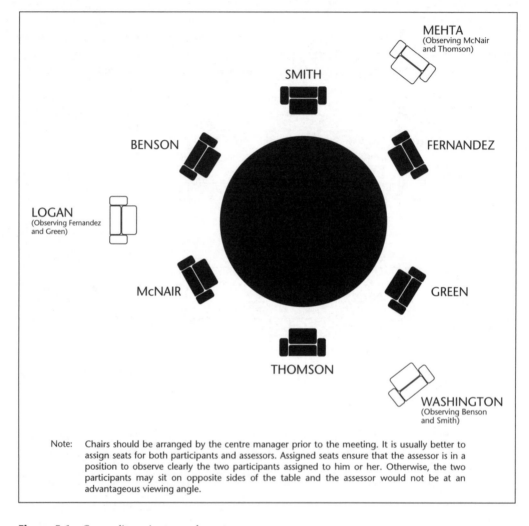

Note: Chairs should be arranged by the centre manager prior to the meeting. It is usually better to assign seats for both participants and assessors. Assigned seats ensure that the assessor is in a position to observe clearly the two participants assigned to him or her. Otherwise, the two participants may sit on opposite sides of the table and the assessor would not be at an advantageous viewing angle.

Figure 5.6   Group discussion room layout

Equipment needs

According to the precise needs of your exercises you will have to consider providing, hiring or checking with the hotel the following items of equipment:

- Overhead projectors. Many presentation exercises require participants to use overhead projectors, in which case one should be provided in every room. As the centre manager on the event you may find it convenient to prepare acetates for standard briefings. If so, you will need an overhead projector.

- A digital or Polaroid camera is a very useful piece of equipment. Even in development centres, when participants are not strangers, a digital or Polaroid photograph of the participants facilitates discussion during the assessor discussion.
- Video tape, player and camera can also be considered. In a development centre, video can support the feedback process and therefore has a clear role to play, particularly where development is designed into the procedures. On an assessment centre, video can be used effectively to supplement an observer, enabling an assessor to roleplay or act as a resource person. The same assessor can later evaluate the participant at (relative) leisure. There has been an increasing trend to video group discussion exercises on the same basis. The principal advantage is that it allows the assessor to note body language in a way that is not normally available while observing directly. Some caution is needed here. The law of diminishing returns takes over so there is no guarantee that the quality of evaluations will improve with this aid. The risk is that assessors will end up doubling the time taken on observation.
- Photocopier. Some clients we have known are extremely conscious of security and, by copying materials as the event proceeds, try to minimise the risk that participants will get advance notice of exercises. Wherever possible this strategy is to be avoided and all materials required should be copied in the week preceding the event. Even so, some photocopying is usually needed, for example, to attain inter-rater comparisons of a participant's work or to give work back to participants to prepare a presentation.
- Laptops, printers and digital projectors. Some assessment centres use business games, which run over a number of rounds and are scored by computer, to simulate interaction in the environment. Equally some centre managers develop their own spreadsheet-based scoring and other mechanisms to keep track of administrative matters. Also, there is often a need to print out various documents, in which case a portable printer is a useful addition to the equipment list.

Services at the facility

Whether you choose to use an hotel or similar conference facility or you have an in-company resource, there are a number of other issues to discuss prior to the event:

- Flexibility over breaks. As noted, the precise timing of breaks is difficult and the most effective solution is to have a refreshment area with a free-access vending machine available at all times. The next most effective is heat-retaining containers which arrive ten minutes before the official break time, and whose contents stay tolerably hot for up to 30 minutes. Buffet lunches are usually the best solution to midday eating for similar reasons.
- Secretarial/clerical help. This is something of a luxury, but you do need to establish in advance whether any help is available, who they are and how flexible they are likely to be. If there is no such assistance it will be you that ends up photocopying, passing messages on to assessors or participants, rearranging rooms, talking to catering staff and trying to brief two groups simultaneously.
- Schedule of extra resources. Establish in advance what arrangements can be made to meet additional resource people and roleplayers and ensure they are appropriately directed when they arrive at the location.

Briefing procedures

Before the assessment centre takes place, all the people involved will need a reminder, preferably in writing, about the venue, their time commitments, travel arrangements, billing procedure, any notes on recreational facilities where appropriate, and dress code.

Assessors should know through their training what is expected of them in terms of their role, their tasks and how to respond to participants. All these issues are discussed in the next chapter. At this stage two groups may need further briefing: the participants themselves and their managers or supervisors. In most cases, it is reasonable to assume that some people will already know that the organisation is about to introduce assessment or development centres. The degree of information required will be affected by the extent of existing briefings. The points that follow suggest the important information to convey. How it is conveyed is a matter of house style, but it should be in writing.

PARTICIPANT BRIEFING

The most important person to brief is the participant. It is important to construct a detailed written brief because they will be the people who are likely to have questions in their mind on a number of topics. A good verbal briefing by their manager, someone in Personnel or a consultant are all viable options but they should be regarded as supplementary, not as a substitute. Issues to cover include:

- Name of the programme.
- Purpose of the centre.
- Who attends.
- The rules about nomination.
- What will happen – general description.
- Description of exercises.
- Other people and their roles.
- How results are used.
- Who uses results.
- Any career implications.
- Nature and timing of feedback.
- Who to address queries to.
- Any preparatory work required.
- How data will be stored and how long.

Clearly, to give this information, your organisation needs to have thought through the issues. If you do use an outside consultant to brief participants, which is quite normal for a first event, they need to be clear about any sensitivities there are to particular pieces of information. Disclosure of the criteria is often a case in point. The trend in many organisations these days is for more disclosure of information and they do explain their developmental criteria in full prior to the event. In the case of pure selection events, the declaration of criteria is comparatively rare. Whatever your organisation's approach, you do need a clear policy line on this and all the issues noted above.

MANAGERS AND SUPERVISORS BRIEFING

The participant's immediate supervisor plays an important role in the success of an assessment centre programme. Nearly always this includes nominating the participant and making arrangements to cover their absence. Many organisations will also expect line managers to deal with questions as they arise and, in the case of a development centre, it is now normal for the line manager to have a significant role in debriefing the participant and arranging career development discussions.

The minimum information required by a line manager is therefore the briefing document given to the participants. In addition managers may need specific guidelines, possibly as a separate document, on the following:

- Nomination procedures. Managers must be able to satisfy themselves and others that the nominee is ready for the event. They should be actively discouraged from sending someone in the mistaken belief that participation in a promotion board will be a good developmental experience. On the contrary, practical experience tells us that weaker participants experience a further blow to their self-esteem as they perceive themselves to have failed, even in a development centre.
- Pre-event briefing. With the exception of managers who are trained and accredited assessors, line managers should be warned of the difficulty for participants of creating expectations that lie outside the brief. The best advice they can be given is to stick to this written brief and ask or refer the participant to an expert source if in doubt.
- Role after the event. The organisation needs to think through and spell out exactly what is expected of line managers. If they are to give feedback, for instance, when are they required to do so? In what format? With a representative of the human resources team? What happens afterwards?

Checklists

None of the issues we have identified in this chapter are difficult in themselves. The difficulty lies in the number of tasks that have to be organised, sometimes at short notice. If it is at all likely that an event is to be repeated, it is clearly worthwhile to have a checklist or two. We have found the following examples very useful in practice: the first, Figure 5.7, is concerned with the centre manager's planning; the second, Figure 5.8, with equipment needs.

Done	

	Assessors trained.
	Information on centre provided to participants and for their bosses.
	Location set and arrangements made:
	  – meeting rooms
	  – meals
	  – breaks
	  – sleeping rooms
	  – transportation to and from centre site.
	Audio-visuals are ready.
	Supplies (assessment and training).
	Name tags, ID tent cards.
	Assessors know location and time of centre
	  – (is a pre-centre assessor meeting planned?)
	Participants know location and time of centre.
	Participants have completed other exercises (In-Basket, Analysis Exercise).
	Participants have pre-centre exercise material (if any).
	Assessors assignments have been made to groups in different exercises.
	Participants have been assigned to seats in Group Discussions and roles in Assigned Role Group Discussions.
	Order in which the participants will be discussed in final assessment discussion has been communicated to assessors.
	Assessment centre schedule for participants ready.
	Assessment centre schedule for assessors ready.
	Assessor/Observer Manual for each assessor available.
	Exercises on hand.
	Material for company-specific exercises (Written Presentation exercise, Interview Simulation).
	Material for training exercises.
	Business Games ready to play.
	Secretary available to type reports (if used).
	Recording equipment for assessors' dictation available.
	People to roleplay Interview Simulation or to be resource persons in Fact-finding Exercise – know time when they are needed and location.
	Participant critique forms for post-centre evaluation are ready.

Figure 5.7   Centre manager's assessment centre planning checklist

Dates _____

Location _____

Method of transport _____

No. of centre managers _____

No. of assessors _____

No. of partipants _____

Additional roleplayers _____

Returned	Packed	Number needed	Assessment centre material
		1	Assessment Centre Planning Checklist *Assessor Manual* (6 in case assessors forget theirs) Criterion Summary Form Programme Participants Evaluation Form Camera (Digital or Polaroid) Film (Polaroid) (enough to take picture of each participant) Audio tape recorder (one for each assessor discussion group) Cassettes (no. of hours_____) Video tape equipment – VTR – Camera – Lights – Monitor – Tape (no. of hours_____) Dictation equipment: – Transcribers – Recorders Overhead projector Digital projector Extra projector bulb Screen Laptop Slides for orientation presentation Felt markers (a variety of colours) Name tags Pencils Erasers Pens Pads of paper (two for each participant and assessor) Paper clips Clipboards Stapler and staples Staple remover Scissors Sellotape® Computer loaded with game software Back-up disks Rubber bands Box of plastic bags for waste paper Sports equipment for free time

Material to be provided by site of centre:

	Confirmed		*Confirmed*
Screen	☐	Photocopier	☐
Overhead projector	☐	Digital projector	☐
Flip charts	☐		
Whiteboard	☐		

Contact person at assessment centre site:_____

Phone:_____

Figure 5.8   Assessment centre materials checklist

6 *Assessor Training*

At the beginning of this book we made the point that one of the key features of assessment centre technology is the use of a team of trained assessors. Together with the advanced identification of criteria through job analysis and the use of a number of well-designed exercises, assessor training is critical to the success of an event. In fact, the assessor training is probably the most critical thing to get right, for reasons we will see shortly, which is why the lack of adequate training observed in a number of studies (Ballantyne, 2000, Lievens and Goemaere, 1999) is perplexing.

On a simple practical level, it is the assessors who will deliver the judgements about a person, whatever the context. The effect of poor assessments can be mitigated to a degree by the chairperson in the wash-up, but it is much better if everyone around the discussion understands the nuances to a similar level. The main point here is that assessor training, or the paucity of it, affects the reliability of assessments, and that assessments cannot be valid if they are not reliable. Reliability, put simply, is about being confident that this person's score is typical or truly representative of their ability, and would not have been significantly different in different circumstances. These different circumstances can include different times, different places, and even, theoretically, the order in which exercises are run over a day, but the most common different circumstance is that different assessors score the same behaviour differently.

You have to be sure that:

- all assessors attribute the same 'label' to the same behaviour, and
- all assessors judge the performance to be at the same level.

Taking any ten people at random in the population, it is very unlikely that such agreement would occur spontaneously and we have to face the fact that some people are just plain bad judges. It should be evident, therefore, that assessors should be carefully selected and thoroughly trained in the relevant skills.

Choosing assessors

WHO TO CHOOSE?

As with most aspects of assessment centre practice, the key issue when selecting assessors is ensuring that they are familiar with the demands of the target job. More often than not this suggests that the ideal choice is for line managers one level above the target job. So, for example, if hourly-paid employees are being considered for the position of foreman, assessors would ideally be general foremen or superintendents. Apart from the benefit of assessors at this level possessing good knowledge of the target job, they are also the people who should have a say in who is appointed to work directly below them. Furthermore, their involvement as assessors gives them a greater understanding and ownership of the process.

Thus assessors are quite often two levels above participants in the organisation. This can obviously pose difficulties when assessment centres are run at very senior levels within an organisation: assessors might have to come from one level above the participants or from staff departments, or in some instances from outside the organisation.

Another reason why assessors are sometimes selected from staff departments such as Personnel is because of the limited amount of time that line managers might be able to commit to the assessment centre. The use of staff assessors has advantages and disadvantages. On the plus side, they may have well-developed people skills enabling them to readily tune in to issues relating to behavioural performance. They can also add a fresh perspective in that they probably won't know the participants as well as the line manager and should be less inclined to allow any personal views about the participants to influence their judgement. On the negative side, they won't be so familiar with the nature and demands of the target job. Despite these observations, there is no evidence to suggest that 'line' assessors are any better, or indeed worse, than 'staff' assessors.

A similar view used to be taken about choosing psychologists as assessors, but a recent study by Sagie and Magnezy (1997) seems to highlight the value of their involvement. They compared the assessor ratings of 39 psychologists with 66 line managers, all of whom attended the same two-day assessor training course. Some 425 candidates were assessed against five competencies (human relations, sensitivity, initiative, organisational acumen and analysis) in three exercises (personal interview, in-basket and a leaderless group problem-solving task). They were keen to see if the different groups of assessor would be able to discriminate between the five different competencies, or would demonstrate convergence to a single factor, in keeping with the 'halo effect'. They found that the psychologists were able to demonstrate high construct validity by discriminating between the five competencies within the exercises. Indeed they had predicted this, on the grounds that psychologists are trained to analyse individual traits and characteristics. However, they also found that although the line managers did not succumb to the one-dimensional 'halo effect', they did view the five competencies as two discrete factors, seeing human relations and sensitivity as a composite interpersonal dimension and initiative, organisational acumen and analysis as a composite performance dimension. This research adds further weight to the idea that regard needs to be paid to the number of competencies being assessed in each exercise. Lievens (1998) went further and recommended that the construct validity of assessment centres could be improved by having psychologists play a key role in assessor teams, acting as a coach to line managers and chairing the assessor discussion. However, it is important to note that not all psychologists have expertise or indeed any interest in assessment centres and, as with staff assessors, they are likely to be handicapped by their more limited knowledge of the target job.

It is for this reason that most organisations try to ensure that the majority of their assessors are line managers. It is therefore apparent that assessment centres will often be staffed by assessors from different management levels. In these cases it is important to ensure that the most senior people are not allowed to dominate the assessor discussion. It is the responsibility of the centre manager to ensure that no such problems arise.

One important factor to bear in mind when choosing assessors is that whilst they need to know the target job, it is desirable that they are not too well acquainted with the participants, otherwise they may find it difficult to assess the observed behaviour in an objective fashion. Such a problem is more likely to arise in a smaller organisation or at a very senior level where people are well known to one another. In these cases, it is important that the assessor training strongly emphasises the need to avoid being influenced by judgements based on prior observations of behaviour outside the assessment centre. Needless to say the onus will be on the centre managers to carefully manage the assessor discussion and to ensure that only valid behavioural evidence collected during the assessment centre is considered.

Some organisations combine the role of assessor and centre manager. Whilst this is possible, it isn't generally desirable as it detracts from the centre manager's ability to fulfil their other tasks which were mentioned in Chapter 5. Furthermore, it means losing the facility of having the centre manager as a contingency fall-back, should one of your assessors fail to arrive, go sick or start to get behind and require help.

HOW MANY TO TRAIN?

A number of factors need to be considered. Firstly, what ratio of assessors to participants will you be employing on your centres? Some organisations go for a one-to-one ratio, so that workloads can be minimised on the centre and a larger number of managers can gain experience as assessors. There may also be a 'political need' to involve a certain number of people. A one-to-one ratio, however, inevitably adds to the cost of the centre and makes it very 'resource hungry'. Most organisations therefore opt for a one-to-two ratio, that is one assessor for every two participants, since this appears to maximise efficiency without impairing the quality of the assessor's work. Indeed, when the ratio goes up to one-to-three, it is likely that the assessors will require more time to complete their evaluations and the overall duration of the event may have to be lengthened. If there are only limited resources available, then a one-to-three ratio can be successfully employed if there is only a limited number of criteria to be observed and little need for extensive documentation. In such cases, some exercises may need to be video-taped for later analysis so as to enable participants to depart without having to wait around for prolonged periods of time. Similarly the heavier assessor workload necessitates a simpler and quicker means of observing and interpreting behaviour, suggesting that assessors will need to be very highly trained.

Secondly, how many participants will attend each centre and how many centres will you be running and in what timeframe? Most organisations run assessment centres for between six and twelve participants, and generally employ the one-to-two ratio, thus necessitating three to six assessors for each centre. The total number of assessors to be trained should be sufficient to provide resourcing flexibility whilst striking a balance between providing enough opportunity for practice and skill development and not over-burdening a few individuals. In general, trained assessors should employ their skills two to four times a year. If they are involved on less than two occasions in a year, they could well get out of practice. On the other hand, it is fairly rare for organisations to enable assessors to be released more than four times during the course of a year.

AT&T took an exceptional approach with their assessment centres at Bell System, by employing line managers on six-month secondments as full-time assessors. This approach enabled them to provide extensive assessor training of three weeks' duration, ensuring very high standards amongst their assessors. The programme was justified because of the very large numbers to be assessed. Midland Bank took a similar approach in the UK in 1988, when they ran three-day 'Career Potential Centres' for about one thousand personnel. Two centres were run each week back-to-back, and this necessitated a large pool of assessors, some of whom were seconded for the duration of the project.

In summary, it is difficult to be precise about the number of assessors to be trained for any given programme. As a rough 'rule of thumb' you should train one assessor for every four participants that might participate in an assessment centre programme during the course of a year. This caters for the 1:2 assessor–participant ratio and assumes that each assessor is likely to be used twice. Naturally if your assessment centre is a one-off event, then you should train enough assessors to enable you to cover the 1:2 ratio, with at least a couple of reserves. Another important issue to consider is that assessors should be given the chance to employ their skills as soon after the assessor training as possible (ideally within a month), so courses should be scheduled with this in mind.

CHARACTERISTICS OF ASSESSORS

Assessor characteristics will vary in terms of job function, work experience, age, race, sex, length of service, and so on. Given the importance of the role of the assessor, it is surprising that relatively little is known about how their characteristics might affect the quality of their ratings. Most research into this area has focused on demographic characteristics. For example, Lowry (1993) investigated the impact of nine such characteristics (gender, age, race, education, rank, tenure, managerial experience, assessor experience and affiliated professional) on assessors' scores. Only age and rank were found to have any impact, with older and more senior assessors giving higher ratings; although in both cases, the overall effects were small. There is also some evidence to suggest that the gender of the assessor can affect ratings; although again the impact is small and the findings are somewhat inconclusive. Gaugler et al. (1987) found that assessor ratings were more accurate when the assessors were psychologists rather than line managers, but as Woodruffe (2000) points out, the risk of losing line manager commitment and involvement would be too high a price to pay for the greater accuracy.

Bartels and Doverspike (1997) took a different approach by examining the personality characteristics of assessors based on the 16PF and how these might impact on leniency in assessor ratings. They found, as they had predicted, that assessors who were more sensitive, warm-hearted and tender-minded, tended to give higher ratings to participants. This finding poses a dilemma, as popular wisdom advocates using assessors who are 'people-oriented' and who would naturally have these characteristics. One possible explanation for this tendency is that assessors are influenced by the context of their role. Kane et al. (1995) have suggested that leniency would be less evident if assessors were anonymous or if they were unlikely to have any future interaction with participants. This therefore suggests that in assessment centres, the old tradition of establishing a little 'distance' between assessors and participants may not be such a bad thing, despite the recent push for such barriers to come down and to be seen as more warm and friendly. Clearly the implications for development centres are quite different, as the accuracy of the ratings is not usually as critical as the need to encourage development. One thing is sure, the research evidence on assessor characteristics is far from conclusive and we are some way from knowing what makes the ideal assessor.

Despite the above observations, we offer a list of personal characteristics in Figure 6.1 which may help when it comes to selecting appropriate individuals. As the list implies, the job of an assessor is a demanding one. The best individuals for the job should be selected, since it is difficult to tell a relatively senior manager after they have been trained that they don't come up to the required standard.

When this does arise, what tends to happen is that those individuals don't usually get picked to act as assessors, resulting in them having wasted the time to be trained and possibly experiencing a sense of rejection. This is the lesser evil when compared to using poorly equipped assessors for an assessment centre which will impact on individual careers. This issue is so important that some organisations make it a policy to regularly assess their assessors! If standards are believed to have declined, then they will either drop those assessors or put them through some form of refresher training.

- Commitment to the assessment centre concept and process.
- People-oriented – able to empathise with others.
- An astute observer of behaviour – a good listener.
- Analytical – seeks to understand cause and effect in behavioural interactions.
- Pays good attention to detail.
- Is systematic and well organised.
- Well-respected as a 'people-manager'.
- Has a track record in counselling and developing staff.
- Has good written communication skill.
- Flexible – receptive to new ways of doing things.
- Good oral communication skill – can articulate viewpoints both in groups and one-to-one situations.
- Displays sound, objective judgement – free from bias.
- Sustains high levels of energy and enthusiasm during long days.
- Is conscientious with high working standards.

Figure 6.1   Personal characteristics for a successful assessor

Assessor training: objectives and duration

Having carefully selected the most appropriate people as assessors, the next step is to ensure that the assessor training comprehensively covers all of the relevant issues. In the US, guidelines for assessor training are included within the *Guidelines and Ethical Considerations for Assessment Center Operations*. These guideliness are regularly reviewed, the last time being May 2000, and whilst they are not enforceable, particularly outside the US, they provide a helpful framework. With regard to the objectives of the assessor training, they recommend that assessors be required to display:

- Thorough knowledge of the organisation and job/job family or normative group being assessed to provide an effective context for assessor judgements.
- Thorough knowledge and understanding of the assessment dimensions, definitions of dimensions, relationship to job performance and examples of effective and ineffective performance.
- Thorough knowledge and understanding of the assessment techniques and relevant dimensions to be observed in each portion of the assessment centre, expected or typical behaviour, examples or samples of actual behaviours, and so on.
- Demonstrated ability to observe, record and classify behaviour in dimensions, including knowledge of forms used by the centre.
- Thorough knowledge and understanding of evaluation and rating procedures, including how data are integrated.

- Thorough knowledge and understanding of assessment policies and practices of the organisation, including restrictions on how assessment data are to be used, when this is a requirement of assessors.
- Thorough knowledge and understanding of feedback procedures, where appropriate.
- Demonstrated ability to give accurate oral and written feedback, when feedback is given by the assessors.
- Demonstrated knowledge and ability to play objectively and consistently the role called for in interactive exercises (for example, one-on-one simulations or fact-finding exercises) when roleplaying is required of assessors. Non-assessor roleplayers also may be used if their training results in their ability to play the role objectively and consistently.

Given the breadth and depth of issues to be covered during assessor training, it usually lasts between three to five days and is generally residential as assessors will invariably have some overnight work.

The duration of the assessor training can often be a bone of contention for many organisations. Whilst they are usually keen to instigate an assessment centre with its associated attractions, they sometimes baulk at the thought of having a number of senior managers go through a further three to five days' training, 'simply to prepare them to be assessors!' Unfortunately this reaction is usually borne out of a lack of appreciation for the complexity of the assessor's task and the need to develop well-honed skills. Indeed, as Woodruffe (2000) rightly says, '. . . it seems a false economy to jeopardize the assessment for the sake of a few hours of training'. If you do attempt to cut back on the duration of the assessor training, you may get prolonged assessor discussions during which inconsistencies in the interpretation of criteria and/or the evaluation of ratings need to be ironed out. Worse still, these problems may be ignored or overlooked, resulting in inaccurate assessments which impact on individuals' careers.

Assessor training strategies

Given the critical impact that assessor training can have on the effectiveness of assessment centres, as mentioned at the beginning of this chapter, quite a lot of attention has been paid to the nature and quality of the assessor training. Woehr and Huffcutt (1994) examined the effectiveness of four different rater (assessor) training strategies, by reviewing 29 different studies dating from 1949 to 1992. We briefly describe their findings below.

RATER ERROR TRAINING

The earliest focus of rater training programmes was to train raters to recognise and avoid undesirable rating effects such as halo, leniency and central tendency. The premise was that this would lead to a reduction of such errors, which in turn would provide more effective performance ratings. Although this rater error training approach has been used frequently on assessor training programmes, the general consensus across the studies was that it did not improve rating accuracy.

BEHAVIOURAL OBSERVATION TRAINING

This approach focuses on raters' observations of behaviour as opposed to their evaluations of behaviour. It entails using processes – which include the detection, perception and recall or recognition of specific behavioural events – as opposed to the evaluation of behaviour, which utilises judgemental processes such as categorisation, integration and evaluation. This training therefore covers methodologies, which enhance raters' abilities to observe and record behavioural events, such as recognising behaviours and note-taking. The research studies suggested that behavioural observation training has a reasonably good positive effect on both rating and observational accuracy.

PERFORMANCE DIMENSION TRAINING

Performance dimension training is based on the premise that the effectiveness of ratings can be improved by familiarising raters with the dimensions (criteria) on which performance is subsequently rated, prior to the observation of performance. Thus the definition of the dimensions, and how they are manifest in operation, becomes the key focus of such training. The research studies showed that whilst such training contributed moderately well to a reduction in the 'halo effect', it had only a limited effect on improving rating accuracy.

FRAME OF REFERENCE TRAINING

This strategy is an extension of performance dimension training. In addition to familiarising raters with the dimensions, it also provides them with a 'frame of reference' (FOR) based on a set of common standards for evaluating performance. The training emphasises the multifaceted nature of performance and it includes defining performance dimensions, providing samples of behavioural incidents for each dimension, along with the level of performance for each incident, and practice and feedback using these standards. In essence, it enables raters to evaluate performance against 'benchmark standards' established by the ratings of job experts, using dimensions as the central ingredient, allowing raters to apply consistent standards across situations, including exercises. The research studies showed that this approach was the most effective single training strategy with respect to increasing rating accuracy and minimising the likelihood of the 'exercise effect' described in Chapter 4.

More recently, Lievens (2001), Goodstone and Lopez (2001) and Schleicher et al. (2002), have all shown that the use of FOR training in assessment centre settings was able to demonstrate improved rating accuracy and higher levels of inter-rater reliability, when compared with the traditional assessor training approach.

Clearly an important aspect of the effectiveness of FOR training is how to define the benchmark standards, as they should reflect the performance levels required in the target job in the context of the organisation's goals and values. Needless to say, a deterrent to this approach is the added time, effort and cost required to define these standards (Goodstone and Lopez, 2001) but this needs to be set against the value and importance of improving the accuracy and quality of assessors' ratings. Also, Lievens (2001) points out that the FOR training approach gives rise to fewer descriptions of behavioural evidence, which could prove a limiting factor when giving feedback on a development centre.

Although there is only limited research evidence to demonstrate it, the commonly held view is that a combination of the strategies described above would increase the effectiveness of rater training. Indeed it is generally the case that the majority of assessor training courses are a mixture of all four strategies, although most emphasis is probably given to the behavioural observation element and not enough attention is given to the added value of the FOR approach.

Assessor training: content

Having determined the objectives of an assessor training course, which may include some, if not all, of the points listed previously, we can now turn to the likely content and sequence for the event, bearing in mind the different strategies that can be employed. Generally speaking a good sequence is as follows:

- Introduction (personal introductions, objectives and timetable).
- Introduction to assessment centres (background, purpose and key features).
- The criteria (the job analysis research, criteria definitions, and so on).
- The behavioural assessment process (observe, record, classify and evaluate).
- Non-exercise components of the assessment centre.
- The assessor discussion.
- How to give feedback.

We will now go through each of these stages in turn.

INTRODUCTION

After the personal introductions, we generally start by clarifying the objectives for the assessor training. This directs delegates' attention to the purpose of the forthcoming assessment centre and enables them to see how the whole process fits within the context of their organisation. We strongly favour giving course delegates an overview of what lies before them on the training. This serves to ensure they recognise the need to commit themselves fully to their task and can start to appreciate its magnitude.

INTRODUCTION TO ASSESSMENT CENTRES

The next session aims to show assessors that the assessment centre process is a well-established and heavily researched method with a proven track record. Thus we generally provide a brief historical background and explain the possible applications and advantages of assessment centre technology in comparison with other assessment methods. We also briefly cover the key features of assessment centres as explained in Chapter 1.

THE CRITERIA

Assessors must be conversant with the criteria being used on the centre. Consequently it helps to explain how the criteria were determined. This usually entails giving a brief explanation of the job analysis process, to ensure that assessors have confidence in the appropriateness of the criteria they are going to be using. Whilst some of the assessors might have been involved during the job analysis stage, or perhaps at the exercise design stage, for others the whole process may be a novelty. Explaining the job analysis process should also serve to clarify how the exercises came to be selected for the centre.

Achieving initial familiarity with the criteria is a very important process which can take one to two hours depending on how it is tackled. At the very least, each criterion and its definition needs to be read aloud and discussed. If assessors are relatively familiar with the concept of criteria and more importantly these criteria in particular, then the focus of the discussion can be on how these criteria generally manifest themselves in the target job. Alternatively, if assessor knowledge of the criteria is limited, then it may be worthwhile including some training exercises to familiarise the assessors with the criteria. One such approach could be to ask delegates to provide behavioural examples from their own experience which would be descriptive of a particular criterion. By asking each delegate to choose a different criterion and having them describe their example aloud, the whole group can gradually acquire an understanding of the criteria.

An interesting point worth bringing to the group's attention at this early stage is that whilst we are seeking to establish how each criterion is uniquely different to all of the other criteria, we rarely if ever, see people behave in a 'uni-criterion' fashion. For example, in attempting to describe leadership, someone might say:

> I had a salesman who wasn't meeting his objectives, so I thought about how he compared with my other team members and identified that he wasn't spending enough time prospecting or planning his sales visits. I called him in and we discussed his performance and we agreed that he would revise his approach. I monitored his performance over the next three months and noticed a significant improvement.

Thus whilst the above example might be quoted as representing good leadership behaviour, the particular incident also suggests abilities in other areas such as problem analysis, planning and organising and perhaps interpersonal sensitivity. Although the definitions for these criteria are distinctly separate, we rarely employ a single criterion exclusively in a given situation. Our behaviour is generally a bundle of discrete behavioural criteria which we have combined for a period of time to deal with a given set of circumstances. This might also be another possible explanation for the high correlations for within-exercise ratings, which gives rise to the 'exercise effect', as discussed in Chapter 4.

However, given the added value provided by the FOR training approach, it is worth including a session here which will familiarise the assessors with each of the criteria in relation to pre-determined standards, defined through the job analysis and related research. This can be done by preparing a list of generic (that is, non-exercise specific) behaviours for each criterion and then converting them into a set of BARS. An example of an exercise-specific BARS can be found on pp. 59–60. These BARS can then be used to facilitate discussion as to how each criterion is manifest and what constitutes varying standards of performance in relation to the demands of the target job. This discussion should be followed by an opportunity for practice and feedback, to ensure that clear differentiation between criteria and consistent agreement on standards of performance have been achieved.

Once delegates have established a strong criterion-based focus, discussion and practice can move to how each of the criteria may be displayed in each of the exercises, again with reference to standards of performance, perhaps supported by the use of exercise-specific BARS. Kauffman et al. (1993) stress the importance of this initial emphasis on the criteria by explaining that assessor training has typically focused on the observation and interpretation of behaviours *within* the exercises. For example, assessors often undertake the exercises as participants and are usually provided with assessor guides for each exercise before practising marking. Although there is little inherently wrong with these steps, they suggest that this approach inevitably encourages assessors to view the criteria in an exercise-specific manner, rather than as global behaviour patterns. This in turn increases the likelihood of the 'exercise effect'. By putting the initial emphasis on the criteria before switching the focus to the exercises, it should be possible to redress the balance and improve assessment centre construct validity.

THE BEHAVIOURAL ASSESSMENT PROCESS

This represents the major element of assessor training, for it introduces assessors to a specific technology that will be applied to each of the exercises that make up the assessment centre.

The assessment of behaviour is essentially a four stage process – Observe, Record, Classify and Evaluate (ORCE) – and can be depicted as shown in Figure 6.2. The reason we like to show it as a pyramid, is to reinforce the fact that each stage of the process is only as solid as the foundation below it. Thus ultimately all evaluations must be based upon observed behaviour and assessors always need to be able to cite appropriate evidence to support their

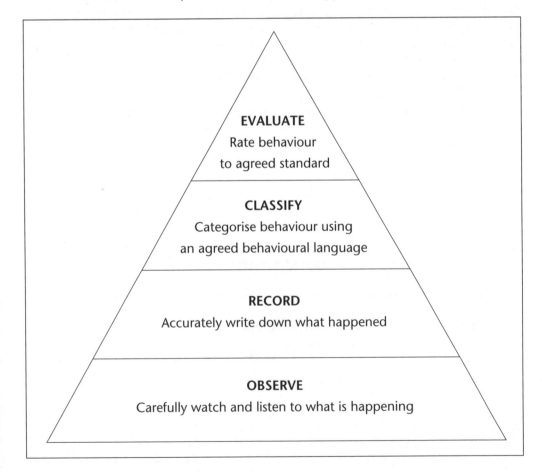

Figure 6.2   The behavioural assessment process

evaluations. This traditional process, which was developed as long ago as 1966, is still the most common approach with more than 80 per cent of centres using it according to Boyle et al. (1995) and Spychalski et al. (1997).

Observe

To observe behaviour, we must first of all be clear about how we define it. Put at its most simple level, 'It is everything we say and do'. Thus although behaviour can be 'observed' through the use of any of our senses, principally we use our eyes and ears. It is astonishing how easily people can be confused about what they truly observe, for many so-called observations are littered with judgemental comments that reflect the biases, prejudices and interpretations of the observer. It is human nature when assessing individual behaviour to jump to conclusions and start evaluating what we are observing. This is the trap that the behavioural assessment process is trying to avoid, for whilst our evaluation may often be correct, we cannot be sure.

Figure 6.3 shows how behaviour can be viewed as the tip of an iceberg (Honey, 1986), which may become visible when people are inclined to express underlying emotions, feelings and attitudes.

The point is that observing behaviour is concerned with *fact*, not interpretation. We often illustrate this point by asking delegates to comment on what they observe, having watched a short cameo from a group discussion, in which a participant says nothing. Their answers typically include remarks such as 'he wasn't interested', 'wasn't listening', 'he was bored', all of which are pure conjecture. We therefore find it necessary to stress that assessors' observations can be likened to the recordings that would be made by a video camera. They simply reflect what happened and are free from the contamination of interpretation. We have yet to encounter a video camera that has passed judgement on someone!

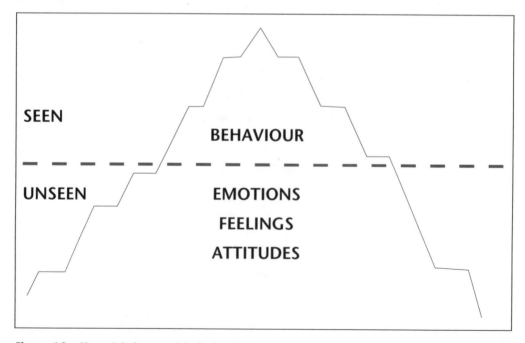

Figure 6.3   Honey's Iceberg model of behaviour

Thus recording observed behaviour, is all about recording what we observe, *not* what we 'think' we observe.

Record

Although the behavioural assessment process is shown as a four-stage process, the first two stages – observing and recording – are barely separable as they go on simultaneously. Consequently the assessor's role during an exercise is not to evaluate the performance of a participant but simply to collect data. Classification and evaluation come later.

Recording copious notes of a participant's behaviour in an exercise is regarded by most assessors as an irritating and difficult task. It is also accepted as being extremely important. The rationale is that the quality of each stage of the behavioural assessment process is dependent upon the preceding stages. For example, the ability to classify a participant's performance will be greatly impaired if the notes of what took place are not suitably accurate and detailed.

When recording behaviour, it is helpful to adhere to the following guidelines:

- Write verbatim quotes wherever possible.
- If it is necessary to paraphrase or summarise, be sure to write key words, so as to be able to reconstruct what was said.
- Note the time at regular intervals, particularly if observing a participant who speaks infrequently in a group exercise.
- Record as much non-verbal behaviour as possible.
- Develop a form of shorthand for speed, for example use initials for people wherever possible.
- When the person being observed is quiet, go back and fill in any incomplete notes, but be ready to resume writing if they start speaking again.

Figure 6.4 shows the format for a behavioural observation sheet that could be used when observing two participants within a group discussion. Figure 6.5 shows the format of a behavioural observation sheet for either observing one participant in a group discussion or a one-to-one roleplay. It also shows how the form might be used. As can be seen, the format is such that the flow of the conversation is tracked in a zig-zag fashion down the page. This ensures that a participant's behaviour is assessed in its full interactive context and the responses of others can be taken into account in the latter stages of the process.

Our usual approach in practising the skills of observing and recording is either to use a generic video which we have previously transcribed, or a video-recording of one of the interactive exercises generated at the exercise trialling stage. Both approaches work quite well. The advantage of a generic video is that it can be thoroughly analysed and used repeatedly, enabling assessors to pick up on fine details of observation and they can practise their technique on an unimportant exercise.

If time is particularly tight on the assessor training course, then it might be preferable to expose the assessors to their first practice at observing and recording on one of the real exercises. This has the advantage of immediately familiarising the assessors with one of the exercises. Given that it is the first practice run, mistakes will inevitably arise and unless the session is to be repeated, subsequent analysis and discussions around that exercise will be impaired.

Needless to say, observing and recording is only necessary for the interactive exercises, since the participant has already done all the necessary recording on the non-interactive exercises such as written analysis exercises and in-baskets.

Exercise		Assessor			Date	

Time	Participant	Others	Participant

Figure 6.4   Example of a behavioural observation sheet

Our normal policy during the practice sessions for observing and recording is to encourage assessors to capture as much factual evidence of what happens as possible. Thus we suggest assessors try to record verbatim notes whenever they can, although we stress that it is rare for an assessor to capture more or less everything. We usually find assessors are somewhat

Exercise .... Assessor .... Date		
Time	**Participant**	**Others or Roleplayer**
10.00	Thanks for coming in. Like to discuss how things are going. Look at objectives, results, any problem, etc. OK?	
		Yes, fine with me.
	We've got 20 mins, then I've got another appointment.	
		Me too.
	How do you think things have been going?	
		Quite good. Sales are slow at present. New product should help when launched.
	What about the NTZ account?	
		Bit of a problem. New buyer – difficult to get on with. Won't return my calls.
	So I understand. In fact I've had a letter. He's not happy with our customer service. Did you know?	
		Well, yes.
	What have you done about it?	
		Spoke to Tom in Prodn. He said there was a mix up in the order.
	Why was that?	
		Actually it was my fault. I put the wrong delivery address on the order.
	Does he know that?	
		No.
	What do you think we can do to improve things?	
		Suppose I could write and explain.
	Yes I think that would be a good idea. Also important to build a relationship – need to get to see him.	

Figure 6.5   Example of a completed behavioural observation sheet for a single participant

anxious about their task, particularly as they tend to take their responsibilities very seriously. However, we have often found that they are quickly able to reach a level of competence, whereby they capture at least 60 to 70 per cent of the relevant behavioural evidence and are in a good position to proceed to the next stage.

Classify

Once an interactive exercise session has finished and the participants have moved on to another task, the assessors can start classifying the observed behaviour against the criteria being measured in that exercise. Generally speaking it is desirable for the assessors to start classifying as soon after the completion of the observing and recording phase as possible. This ensures that the assessor has a relatively fresh recollection of what transpired during the exercise and is in a position to 'flesh out' their notes if necessary. By 'flesh out', we mean to recollect incidents, events or comments that might have been forgotten. We are not seeking invention. Assessors must always remember that they are only asked to report facts and must all the time guard against allowing their own interpretation to cloud their judgement of reality. Sometimes the scheduling of the exercises necessitates the assessors moving from one session of observing and recording to another, in which case a brief interval is often helpful to allow the assessors an opportunity to finalise their recordings before moving on. Ideally the timetable for the assessment centre will be designed to minimise such circumstances as was discussed in Chapter 5.

Some people – Woodruffe (2000, page 202) for example – encourage assessors to classify during observing and recording. Whilst this is just about possible for very experienced assessors, our normal recommendation is to avoid doing so, as it is highly likely that it will distract attention from the task of observing. Furthermore, classifying is by definition a judgemental process, requiring the assessor to judge a piece of behaviour and relate it to one or more criteria and for each, to determine if it is a positive or negative display of that criterion. This is in sharp contrast with the process of observation which is supposed to be strictly non-judgemental. As such, we believe it is highly dangerous to try to carry out both these tasks at the same time.

The actual process for classifying and some of the related issues are described below:

- Ensure that you are familiar with the criteria that may be displayed within this exercise, making particular reference to any guidelines that explain how the criteria might manifest themselves.
- Starting at the beginning of your notes, identify the first piece of behaviour you observed from the participant you were watching. This piece of behaviour can be a very short sentence, a single word or a long paragraph.
- Attempt to relate criteria to the piece of behaviour in question. Note, as explained earlier, that it is quite common for several criteria to relate to a single piece of behaviour. Another point to recognise is that the omission of behaviour can also constitute important evidence. For example, if a participant were to be asked a direct question and to respond with silence, then this is still behavioural evidence which should be noted and classified, even though its interpretation may prove difficult.
- For each criterion that is related to the piece of behaviour, decide if the behaviour is a positive or negative example of that criterion and annotate as shown in the example in Figure 6.6. Remember that a single piece of behaviour (for example, a sentence) can contain a combination of positive instances of some criteria and negative instances of other criteria.
- Repeat the process for each piece of behaviour as you work through the transcript of your notes. See Figure 6.6 for an example of a classified transcript.

Sufficient time must be allocated during the assessor training to practise the skills of classifying. Typically we find that the first attempt at classifying an exercise requires about 45 minutes to one hour. With practice over time we have found that assessors can usually complete the classification of an exercise in about 30 minutes. We also find it helpful to have assessors observe, record and classify the same behavioural evidence from a video or a live observation, so that they can compare notes afterwards. This helps to identify areas of

Time	Participant	Others
	What really happened today, did he tell you? **PA+ (Seeking information)**	No, I didn't pursue it, he's got tomorrow's deadline ahead of him.
	What did you make of it? **PA+ (Still seeking information)**	Hard luck I guess, there's always some team that picks up a jinx.
	You don't believe that ... get yourself a drink. **D+ J+ IS+** **(States his (Sensitive to Mike's** **opinion) need for a drink)**	Thanks.
	I don't believe in hard luck, there's always a reason ... What have you got on your mind Mike, spill it? **D+ IS+ T+ PA+** **(Senses Mike holding back)**	I'd rather not.
	Let's have it, warts and all. **T+ (Persistent)**	Well you won't like it, I don't. It's the Account Manager.
	Steve? **IS+ (Listening)**	Well, it's always the Account Manager, it's his job isn't it?
	A little funny coming from you, he's your friend. **POC- IS- (Poorly phrased and insensitive)**	I didn't ask you to ask me.

Where:
  1) PA = Problem Analysis
  2) D = Decisiveness
  3) J = Judgement
  4) IS = Interpersonal Sensitivity
  5) T = Tenacity
  6) POC = Persuasive Oral Communication

Figure 6.6   Example of a classified transcript with criteria annotations

misunderstanding and often demonstrates to different assessors the richness of the criteria. In many ways the process of classification can be likened to translating from one language to another, for what we are doing is translating real observed behaviour into a 'behavioural language' defined by a set of criteria.

As mentioned earlier, apart from practising on the exercises themselves, it is also possible to use additional training exercises aimed at refining the skills of classification. These entail providing samples of behavioural evidence that might have been gathered by assessors and asking delegates to comment on which criteria are portrayed. Assuming these samples have been 'pre-marked' by an 'expert', it provides an opportunity for a useful discussion around the interpretation and understanding of the criteria.

Evaluate

Evaluating the behavioural evidence that has been gathered for each criterion on a given exercise ought to be a straightforward process. It entails looking at all of the evidence, both positive and negative, for that criterion and then awarding a rating which summarises the participant's ability on that criterion within that exercise. This process is then repeated for each criterion in turn.

It is self-evident that all of the assessors must use the same rating scale and must of course attempt to interpret the scale in the same way. There are numerous possible rating scales that can be used and the following is a fairly popular one:

5   Very high level of ability.
4   More than acceptable level of ability.
3   An acceptable level of ability.
2   Less than acceptable level of ability.
1   Unacceptable level of ability.

The process of applying a rating to a set of behavioural evidence relating to a criterion is complicated by what we refer to as the need to 'benchmark'. In simple terms, it means that when an assessor awards a rating of, say, 3 on a criterion such as leadership in a group discussion exercise, they are actually saying 'this participant displayed an acceptable level of leadership in this group discussion exercise, *when compared to the likely demands of the target job'*.

This caveat about the demands of the target job is fundamental to the success of the assessment centre's ability to predict future job potential. Assessors have to continually remind themselves about this caveat, in order to ensure that they maintain appropriate focus.

Thus time needs to be allocated during the assessor training to ensure that the assessors are all working with the same benchmark standards and that one assessor's rating of 3 is the same as another's. It is quite commonplace during the early stages of training to find that one assessor evaluates a set of behaviour as a 2 or a 4, whilst others might rate it as a 3. These inconsistencies must be discussed and cleared up if inter-rater reliability is to be achieved.

In terms of the mechanics of evaluation, we recommend that the assessors take a balanced view of the quantity and quality of their evidence for each criterion. To help them do this, we use an assessor report form formatted as shown in Figure 6.7. Assessors are encouraged to count up the number of positive and negative examples they have noted for a criterion and to cite key examples of each. They then need to review the total evidence for

Participant	Exercise
Assessor	Date

Criteria	+	Key Observations	−	Evaluation
Problem analysis + −				
Judgement + −				
Decisiveness + −				

Figure 6.7   Assessor report form

that criterion, recognising that the quality of some of the examples may well outweigh issues relating to quantity and then finally they decide on a rating as previously described. Typically we have found that the evaluation process can be very quick, although we tend to stress the need for the application of careful judgement.

Alternatives to traditional ORCE methods

Hennesey, Mabey and Warr (1998) have investigated two alternative procedures to the traditional ORCE method. The first variation from the traditional approach entailed providing assessors with a behavioural checklist of ten positive and ten negative indicators for each criterion, for the assessors to use after observing and recording evidence in the traditional way. This approach is not a major departure from the traditional method, as it is quite common to provide assessors with a guide which lists behavioural indicators for each criterion. The primary difference was that the checklist provided a more prescriptive basis for classifying evidence, as assessors were restricted solely to these indicators and were not allowed to include others they may have observed. A comparison between the use of the behavioural checklist and the traditional approach revealed little differences in accuracy, although it did help to reduce variability between assessors, suggesting that this extra structure could prove particularly helpful to inexperienced assessors.

The second variation from the traditional approach required assessors to use a behavioural coding sheet during their observations of the exercise, instead of taking detailed notes in the usual fashion. Assessors were furnished with a coding scheme comprised three positive and three negative broader constructs for each criterion, which had been derived from the behavioural indicators used for the aforementioned checklist. Their task was simply to tally (using a 'five-bar gate') each occurrence of these behaviours during the exercise. Contrary to expectation, they found that this approach produced equally accurate results as the other two methods. This was regarded as an important outcome, as assessors have long been advised against classifying behavioural evidence whilst observing an exercise. The most obvious disadvantage of the behavioural coding approach is that it could result in assessors not being able to write accurate summaries of behavioural evidence for the assessor discussion or subsequent feedback. It was noted, however, that this was not a problem if assessors were able to write up these summaries immediately after the end of the exercise; although it was noted that this places a reliance on the assessor's memory.

Whilst the idea of behavioural coding is worthy of consideration, it is perhaps still too early to suggest that it is a totally safe approach. The concerns relating to it include: the need to be highly confident that the right constructs have been defined for the coding sheet; the fact that other relevant behaviours could be disregarded, and the reliance on the assessor's memory to produce good quality narrative summaries to support ratings.

NON-EXERCISE COMPONENTS OF THE ASSESSMENT CENTRE

It is usual to include in this session the use of interviews and/or psychological tests as was explained in Chapter 4. If they are to be used, then the assessors need to be clear about their own involvement with these methods.

It is quite common for the assessors to have to conduct one or more interviews with some of the participants, in which case they need to be given appropriate training. If a CBI is to be used, then at least one day's training needs to be provided, assuming delegates have had previous interview training. Where delegates have had no previous interview training and CBI is to be employed, it is advisable for them to attend a separate two- to three-day CBI course. Once again this is an area where there is a strong temptation to try and 'cut corners'; however, in our experience this usually results in a less than satisfactory outcome in terms of the quality of the assessors' contribution on the assessment centre, the consequences of which have already been outlined.

If a different type of interview, other than CBI, is to be employed then care needs to be taken to ensure the assessors understand how the data gathered in the interview can be related to the rest of the assessment centre evidence. The interview training will therefore need to address this issue to ensure effective integration of data at the final assessor discussion stage.

As far as psychological tests are concerned, it is unusual for assessors to have any particular involvement. Thus what they will need to know is what tests are being employed and how the resulting information might be used as part of the overall process.

THE ASSESSOR DISCUSSION

The assessor training needs to explain how the assessor discussion, often referred to as a 'wash-up', will run on the assessment centre. In particular, it should help to give assessors a feel for the shape of the final output from the centre. We find it helpful to warn assessors that we will be spending a certain amount of time discussing each candidate and that they may have to justify their ratings with behavioural evidence.

Furthermore, if the final evaluation procedure is going to include deciding on an Overall Assessment Rating (OAR), then the assessor training needs to explain the procedure that will be employed. This issue is discussed in further detail in Chapter 7.

Finally, if assessors are going to have to write up an overall report on a participant during the assessor discussion, then the format of the report and the mechanics for writing it must be explained during assessor training. The nature of such reports is discussed in Chapter 8.

HOW TO GIVE FEEDBACK

If assessors are going to be involved in giving feedback to the participants, then they should receive the necessary training. Such training needs to emphasise the structure and mechanics of the feedback session, as well as the basic principles of counselling. (The main aspects of providing useful behavioural feedback are covered in Chapter 8.) The amount of time that needs to be dedicated to this training will be determined by the level of feedback needing to be provided, the experience of the assessors in giving feedback and the time available on the training course.

The benefits of assessor training

Although the main purpose of assessor training is to equip delegates with the ability to act as assessors on an assessment centre, they also gain additional 'spin-off' benefits. As Dulewicz (1991) points out, these benefits can be applied in the everyday management responsibilities of the assessors. The benefits will include the following:

- Heightened ability at observing behaviour (enhanced listening skills, more aware of non-verbal behaviour, greater objectivity, less likely to succumb to the 'halo-effect', and so on). Indeed, Lorenzo (1984) found that previously trained assessors were more effective than managers with no assessor experience at acquiring information about people, verbally presenting and defending it, and communicating it in written reports.

- More effective interpretation of behaviour through the use of behavioural criteria. Tony Glaze (1989) at Cadbury Schweppes reported that 'the most fundamental effect of the use of assessment centres has been their contribution to the behavioural literacy of many of our managers'. This benefit is commonly experienced in organisations where they use behavioural criteria to underpin many of their human resources procedures such as within the appraisal process.
- Increased appreciation of a variety of methods for handling different situations, for example different leadership styles in group and one-to-one situations, various approaches to completing an in-basket and so on.
- Enhanced one-to-one interviewing skills which can be applied to selection, performance review, appraisal, feedback and counselling situations.

The spin-off benefits from assessor training are so valuable that some organisations such as General Electric (Byham, 1971) have increased the ratio of assessors to participants in their programmes, in order to expose more assessors to the experience.

Roleplayer training

If one-to-one interactive exercises form part of the assessment centre, then some form of roleplayer training is necessary. This may or may not be included as part of the assessor training. If the assessors are also going to act as roleplayers then combining the two forms of training makes much sense, although it should be appreciated that it adds to the burden for assessors and will probably necessitate slightly lengthening the course. We therefore prefer, wherever possible, to use independent roleplayers, so as not to over-burden the assessors and favour training them as a separate group if possible.

Roleplayer training needs to ensure that all of the roleplayers reach a common understanding of the exercise(s) in question and are equally able to carry out their role(s) in a reasonably consistent manner. The key aspect of roleplaying is to act as a catalyst for the participant's behaviour and to present a consistent set of stimuli to each participant, allowing the participant to respond as he or she chooses. The exception to this 'rule' would be if a participant initiated a certain behaviour pattern which did not warrant the planned or consistent response. For example, if the roleplayer is briefed to behave in a reasonably co-operative manner, albeit slightly defensive, then it would be inappropriate to continue to do so if the participant adopted a highly aggressive manner towards the roleplayer. We normally tell roleplayers that they need to remember the maxim that 'Behaviour breeds Behaviour' (Honey, 1986) and they should allow their behaviour to develop in response to the participant's behaviour. Having said that, it is not uncommon for some exercises to have built-in traps and responses aimed at testing participant behaviour.

Boddy (2002) points out the merits of video-recording a roleplay session, as this can be used to provide a 'standardised' roleplay for training other roleplayers, as well as practising assessor calibration during their training. The following important points also need to be stressed during roleplayer training:

- They need to draw the participant into the situation as if it were real and within reason, need to help settle a nervous participant, but without providing undue help.
- They should not create unwarranted pressure or put the participant under undue stress, unless it is part of the exercise or legitimately provoked by the participant's behaviour.

- They need to be fully conversant with the exercise content and any necessary briefing instructions or administrative matters for which they are responsible.
- They need to appreciate the criteria that the exercise is attempting to measure and must be aware of the types of behaviour that might be elicited.
- They must help maintain security of all appropriate assessment centre materials and the confidentiality of exercises and any issues arising.

Given the powerful impact of roleplay exercises within an assessment centre, we have adopted the policy of asking roleplayers to share with the assessor their personal observations and feelings about the exercise in which they have just participated. Both assessors and roleplayers should be briefed/trained to have this short discussion and we usually use a simple 'roleplayer report form' to facilitate this discussion. We believe this approach to be helpful and legitimate. In our experience good roleplayers become highly engaged in the exercise and their emotions and feelings are a real consequence of the interaction that has just occurred. Clearly assessors need to regard this additional data with some care, but it can be invaluable when interpreting a participant's performance and also when providing feedback. For example, if an assessor has just witnessed the poor handling of a performance review session and it is obvious that the interaction between the participant and the roleplayer did not go well, then it is helpful to ask the roleplayer about their level of motivation. So long as the assessor does not ask a leading question, the answer can help confirm a suspicion or can provide evidence which can be used to prove a point in feedback, particularly if the participant is in denial.

7 Running the Assessment Centre

Readers who are used to running their own assessment centres may think that our references to a dedicated 'centre manager' is excessive, because many centres are run by one of the assessors in addition to their normal work. Clearly, that approach can have advantages when budgets are stretched, but it is generally a false economy. At best, this arrangement can only work if the person keeps to simple administrative duties such as briefing participants as each exercise starts. We hope that by the end of this chapter you will be convinced that there is potentially much more to the role than simply ensuring that the centre runs efficiently. The efficient running of the centre is a direct consequence of a good plan. While there are some points to make about the running of the assessment centre, we want to give some attention to two additional aspects of the centre manager's job: quality control and managing the assessor discussion.

Starting the event

There is a logical continuum between planning and running the centre and the cut-off point is always a little arbitrary. The issues discussed in Chapter 5 can all be actioned well in advance, in some cases years previously. The following points relate to the night before or the early part of the morning of the centre.

- Check the facilities. Especially if this is your first visit to a particular location, you need to know the location of every room and be satisfied that your layout instructions are complied with. Make sure you meet the person who is responsible for all logistics, know how to get access to them and who else to speak to in out-of-hours situations. If the information is not volunteered, you also need to establish any emergency procedure and how you are expected to respond.
- Label clearly all rooms that you are going to use. The need to do this will vary according to the facility. Some hotels will do this for you quite satisfactorily as will many in-house training centres. If there is any doubt, it is better to over-label rooms using simple titles which help both participants and assessors find their way round, for example 'Interview 1'.
- Finalise the timetable. When the names of all participants and assessors are known, insert this data into the master schedule and arrange sufficient copies for all assessors. There are a number of alternative ways of showing the information that is required. The Assessor–Participant–Exercise Matrix (see Figure 7.1) is one. Its use as a planning document is obvious, as a means to ensuring that every assessor sees every participant. In the centre itself, it informs each assessor whose work they will be assessing in each exercise. To complete information for assessors, this information needs to be combined with details of

the timing and location of each exercise to provide each assessor with a personal schedule. Figure 7.2 shows a pro-forma assessor schedule for the same event.
- Lay out the assessors room. Lay out any stacks of paperwork that are required in the order they will be used. This will include observer sheets, CBI pro formas and usually Assessor Report Forms. Prepare a wallet file for each participant with a paper copy of the participant performance matrix in each.
- Arrange for participant photographs. Participants should be photographed on arrival if possible and definitely before the centre starts in full.

	Exercises					
Assessor	Non-assigned role group discussion	Assigned role group discussion	1st criteria based analysis interview	2nd criteria based analysis interview	Written/present analysis exercise	In-basket exercise
A	1 7	2 4	3 9	5 11	6 12	8 10
B	2 8	1 3	4 10	6 12	5 11	7 9
C	3 9	6 8	5 11	1 7	4 10	2 12
D	4 10	5 7	6 12	2 8	3 9	1 11
E	5 11	10 12	1 7	3 9	2 8	4 6
F	6 12	9 11	2 8	4 10	1 7	3 5

Participants	
1.	7.
2.	8.
3.	9.
4.	10.
5.	11.
6.	12.

Figure 7.1 Assessor–Participant–Exercise Matrix

Time	Activity	Participant	Venue
13.00	Assessor Conference/Lunch		
14.15	Welcome and Introductions		
14.30	Observe and Record Non-Assigned Group (1–6)		
15.30	Classify and Evaluate Non-Assigned Group		
16.15	Observe and Record Non-Assigned Group (7–12)		
17.15	Conduct Interview (1–6)		
18.00	Conduct Interview (7–12)		
18.45	Company Presentations		
19.45	Drinks and Dinner		
21.00	Classify and Evaluate Analysis Exercises		

Figure 7.2   Assessor schedule

BRIEFING ASSESSORS

Most assessment centres that we have conducted start with a briefing for assessors. The only exceptions we are aware of is where assessment centres run continuously and assessors are seconded for several weeks at a time. Even with the highest standards of training, one must bear in mind that most assessors are busy line managers who are likely to come to the centre with very little done by way of advanced preparation. The assessor briefing is therefore an important opportunity to recap on several points covered in the training programme, as well as dealing with the logistics of the event. To deal with the logistics first, the issues to cover include:

- The timetable. This should start with a complete overview to remind them of the general run of events, with appropriate emphasis on their time use and allocation.
- The facility. Time permitting (which is up to you!) it is a good idea to walk the assessors round the facility. No doubt they will ask again, but the objective just now is to orient them to their surroundings.
- Assessor–Participant–Exercise Matrix. Brief assessors on who they will be observing and evaluating in each exercise and issue them with a personal schedule as discussed above. Alternatively they can locate themselves on the master schedule (see Figure 5.5) and highlight the appropriate information.
- Issue and talk through Assessor Manuals. These should contain everything an assessor needs including timetable, criteria–exercise matrix, definitions of criteria, guide for

assessors for each exercise, sample interview questions if using CBI, and any final report forms that may be required.

- Demonstrate any paper stacks in the room. Point out what and where things are and indicate that after the briefing they can start preparing by putting participant names on observer sheets and interview pro formas for the first day.
- Indicate how assessors should handle work completed by the participant and where they should leave their completed evaluations.
- If interviews are being conducted, issue job application forms and any previous notes on participants to the appropriate assessor.

This ends the logistical points for assessors. In addition we would recommend an element of retraining as part of the briefings as follows:

- A reminder of criteria and their definitions.
- A reminder of each of the exercises to come, including the criteria that are likely to be elicited in each exercise.
- A reminder of the skills of observing and recording, in particular to record key words verbatim and use silent time to fill in any gaps.
- A reminder of behaviourally specific observations.
- A reminder to respect the integrity of the process and avoid interchange of views about particular participants.
- A reminder of their duty to help the centre run to time, particularly where they do effectively control it in interviews and other one-on-one situations.
- Related to both the last two points is the need to keep up with the process and write up reports at every available opportunity.

Close the briefing for assessors by quickly recapping on the hints on being an assessor (Figure 7.3) and encouraging them to use any remaining time before they meet participants by recapitulating on exercise content, preparing for interviews and annotating observer sheets with participant names.

BRIEFING PARTICIPANTS

The need to brief participants will vary according to the amount of detail that has previously been available to them. For most in-company events, such as a promotion board or development centre, it is probable that prior briefing will have been extensive. With selection events, participants may arrive with no real idea about what is expected of them except that they have been asked to give up one or two days of their time. For all, it is worthwhile to brief participants before the event proper on the following:

- The nature of the exercises. There is no need to go into detail, but it does help participants to know that some exercises will involve them in working in groups to discuss various issues, that they will/will not be interviewed again, and that they will be doing some written work. Explain that the exercises have been constructed to reflect the kind of work they would do in the target job.

- Consult the centre manager about which participants to observe.
- Keep the programme on time; report any emergency deviation from the programme schedule to the centre manager.
- Be prepared before the scheduled time of each exercise; write the name of the participant(s) to be observed on the forms, listing criteria to be assessed, reading background materials, and so on.
- Check to see you have the appropriate forms before each exercise.
- When observing a group exercise position yourself so as to be as inconspicuous as possible, whilst still being able to see.
- Never indicate to a participant he/she is doing well or poorly during an exercise by smiling or nodding, but do put them at ease whenever possible.
- Do not give personal feedback on performance. If necessary make general references to exercises but do not evaluate.
- Do not show particular friendliness or attention to individual participants; for example, do not spend all of your breaks together, do not continually ask about their progress.
- Always wear name tags and look like you know what you are doing!
- Do not leave your Assessor Manual lying around; be aware of security of exercises and all forms.
- Complete Assessor Report Forms as soon as you possibly can.
- Do not discuss with other assessors detailed information on the performance of participants observed lest it bias their observations of subsequent exercises.
- Do not make/receive telephone calls except during breaks.
- Maintain a friendly and helpful attitude toward participants; help them to enjoy the experience and to feel that it is 'fun'; but be serious during exercises even when things are amusing.
- Ask the centre manager if you need help – things can get confusing.

Figure 7.3   Hints on being an assessor

- The role of the assessors. Participants should be told that most of what they are doing will be observed directly and that the role of assessors is to record behaviour. The data recorded will later be integrated. Ensure that participants understand that assessors have no other role and that they should not interact with them in any way.
- Expectations of them. Having just said that they will be observed, it is important that participants understand that they are not expected to play any kind of role. There is no mileage in trying to second-guess what assessors are looking for; on the contrary, the best advice to participants is to 'be yourself'. The only way in which they can help themselves is to give voice to their thoughts and speak audibly when they are being observed.

Finally, emphasise that many exercises are conducted under time pressure. It is important, therefore, that participants listen carefully to their briefing and respond immediately if they have any doubt or if the instructions are not clear. Equally they should know whether or not they willl be getting any time checks during exercises.

Administering exercises

ADMINISTRATION INSTRUCTIONS

There is evidence that poor administration can affect the way that people perform in the exercises. Most importantly, inconsistent administration can be a source of bias, though this is not usually intended and is intrinsically unfair. Consider, for example, how you might feel if you were in a group that had no instruction about time compared to another on the same centre where the finish time was displayed on a white board and clearly pointed out by the person who briefs the exercise. For this reason, we always prepare administration instructions (as explained in Chapter 4) and anyone involved in administering exercises is strongly advised to use such documents to evolve a consistent approach.

DURING THE EXERCISE

For most exercises the centre manager's role is mainly to invigilate to ensure that, for example, participants do not discuss any briefing material they have during a preparatory period. As exercises proceed, the centre manager might well act as a supernumerary assessor and should do this, particularly in group discussions, to increase their contribution to the assessor discussion. In general the centre manager, like the assessors, should not intervene in the process with the following exceptions:

- Timing announcements. These should be carefully confined to circumstances where a group discussion has clearly lost sight of the time and should be given in the form of saying 'x minutes have elapsed since you started your discussion'.
- Clear misinterpretation of the rules. Certain types of exercise have a negotiating component or, as in all assigned-role exercises, people are required to compete for resource in some way. Clearly the exercises will not work as designed if an early decision is arrived at to split the pool equally and call it a day. Normally it is sufficient, and it is always best practice, to re-read the participants' instructions without giving any further interpretation.
- Answering questions as the exercise proceeds. This does not happen often, but participants do sometimes ask for guidance during an exercise, asking for example 'How much time is left?' or 'Should we be writing this down?' Centre managers should use their own judgement but, as a general rule, answering process questions like the ones cited is fair, although strictly speaking outside the rules. Anything to do with arguments should be ignored, if possible. If that is not possible you should reply neutrally, such as 'The assumption you are making about that is/is not correct.' Again it is usually sufficient to re-read specific instructions from their brief.

AT THE END OF EACH EXERCISE

Most exercises, once completed, will require participants to complete a Participant Report Form. The precise nature of the form will vary but participants should be allowed to spend time completing these forms without any added pressure. For many events, particularly graduate selection centres, participants do take a lot of care completing these documents and it is often a sore point between centre managers, trainers and assessors that assessors often neglect this information. Centre managers should make it their business to read all Participant Report Forms quickly with a view to noting any information that may be useful in the evaluation of that participant. This contributes to the centre manager's ability to monitor the quality of assessors' work. There is also a need in discussion exercises to monitor the participants' responses, as we shall see.

ADMINISTERING SPECIFIC EXERCISES

In addition to the general comments above, there are some specific points relating to particular exercises:

- In-basket exercises. Read instructions aloud and encourage participants to follow through with you. Read slowly and always ask if there are questions before everyone starts. The objective is to stop participants rushing to get a head start without an adequate understanding of what they have to do. These exercises are always quite lengthy and consequently it seems appropriate to give periodic time announcements at half-hourly intervals.
- Analysis exercise. If the analysis exercise is simply being administered as a written exercise then the administration requirements are the same as for an in-basket. There are often presentations to follow and there may well be a group discussion after that. Again, some analysis exercises may require the participant simply to undertake enough preparation to make a presentation, where others ask participants for a full written report. A further variant is to make one- to-one presentations or have groups of participants present to one another and (usually) two assessors. Finally, the degree of formality can vary considerably. From the centre manager's point of view the main points are to ensure that participants have the correct instructions and to ensure security of material between sessions. The latter is particularly important where the presentation is handled as a surprise briefing of a boss on the next day.
- Written presentation exercise. Much like the analysis exercise, this type of exercise can take multiple forms. A common form that is used in-company for senior people is to have participants address the strategic issues that face the company over the next five years. More often than not, this is followed by a group discussion, which may or may not be assessed. As the issues have very real interest for the participants, not having a group discussion runs the risk of alienating participants. They may feel they are missing an important opportunity to express their views to senior managers and are always interested in the views of others. Many companies see this as sufficiently important to arrange for a group spokesman to present their findings to a senior executive after dinner. As the centre manager, the main concern is to ensure that instructions are issued correctly in the appropriate sequence. If there is a group discussion they should ensure that it runs to time and that a representative is clearly identified.
- Group discussions. The administration of group discussions is usually simply a matter of giving a brief, being aware of finishing times and, wherever possible, making one's own direct observations. Experienced centre managers find that with practice they can notice and classify contributions sufficiently well to contribute data to the wash-up, if needed. One of the greatest disasters that can happen is when a centre manager mixes up the briefs in an assigned-role group discussion so that two or more participants get the same brief. This is easily avoided by ensuring that you only have fresh complete sets every time

the exercise is run. Avoid the temptation to keep spare discussion briefs by destroying them.

- One-to-one exercises. The main objective for the centre manager is to ensure that roleplayers (or assessors) play their parts with consistency. Although relevant to fact-finds and presentations, this issue is crucial in interview simulations where the objective for the roleplayer is to respond appropriately to the interpersonal skills being displayed by the participant. Faced with playing a role three or four times, many roleplayers are tempted to drop out of role or to make the next interview harder than it was intended to be or to steer participants who are struggling. If any of these should happen, some participants will be relatively disadvantaged. Training should be aimed at overcoming inconsistency, but if it happens the roleplayer should be advised immediately after the observed session and requested to 'play with a straight bat'.

Quality control

There will almost always be a blend of experience and ability among assessors at an assessment centre. With the rare exception of organisations like AT&T who assign assessors on temporary secondment for months at a time, most assessors will be assigned away from their normal place of work for a few days at a time and may only put their skills into practice two or three times a year. Even where assessors become reasonably practised, their performance will vary, just like in any other human task response, according to the level of their commitment to the process, how clearly they identify the criteria, how much time they have had to revise and prepare for the assessment centre and a host of other factors. Although the assessor training will have aimed to get every assessor to attain certain minimum standards, it is up to the centre manager to ensure that those standards are attained in the live situation. Naturally the assessor discussion will enable assessors to come to a shared view of all the participants at the end. The following hints suggest where there are opportunities to make running adjustments as the centre progresses.

- Periodic rebriefing. Depending on the length of the centre, there is often an opportunity when assessors are together to remind everyone of an upcoming exercise or two. The points to cover include the exercise content, typical behaviours that are observed, and the criteria that are likely to be exhibited with some example standard behaviours.
- Start and end of the day. In a centre spanning more than a day it is always worthwhile having a session each morning to talk about the day ahead and having a debrief at the end of the day. The end of the day briefing particularly emphasises any expectations that you have for overnight marking and presents an opportunity to recap on common errors that have been detected during the day.
- Immediately before each exercise. New assessors particularly welcome this kind of intervention at least at the beginning of a centre. All that is required is a quick check that they know who to observe in a particular situation.
- Screening completed work. In most assessment centres there will be at least one opportunity to spend time going over work that has been completed by assessors. We find the best approach is to take all the work related to an exercise together with our own observations and briefly examine the classification examples and the evaluations. The objective is to identify some of the most obvious 'howlers' such as totally inappropriate

classifications and evaluations that make no sense, for example, no evidence for written communication on a piece of written work, or a 'less than acceptable' evaluation for planning and organising where there is no evidence of poor planning. Another common shortfall is not taking account of important information on a Participant Report Form (PRF) – a clear indication that it hasn't been read. Any findings of this kind are fed back to the assessor with a request to reconsider their position.

Centre managers should not assume that something is known and understood by assessors just because it was covered in the assessor training. Assessment centres can be very confusing on the first occasion and most assessors welcome help and guidance as the programme evolves. That said, one should seek to avoid an approach that is too didactic – after all assessors will mainly be senior managers who are willingly contributing to this process. When you are handing work back for re-evaluation, the written notes that accompany it, in particular, and the tone of your approach, in general, should be non-evaluative and discreet. Otherwise, you may find you are running out of assessors in the future.

As a final point, despite everyone's best intentions to keep up with the process, there will be occasions when you have to intervene and help an assessor directly because they are falling far behind. As a general rule, assessors are least confident evaluating written exercises and a negative response is unheard of if you volunteer to evaluate an in-basket.

PARTICIPANT QUALITY CONTROL

Because one is seeking to observe participant behaviour that is as natural as possible, the idea of quality control of participants runs contrary to a principal design point. There is one point on which you can ask participants to be thorough and that is in completing PRFs. We recommend that, much like scanning assessors' work, you should attempt to briefly scan participants' PRFs. This is most important the first time they are used because, if corrected at this stage, most participants will get the message next time they are used. Generally this isn't a problem, but watch out for the following:

- In group discussions, participants refusing to rank the discussants from most effective through least effective, as they are often asked to do.
- Participants saying that everyone has contributed equally. In effect this is the same thing as the above.
- Remarks that are so brief that they give no real insight into how the participant has attempted the task.
- Not completing the reverse side of a document.

The solution to all of these is to hand the form back to the participant with an indication of what is required, for example, 'I notice you haven't answered question 4 fully.'

Closing remarks to participants

There is a natural tendency among assessors to want to push on to complete their evaluations when the last exercise is finished. It is discourteous to participants, however, not to have a formal goodbye session with everyone present. This is normally timed to coincide with the arrival of a natural break for refreshment at which everyone can say goodbye less formally. The points to cover at this stage include:

- Ask participants to complete an instant appraisal form.
- Explain that results cannot be given until after the assessors have met. Talk briefly about the wash-up to come and emphasise that it is a multiple assessment process which takes some time to complete.
- Explain what feedback will be given and its timing.
- Make any housekeeping announcements, such as payment of bills and expenses.
- Bring up the issue of discussing the results with colleagues on return to work. The best advice is not to, since it will probably confuse those colleagues and may set up false expectations.
- Stress the value of attending the centre as a training opportunity and a chance to see what working at the target job level might be like.
- Describe any evaluative questionnaires or other methods of follow-up that you intend to use.
- Thank participants for putting in so much effort.

Preparing for the assessor discussion

There are a number of tasks that should be completed prior to the assessor discussion to ensure that time is used well when it does actually start. These include:

- Complete matrices of evaluations by criteria and exercise type for each individual. Much of this should already be done as assessors hand in their completed reports while the centre progresses. (See Figure 7.4 for example.)
- Establish a clear procedure so assessors know where to leave the work they have evaluated before the details are entered on to the participant performance matrix.
- Note on each matrix which assessor is responsible for each exercise in relation to the participant. This serves two purposes. Firstly, it helps to keep track of any assessor who is falling behind with their workload and/or is retaining completed work without handing it in. Later it will serve as a reminder about who assessed each participant in each exercise.
- Complete participant files and, if appropriate, lay them out in some logical discussion sequence. It may be possible in a selection event to detect a pattern of evaluations which lends itself to sorting participants into accept, hold or reject piles. In a development centre this is less likely to apply. The objective is to have easy access later on when assessors may want to refer back to original Assessor Report Forms in the course of debate.
- Keep an eye on assessors' use of time. Despite advice to the contrary earlier on, try to avoid giving yourself an excessive workload of report-writing at this stage. If, as is almost invariably the case, some assessors are falling behind with their reports, try to encourage those who have finished to assist them by giving advice or undertaking to evaluate additional work.

Participant							
Criteria	**Exercises**						**Overall rating**
	Non-assigned group discussion	Assigned role group discussion	Interview simulation exercise	Fact find exercise	In-basket exercise	Criteria-based interview	
Planning and organising	■					■	
Problem analysis			■			■	
Judgement		■	■				
Decisiveness	■					■	
Initiative				■	■		
Leadership			■	■			
Interpersonal sensitivity		■		■		■	
Persuasive oral communication				■		■	

Figure 7.4   Example participant performance matrix

The assessor discussion

The assessor discussion represents the high point of the assessment centre for most centre managers and assessors. The precise format of the meeting will vary according to the nature and purpose of the centre, but the almost universal approach is to hold a discussion where assessors pool their judgements and reach consensus about participants' performance on the criteria.

However, despite the significant volume of research into different aspects of assessment centre practice, there is curiously little firm guidance as to how best to run the assessor discussion, other than the general recommendations provided in the 'Guidelines and Ethical Considerations for Assessment Center Operations' (2000), which state:

- The integration of behaviours must be based on a pooling of information from assessors or through a statistical integration process validated in accordance with professionally accepted standards.
- During the integration discussion of each dimension (criterion), assessors should report information derived from the assessment techniques but should not report information irrelevant to the purpose of the assessment process.

- The integration of information may be accomplished by consensus or by some other method of arriving at a joint decision. Methods of combining assessors' evaluations of information discussed in the assessors' integration sessions must be supported by the reliability of the assessors' discussions.
- Computer technology also may be used to support the data integration process provided the conditions of this section are met.

Although these might appear somewhat prescriptive, they still leave a lot of room for different approaches to be employed.

Some concerns have been raised, both with the idea that criteria operate in a stable way in different circumstances (Sackett and Dreher, 1982) and with consensus as a process (Feltham, 1988b).

On the first issue, Herriott (1986) concludes that the rationale of rating by criteria is unsound and that it would be better to ensure that each exercise represents a valid work sample and then rate performance on each exercise separately. No doubt this argument has its merits but assessors' comments are nearly always mediated by criteria. In a development context we frequently find that specific feedback is often given in such a way as to discriminate between performance on the same criterion in different exercises. People have to know that it is, for instance, their planning skills that let them down in the in-basket in order to make sense of the data and make progress on their development. Indeed these reasons probably explain why Boyle et al. (1995) found that 81 per cent of a sample of UK assessment centre practitioners awarded overall ratings against each criterion which, as they pointed out, was usually driven by the purpose of the centre and the nature of the required output.

As to concern with the consensus process, a number of researchers have demonstrated that the final decision could be correctly predicted by a formula applied to their ratings prior to the assessor discussion as much as 95 per cent of the time (Sackett and Wilson, 1982). There are even claims that applying a formula might give a better result than an assessor discussion because the tendency is for more powerful assessors (that is, more senior people in the organisation) to hold sway in discussion.

It is difficult, without conducting further research, to refute this argument. We can agree that centre managers do need to be vigilant about the extent to which more senior views prevail in an assessor discussion. The implication that a simple mechanical pooling of ratings would have no detrimental effect on validity is counter-intuitive. Even if one could persuade assessors to forego the opportunity to discuss the participants in detail, which is doubtful, it seems a gross waste of such a high volume of rich data. So perhaps unsurprisingly, consensus was found to be the preferred approach of 76 per cent of the UK practitioners sampled in the research conducted by Boyle et al. (1995), with only 20 per cent favouring an arithmetic approach.

OVERALL ASSESSMENT RATING

As indicated above, the precise format of the assessor discussion will vary according to the purpose of the centre. One particular variant that is frequently mentioned in the literature is the OAR, in which the culmination of each discussion is to award the participant some form of numeric score. In its most obvious form, this is simply putting a number to the participant's performance to account for a decision to offer an appointment or to reject the participant. This has the advantage that it facilitates later research, because numbers are easier to manipulate, but otherwise seems to have little merit over simply making the decision.

Wigfield (1997) reports on a particularly interesting attempt to ensure a highly standardised approach to the 'wash-up' discussion, which used arithmetic scoring for an assessment centre run for one of the UK police forces. Assessors produced ratings using a 1–5 scale supported by written evidence for each of the ten criteria assessed across the five exercises. Overall criterion (OC) ratings were then awarded to each criterion by calculating mean scores, as well as calculating an overall OAR, based on the mean score of all the ratings. As this was a promotion assessment centre and it was essential that the process was to be seen to be fair and equitable, a set of decision-making rules were drawn up and publicised before the centre took place. These rules were used in the 'wash-up' discussion to determine who would be promoted, rejected or invited to attend a further interview in the case of borderline candidates. The rules stated that to be promoted a candidate must:

- Achieve an OAR ≥ 3 (where 3 is an acceptable standard)
- Achieve an OC ≥ 3 in at least 7 of the 10 criteria being assessed.

However, to aid the discussion candidates' scores were placed into five bands:

- Band A = OAR ≥ 3 and all 10 OCs ≥ 3
- Band B = OAR ≥ 3 and 9 OCs ≥ 3
- Band C = OAR ≥ 3 and 8 OCs ≥ 3
- Band D = OAR ≥ 3 and 7 OCs ≥ 3
- Band E = OAR < 3 and/or 4 or more OCs < 3.

Given sufficient vacancies, Band A candidates were automatically selected for promotion without any discussion. Similarly, Band E candidates were automatically rejected. This allowed debate to focus on the other three bands and consideration was given to which criteria were deficient and, should a candidate fail consistently across a criterion, then they would most likely be rejected as it would suggest they are unable to perform an essential aspect of the role. Wigfield reported that this approach saved a lot of time (30 candidates could be reviewed in as little as 1½ hours), whilst at the same time protecting the integrity of the process.

Indeed he stressed the need for practical expediency with such a process and pointed out that this was aided by careful consideration being given to the composition of the team chosen to review the data. Thus the review team who attended the 'wash-up' included a senior police officer, an occupational psychologist with responsibility for the design of the centre, an experienced police assessor with a remit for quality control within the centre and none of the assessors! The rationale behind this unusual approach was to ensure a balanced and objective review of the data relating to the borderline candidates and to have a transparent process which was free from any bias. Needless to say the review team needed to justify their decisions regarding the borderline candidates, 10 per cent of whom would typically be invited to attend a further interview. Wigfield does not go into any detailed explanation as to why assessors were excluded from this process, or how they felt about having their involvement curtailed. However, one thing is certain with this approach: the quality of the data captured during the centre must be well recorded so that the review team are able to interpret this information in the absence of the assessors. This requirement may well benefit from the occupational nature of police work, as having worked with police force assessors ourselves, we have noted that they are very particular in the way they record evidence!

Another interesting approach linked to the use of an OAR is the one adopted in, for example, Shell and AT&T. Although the OAR is still a one-numbered approach it is expressed as an organisational grade or level that the assessors expect the participant to attain over their career. From the research point of view this provides a much more interesting validation challenge, because the outcome may not be known for 10 or even 20 years.

In contrast with the single score indicated by an OAR, many of the more sophisticated development centres need a more detailed breakdown of the participants' performance against each of the criteria. This will require someone, usually a specified assessor, to complete a full report on the participant concurrently with the wash-up discussion. The amount of time spent on each participant can be as much as two hours, sometimes more. The contents of such reports and other follow-up issues are dealt with in the next chapter.

RUNNING THE ASSESSOR DISCUSSION

In terms of administration, the technique is almost invariably to take each participant in turn, then proceeding in criterion order to discuss their performance in each exercise with a view to achieving the consensus score on all the criteria. However, Boyle et al. (1995) point out that there are numerous different ways of doing this, of which they list three:

- Assessor reports evidence and then gives own rating – other assessors are invited to discuss the evidence and agree or amend if appropriate. This is perhaps the most traditional approach and was used by 60 per cent of their UK practitioner sample.
- Assessor reports evidence and then the group agree the rating – other assessors discuss the evidence and jointly agree a rating. This approach was employed 19 per cent of the time.
- Assessors report evidence and then assessors individually assign ratings, then group agree – other assessors assign their ratings which are then announced and discussed prior to a group decision by consensus or averaging. This approach was also employed 19 per cent of the time.

They note that whilst the first approach is clearly the most popular, it is less likely to lead to a thorough review of the evidence, as assessors will be less likely to challenge one another when they have not had the opportunity to directly participate in the process. They also point out that assessors are more likely to remain attentive when they know they will be asked to award a rating. Despite these observations, they do not go on to recommend either of the alternative approaches, perhaps because there is merit in all of them and at this stage there is no evidence to suggest that one approach is any better than the other.

As already stated, we favour taking each candidate in turn and discussing his or her performance criterion by criterion, until an overall picture of the person is built up. We also try to design the process so that every assessor can comment on every participant and therefore contribute to the consensus. However, there are several variants on this approach that we have come across as follows:

- In selection events, the marked grids are presented anonymously and the assessor group decides on that basis alone whether there should be an accept/reject or hold decision before they look at any individual record.
- Double marking is dominant in the academic sector but has crept in elsewhere, such as in the Civil Service, where it features within their Recruitment Code on the grounds that it reduces the likelihood of bias and increases objectivity and fairness. In the wash-up, both assessors are asked to put in their evidence. The centre manager has to be careful to rotate who is asked first, because the second marker can feel they have little to add.
- Integrating all the scores around an exercise can be very useful with a team of assessors who are 'bedding down' to their standards, particularly around a group discussion when every assessor will have seen all the participants to some extent. The rationale is less clear with other exercises, as it is the person who is the focus of the selection/development decision, not the exercise.
- Expert versus line assessors. Some consultancies train line assessors in relation to the live/observable/interactive exercises and provide or train other resources to mark written exercises, which are subsequently integrated in the wash-up discussion. This can speed up the process, but the centre manager needs to be conscious that expert opinion can be overly influential. There is also the risk that the other assessors never fully understand the input and the judgement if they don't know the exercise content themselves.

Although the process sounds relatively easy, it is at this stage that its integrity can come under attack. As noted earlier, the centre manager should avoid a tone that is excessively didactic or patronising, but they must retain control of the process. The following points should be noted:

- Insist on adequate time for discussion of each individual. Even in a selection event, where the summary of evaluations immediately suggests that the participant should be rejected, there is a need to ensure that the evidence is valid. It is not often the case that a participant is universally poor across all criteria. Even where that is the case, there is a need for a fuller explanation on two counts. Any selection decision must be legally defensible: the evaluations in themselves will not be enough to meet this need. Secondly, as we have noted elsewhere, the trend is to give some degree of feedback to participants even in selection events.
- Take notes as the evidence is presented. The extent to which you keep notes is a matter of personal style and the requirements of the centre. You should be satisfied that there are sufficient behavioural observations to back up the evaluations, before the group discusses the next participant. Keep on asking 'why' until the data have been procured.
- Delegate report-writing to assigned assessors. In centres with a developmental content, often for example in internal promotion boards, there will be a need to write a report of some sort. It is best if notes are committed to paper immediately following the discussion under criterion headings. In the normal format, one assessor would write up two participants as the wash-up proceeds. There is a need to be sensitive to the needs of individual assessors, occasionally paraphrasing discussions and suggesting written content to them.
- Timing and spacing discussions. We have already noted that wash-up discussions can take as much as two hours for each participant. What is much more likely in practice is that the first discussion takes three hours, the next couple about two hours each and following

discussions about one and a half hours each. This is because all new groups need to settle in to their own group dynamics. They need to become accustomed to the procedure and, most importantly, the first discussion almost always involves a considerable amount of calibration of standards. Try to arrange breaks at sensible points so that assessors can take a breather between participants.

- Taking the chair. In general the centre manager should aim for minimal personal input by acting as a catalyst of discussion, being timekeeper and clarifying points that may be at issue. Unless you are perforce an assessor, the role to avoid is that of the expert. During discussion, these are the centre manager's functions:

  - Aid assessors in recording behaviour by, for example pointing out if the evidence is inadequate and asking for more.
  - Enable assessors to communicate with each other. Encourage assessors to read verbatim from the Assessor Report Form, citing their evidence. This is very important for the first participant as it provides a model procedure for assessors thereafter.
  - Ask questions to clarify points. Only intervene if other assessors do not challenge evidence first. Then ask friendly open questions which help the assessor articulate why they have assigned this piece of evidence or that evaluation.
  - Watch the timing of the discussion and maintain focus. You have to use your own judgement as to the extent of drift that is tolerable. Beating an issue to death after a decision is as much a problem as digressions during a discussion. Periodic reminders of the number of participants left and the time available are usually enough to keep reasonably on track.
  - Minimise the impact of high-status assessors. This is rarely a problem but, when it does appear to be happening, one way of controlling the situation is to ask significant influencers for their contributions after everyone else.
  - Keep outside knowledge out of discussions. One of the main points of doing assessment centres is that judgements are made on the basis of what is seen at the centre. To ensure that all participants are treated equally, any previous knowledge of their performance should not be permitted. One of the very real pleasures of an assessment centre is in identifying talents and abilities that were previously undiscovered. Equally, although it is naturally disappointing when a protégé fails to meet the required performance standard, assessors must stick with the evidence they have before them.

RESOLVING DEBATES

Notwithstanding the comments above, there are times when the centre manager is the expert, very often because of their considerable experience as an assessor, and that can help to resolve questions. On process issues, questions should simply be responded to. On content questions the centre manager can offer their own observations from group discussions, for instance, but only after it is apparent that important data have not been volunteered by any of the assessors who observed that discussion. The best procedure is to ask whether anyone noticed a particular incident or item of behaviour that you believe has been overlooked. Quite often this will resolve a debate that is in danger of going round in circles. Even so, one must take time to check that everyone is happy with the resolution.

It is tempting to fall into the trap of responding to requests to give your own observations or evaluations as the wash-up proceeds. Although tempting, this should be resisted because you will be over-influential in the judgements that are made. This assessor behaviour is driven by lack of security in their role and in their judgement. Taking a longer-term view, their maturity will increase with increasing opportunity to use their judgement, not because you say what the answer should be.

You should also try to avoid giving a personal view of summary ratings, either by criteria or on the individual. If, having listened to the evidence and the debate, you feel that this participant merits no more than '2' and yet the assessors are agreed on a '4', then it is likely that standards on this criterion need discussion. It is clear that if a centre manager does not understand how the assessors are evaluating information then further discussion is necessary, to get to the point where common standards of judgement are reached. It doesn't actually matter who moves in which direction. What does matter is that a benchmark is worked out and applied consistently.

One final thought. Assessor evaluations should work on the basis of a standard that is absolute. In the most commonly used five-point scale, it is usual for the evaluation point '3' to indicate behaviour that is acceptable for performance in the target job or at the target job level. While all participants should be evaluated against an absolute, it can happen that assessors' views drift over the course of the assessor discussion. As a final check against that possibility, all final evaluations can be compared across the range of participants. There is a risk of reopening debate for the sake of it but, on the other hand, if it is evident that dissimilar standards have been applied over time, that issue must be resolved.

8 Life after an Assessment Centre

An assessment centre is such an all-embracing event for everyone involved that it is often easy to forget, during the planning stages and particularly during the centre itself, that there is life afterwards! In particular, thought must be given to the type of report that will be generated by the assessment centre, the means by which feedback will be provided and, if appropriate, how any development needs will be addressed. Although these events occur during and after the centre, they must naturally be planned for before the centre is run.

The assessment centre report

The nature of the assessment centre report is a function of the purpose of the assessment centre. If the centre is being run in order to make an external recruitment decision, then the report is of secondary importance when compared with the primary need of reaching a Yes/No decision and as such any report tends to be brief. If, on the other hand, the event is more of a development centre where all of the participants are internal, there is a greater need for a detailed report which is in fact the primary output from the centre.

WHAT FORMAT SHOULD THE REPORT TAKE?

As already indicated there is no one answer to this question, since the purpose of the event inevitably influences the outcome. Generally however, assessment centre reports will include some or all of the following:

- A summary of the individual's performance at the assessment centre.
- Some form of concluding remarks, possibly including recommendations.
- A summary evaluation of each criterion, including an overall evaluation rating if appropriate and an explanation of the behavioural evidence to justify that rating.
- A summary comment of the individual's performance on each of the exercises. This may or may not be accompanied by an overall evaluation rating for the exercise.
- Training and development recommendations and issues for further discussion.

The length of the report will therefore vary, depending upon which of the above elements are included. We have been associated with centres where the reports have been as short as one page, or as long as 15 pages! Our preferred stance is that whilst one doesn't wish to 'over-egg the pudding', it seems a shame not to capture as much useful evidence as possible from an event that is likely to be one of the most revealing experiences within an individual's working life. Indeed on many development centres, we believe the participant is entitled to a detailed report, having undertaken what is generally a very challenging experience. We usually therefore tend to recommend the following report format:

1. Personal Profile by Criteria
   1.1 Description of Performance on Individual Criteria
       (This usually runs to about half to one page per criterion.)
   1.2 Overall Performance Summary
       (This is a copy of the participant performance matrix referred to in Chapter 7.)
2. Personal Profile by Type of Exercise
   2.1 Group Exercise(s)
       (This section summarises the individual's performance when working with others. It will also highlight how the individual seems to perform in different types of group exercise or indeed different group sizes, if such data are available.)
   2.2 One-to-One Exercises
       (This section describes the individual's performance across the range of such exercises, again highlighting any variations where appropriate.)
   2.3 Working alone Exercises
       (This would typically include the In-Basket and/or Analysis Exercise and would again summarise the individual's overall performance on such tasks.)
3. Summary of Strengths and Weaknesses
   (This section highlights the individual's main strengths and their most significant weaknesses, usually two or three. It is generally about one page in length.)
4. Development Needs and Action Plan
   (This section, usually about one page, highlights the key development needs and outlines actions that need to be undertaken to address those needs. It will also include any job-related recommendations, or if necessary these can be shown under a separate heading.)
Appendix: List of Criteria and Definitions
   (We generally include these in the report in an attempt to reinforce the need to continually refer back to the criteria, as the basis of the behavioural language.)

Thus the level of detail in such a report would be similar to that given in the extract in Figure 8.1.

The time required to write an assessment centre report ranges from half an hour for a one-page report, through to two to four hours for a 15-page report. The latter will vary depending on the level of experience the individual has in writing such reports.

WHO SHOULD WRITE THE REPORT?

Essentially there are three options: the centre manager, an assessor or the participant. Needless to say there are advantages and disadvantages with each.

The centre manager

The centre manager is often expected to write the final assessment centre reports. The advantages stem from the fact that he/she should be an expert in assessment centre matters and having chaired the wash-up, will be familiar with all of the relevant details. Thus the reports should be of a high quality and will be written in a consistent style. The disadvantages relate to the fact that it will take a fair amount of time for one person to write

---

JUDGEMENT (J) - 2

* *Group Discussion* – Here Smith showed some evidence of good judgement: 'I think you (Mike) should become involved in that'; (taking notes - it was Mike's call next); 'Yes, I say that it is too early to mention products yet'; 'They would not want to compromise when they are spending £7 million'. Occasionally, his weak arguments caused him to back down against his better judgement; 'Those are not going to be the opening objectives?'; ('Yes, they are') 'Oh, all right'.
* *Sales Call* – Here Smith showed evidence of poor judgement: 'You are speaking to us because we are a PC supplier' did not help the objective of getting the customer to see the company as a broad-based supplier. When asked how much it would cost, and knowing the budget was £7.75 million, he said, '£8 million'. When the customer reacted to this, he said, 'A small increase in budget is justified'. (The customer was the 'number two' in a large Building Society and would not expect a salesman to react in this way.)
* *Written Proposal* – Here Smith gave good valid reasons for recommending his solutions, including central control, allowing instant access and the importance of protecting the investment.
* *Presentation* – Again, Smith showed poor judgement by saying to a Board of Directors, 'We will only progress if you agree to progress', and 'The next section is provisional on your doing business with us.'

Smith's overall performance indicates that while he can make some very sound judgements on occasions, he can also come to ill-thought-out conclusions and statements which could, in some circumstances, have a significant negative impact overall. Whilst generally his data analytical judgement is good, his people-judgement can be flawed.

Figure 8.1   A sample extract of a final assessment centre report

all of the reports and this may impact on the timing of the feedback. It is for this reason that organisations sometimes bring in further resources to assist with the task. If they are external consultants, their lack of knowledge of the organisation and its systems may adversely impact on the nature of the recommendations that ensue.

The assessors

Using assessors to write the final reports is often the preferred option. The advantages are that it allows the workload to be shared, thus enabling the task to be completed in a short timeframe. The assessors will not only be aware of all the relevant information from the wash-up, but will also have had the advantage of having seen the participants in action during the event. Furthermore, as the assessors are often the preferred choice for giving feedback, it makes sense for them to write the reports, enabling them to see the process through in its entirety.

The main disadvantage of having the assessors write the reports is the extra time commitment required from them. As each assessor is generally only asked to write one or two reports, this should not represent a significant problem. It is highly desirable to have the assessors write the reports before they return to their normal duties, otherwise other things may start to intrude and any delay may impair their ability to recollect specific details.

The participants

This is a rare alternative which has been undertaken on Self-Insight Assessment Centres (SIACs) which are explained in Chapter 10. The advantages are that the participant should be enthusiastic and committed to the task, since it is about them. Some people are more inclined towards such introspective analysis than others and consequently the level of detail and thoroughness often varies.

Again it is important to get the report completed before the event is concluded, otherwise it may slip as a priority once the participants return to work. The obvious disadvantage of this approach is the danger that participants may lack objectivity, or worse still may attempt to distort the truth. In our experience this rarely happens, particularly if there are procedures in place whereby the report has to be submitted to the centre manager who can verify the validity of the content, before it is presented to the participant's manager for discussion.

WHEN AND HOW SHOULD THE REPORT BE WRITTEN?

Once again there is no one definitive way of doing this but it may be helpful to describe how we generally approach the task. Given that we usually opt for the 1:2 assessor to participant ratio, we tend to ask each assessor to write two reports and to give feedback to those same two participants. During the wash-up, the appropriate assessor is encouraged to make notes on their participant. Whilst these rough notes can slow the process down a little, they provide useful summary comments which can then be developed into a reasonable draft report.

The centre manager has to ensure that the wash-up is not only thorough, but that the assessor in question has had the time to note comments as appropriate. Thus the challenge for the centre manager is to control the pace of the discussion without allowing the process to get bogged down. At the end of the discussion on that participant, the assessor is given all relevant documentation about that participant for subsequent reference. A period of time is set aside later for the assessors to generate their initial draft reports, which are normally perfectly adequate as the basis for feedback.

After the feedback session, assessors make any necessary final amendments to the report before submitting it for typing. The final draft of the report is then used for subsequent discussions and copies can be sent to the participant, their manager and/or their personnel file, depending on the organisation's policy.

Feedback

If the final report constitutes the main output from the assessment centre, then feedback can be seen as the process by which the assessment centre achieves its purpose. In most if not all cases, that purpose is to facilitate the personal development of the participants. Thus feedback should be a part of every assessment centre, even if the event is being run purely to help make a Yes/No hiring decision, for it would be a missed opportunity not to provide feedback to the successful job applicants. Indeed it is even worth considering giving brief feedback to unsuccessful external applicants and a number of organisations are now beginning to provide this facility. When assessment centres are run for selection purposes – such as with graduate recruitment or some form of internal selection – it is important to provide feedback as soon as possible. This is obviously true in terms of conveying the ultimate Yes/No hiring or promotion decision, as candidates will be anxious to hear how they got on. However, it is also true about why they were successful, or unsuccessful, so the feedback should take place preferably within a day and certainly within a week of the event itself.

In fact the position regarding the importance of feedback is underlined by the recommendations made by both the International Task Force on Assessment Center Guidelines (2000) and the British Psychological Society's *Best Practice Guidelines* (2003), (see Appendix at the end off this book) which state: 'All candidates/participants should be offered feedback on their performance at an assessment/development centre and be informed of any recommendations made.'

Feedback will inevitably be more detailed for a development centre, where the purpose is to motivate and enable the participant to do something meaningful with the information from the centre. Therefore, our focus in the remainder of this chapter is on the development centre type of event.

There are a number of different people who can provide the feedback, namely the centre manager, one of the assessors, a local HR representative, or an external consultant. Whoever it is, they need to be well trained in how to conduct this type of feedback and must be conversant with all aspects of the assessment centre in question. Thus if a local HR representative is chosen for the task, it is essential that they should have already been trained and have acted as an assessor.

One person who certainly should not give the feedback is the participant's manager. Although they may be well trained and very adept at such matters, the problem is that they are unlikely to be viewed as totally objective and the participant will probably suspect them of basing their observations and conclusions on events outside the assessment centre. Furthermore, the participant should receive regular feedback from the manager anyway, so it would be a lost opportunity for a fresh perspective. More often than not, the assessors are the best people for the job, for although they may not be as well trained as the centre manager, they should have a good knowledge of the target job or job level and they can share the workload.

Most feedback is carried out face to face, mainly because the nature of the task requires a high level of contact, the need to build a relationship of trust and to generate empathy. Furthermore feedback sessions usually last from one to two hours and it is difficult to effectively carry them out by other means. The main exception to the face-to-face approach is where telephone feedback might be provided to unsuccessful external applicants after a selection assessment centre.

PLANNING THE FEEDBACK SESSION

The first thing to be remembered when planning a feedback session is to be clear about the goal or objective to be achieved. In general, this will always be the same, namely to gain the participant's commitment to take action to develop their abilities in certain areas. In this respect the feedback interview is a type of selling situation. The participant should be motivated to want to take action and feel a sense of obligation, for there are far too many instances of people seeming to respond positively to feedback, only for them to take no subsequent action. To continue with the sales analogy, the customer hasn't bought until the contract is signed. So keeping this fundamental point in mind, we can list some of the issues to be considered during the planning stage:

- Establish a clear agenda for the feedback session. This will ensure consistency in approach for each feedback session and reduces the likelihood of anything being overlooked.
- Time will need to be allocated at the beginning to explain that the assessment is based upon a set of criteria which may need to be explained, if not already done so. It is also

useful to explain that the criteria and the simulations are linked to the demands of the target job or job level. Finally it helps to state that the feedback is based upon the collective views of the assessor panel and is not based on the views of any one individual.

- Think about whether the emphasis for the feedback session will be in relation to performance against the criteria or the exercises. In most cases the criteria act as the basis for providing feedback, as they represent discrete skill areas which can be targeted for development. On other occasions you may wish to highlight performance issues within a particular exercise. This is generally helpful if the participant has performed very well or very poorly in a given exercise.
- Plan the sequence of the feedback interview for each participant in such a way as to ensure that the interview commences and concludes on a positive note.
- Think about any specific points relating to the participant that need to be planned for or anticipated in advance. For example, sometimes a participant's self-report form, which is completed after each exercise, indicates that they believe they performed well, whilst your feedback is going to challenge that perception. In such cases you need to prepare carefully how you will present the evidence to enable them to appreciate the point you are trying to make.
- When selecting the evidence you intend citing to illustrate a behavioural characteristic, try to use a few good quality examples rather than a mass of incidents, some of which might be spurious. Aim for quality rather than quantity. Furthermore, make sure you have all of the relevant evidence available should you need to refer to it.
- Ensure that the logistics are in place for the feedback interview. As with any interview you will want a quiet room, free from interruption and available for the duration of the session.

CONDUCTING THE FEEDBACK SESSION

As already mentioned in Chapter 6, the givers of feedback, who in most cases will be the assessors, need to be thoroughly trained in how to handle the feedback process. Giving feedback and the associated area of counselling are significant topics in their own right and we obviously cannot attempt to cover them adequately within this book. There are many generalised recommendations about feedback, most of which in broad terms suggest the following:

- Be specific, not general – use behavioural evidence to focus on tangible facts, not generalised comments and opinions.
- Focus on behaviours – indeed focus on behaviour that can be modified rather than shortcomings that cannot be changed.
- Be descriptive, not evaluative – whilst evaluative comments are sometimes necessary, they can also get in the way and it is generally more helpful to focus on factual observations which will allow the recipient of feedback to reach their own conclusions.
- Check and clarify the recipient's perception. Do they see things in the same way, do they understand the points being made? Similarly try to anticipate their position and put things in their terms, rather than your own.
- Provide feedback with manageable amounts of information. The process can be impaired if the recipient is expected to absorb too many points at one time. This is why it is usually helpful to deal with only the most significant areas needing development, even if there are

more development needs. Don't bury the recipient, otherwise they won't know where to start when it comes to taking remedial action.

- Provide feedback with care and genuine concern. The recipient should feel that the provider of feedback genuinely wishes to help them. Thus it is essential to develop a degree of empathy with the recipient when providing feedback.
- Encourage the recipient to be open and receptive to feedback – it is much more constructive when an individual invites feedback and can be encouraged to enter into a process of self-evaluation.
- Express your own feelings – this can help to build trust and empathy within the relationship, especially when coupled with the use of self-disclosure. We have often found it beneficial when providing feedback to young management trainees to share with them our own mistakes in similar circumstances and we often finish up by saying 'Welcome to the human race!'
- Help the recipient to explore solutions – remember that the ultimate purpose of the feedback is to bring about a constructive change in future behaviour. Sometimes people cannot see how they could have done anything any differently, in which case it is useful to help them to see different possibilities. This is usually best achieved by asking questions like 'How else could you have...?' or 'Could you have tried...?', or if necessary making suggestions like 'Well you could...'

None of these suggestions should be regarded as directives. Indeed, as Wood and Scott (1989) explain in relation to a similar list of their own, you can break any of the rules of feedback providing you understand the purpose of the rule and assuming your course of action will achieve the goal more efficiently with due regard to the individual.

For a more detailed appreciation of feedback, consult such texts as *The Manager's Guide to Counselling at Work* (Reddy, 1987).

When it comes to sequencing the feedback interview, it is important that all of the issues raised previously are built into a coherent structure. Goodge (1989) suggests a useful outline framework called BRINK which depicts the following sequence:

- Background
- Results
- Implication
- Needs
- 'Klosing'.

Thus the process starts with some general *Background* points which include establishing the purpose and agenda for the session, gauging the participant's overall perception of their performance and starting to get a feel for their aspirations. The next stage is to discuss the *Results* from the assessment centre, which constitute the 'meat' of the session. This leads on to the *Implications* for the individual's development and career decisions. The individual is then encouraged to identify what *Needs* to happen next. (It is important at this stage that they begin to take ownership of these actions.) Finally, the provider of feedback should seek to *Klose* the session by getting some form of clear commitment to action. It is in this manner that the feedback session is likened to a sales situation, in which 'the close' is the final step in the sales process. Within the context of the feedback interview this might entail getting agreement to specified actions and defining at what point progress will be reviewed at some future stage.

Our own preferred approach to the feedback interview is very similar to this and a typical example of an outline agenda is provided in Figure 8.2.

1. Ask them how they felt it went. Encourage them to express their views. Use this as a gauge of how accurately their self-perception matches up with the feedback you are about to give.
2. Explain:

   - The feedback is based upon the collective views of the Assessor panel, who were all involved in reviewing all of the available information about the individual's performance.
   - The rating scale that was used (only necessary if participants will be shown their ratings).
   - The criteria that were being used on the assessment centre; just check they are familiar with them as these will be discussed in further detail as you proceed.
   - They will get a copy of the report for their own retention; however, they may wish to make notes to assist them with their Personal Development Action Plans.

3. Go through the criteria in your predetermined order:

   - Restate the definition of the criterion.
   - Provide positive and negative examples of behaviour from different exercises.
   - Check for understanding and agreement; seek reactions.
   - Give them the Assessors' performance evaluation on that criterion.
   - Repeat for each criterion in turn.

4. Provide an overall summary of their performance on the assessment centre (this sometimes includes showing a matrix of their ratings).
5. Discuss major strengths; do not skip over these as it will give the participant the feeling that their strengths are not really important.
6. Discuss major areas of weakness; if the participant has many weaknesses then it is helpful to focus on a few of the major ones for developmental purposes.
7. Explain that the report needs to be finalised with the addition of Action Plans and, once typed, copies will go to the individual, their manager and to personnel for record purposes (lifespan of about 2–3 years).

Figure 8.2   An example of an outline agenda for a feedback session

WHO SHOULD BE PRESENT WHEN FEEDBACK IS GIVEN?

Organisations often wrestle with the question of who should be present on the grounds that an individual's development is generally accepted as being one of the responsibilities of his or her manager. Clearly organisations do not wish to undermine the manager's role; however, it is generally felt that the presence of the manager at the feedback session may serve to hinder the process. This may occur for several reasons: for example the participant may feel embarrassed or even outnumbered, depending on the relationship they have with their manager. The manager may become defensive on behalf of the participant, particularly if they feel things reflect on them personally.

So whilst there are no right or wrong answers, general practice would seem to support the view that the manager should not be present during the feedback, although naturally there are exceptions. For example, if the feedback is going to be very positive and it is felt that there is an opportunity to galvanize the two to work together on the individual's development, then it may be worth considering. There is of course the concern that different participants may be seen to be treated in different ways.

If the decision to exclude managers from the feedback session is adopted as a general rule, then the question arises of how to convey the information to the manager?

In our view this is an important step within the developmental process because the individual and his/her manager will need to work closely together in addressing identified needs. There are a number of ways of tackling this issue: for example, the participant might be encouraged to talk through the results of their report with their manager. Alternatively, as mentioned earlier, the manager may receive their own copy of the report; however, this can be dangerous in that the interpretation of the results from an assessment centre could be adversely influenced if one doesn't have a good understanding of the process.

It is for these reasons that it is generally recommended that either the centre manager, or preferably the assessor who provided feedback to the participant, should talk through the report with the manager. In this manner, on-the-job performance can be compared and contrasted with the findings from the centre, although it needs to be remembered that the assessment centre is focusing on a higher job-level with its associated demands and responsibilities. Such a discussion should take place before the participant meets with their manager, so as to maximise co-operation, avoid misunderstandings and ensure the manager is not at a disadvantage. When the participant and his/her manager do finally meet, they should be aiming to identify development actions for implementation and should agree a schedule for reviewing progress. It will also be likely that some form of progress report will be required by the centre manager of the assessment centre, or some other co-ordinating body such as the training and development function.

FEEDBACK ON THE FEEDBACK

Whilst this might seem somewhat incestuous, it provides an opportunity for establishing the likely level of commitment that the participant has towards their on-going development. This should be viewed as a 'crude measure' for, as Goodge (1989) points out, the extent to which people agree with the feedback is a poor measure of how effective it has been and the best measure will be the degree of subsequent behavioural change that arises from the feedback.

Thus the more useful benefit of this process is that it will highlight any quality control issues that might need to be addressed, with regard to the way in which the feedback session was conducted. This in turn will assist in the process of monitoring assessor standards as referred to in Chapter 6.

The recipient's views on the quality of the feedback can be obtained by using a questionnaire such as that shown in Figure 8.3.

Actioning the development plan

Once the feedback has been concluded and the development needs have been agreed in principle, the means by which they are to be addressed should be considered. An important factor in this is the extent to which a multi-faceted approach is adopted for it is all too easy to simply point the participant in the direction of the training department, expecting them to

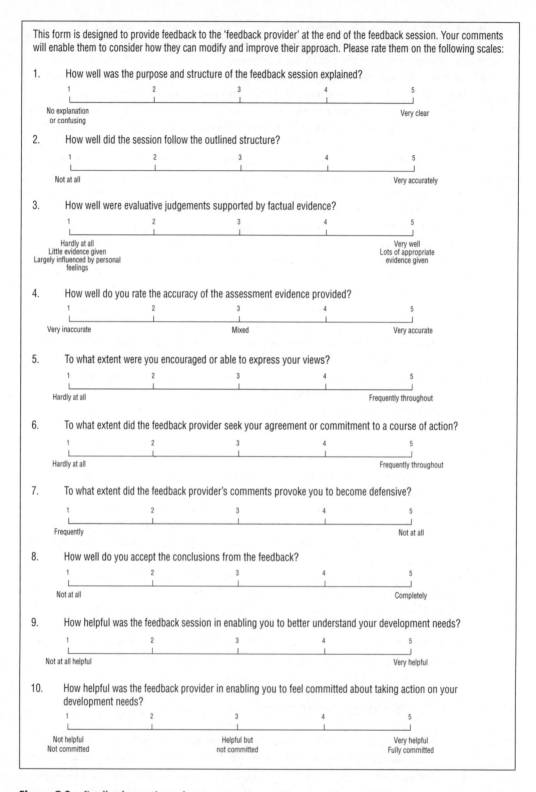

This form is designed to provide feedback to the 'feedback provider' at the end of the feedback session. Your comments will enable them to consider how they can modify and improve their approach. Please rate them on the following scales:

1. How well was the purpose and structure of the feedback session explained?

    1   2   3   4   5

    No explanation   Very clear
    or confusing

2. How well did the session follow the outlined structure?

    1   2   3   4   5

    Not at all   Very accurately

3. How well were evaluative judgements supported by factual evidence?

    1   2   3   4   5

    Hardly at all   Very well
    Little evidence given   Lots of appropriate
    Largely influenced by personal   evidence given
    feelings

4. How well do you rate the accuracy of the assessment evidence provided?

    1   2   3   4   5

    Very inaccurate   Mixed   Very accurate

5. To what extent were you encouraged or able to express your views?

    1   2   3   4   5

    Hardly at all   Frequently throughout

6. To what extent did the feedback provider seek your agreement or commitment to a course of action?

    1   2   3   4   5

    Hardly at all   Frequently throughout

7. To what extent did the feedback provider's comments provoke you to become defensive?

    1   2   3   4   5

    Frequently   Not at all

8. How well do you accept the conclusions from the feedback?

    1   2   3   4   5

    Not at all   Completely

9. How helpful was the feedback session in enabling you to better understand your development needs?

    1   2   3   4   5

    Not at all helpful   Very helpful

10. How helpful was the feedback provider in enabling you to feel committed about taking action on your development needs?

    1   2   3   4   5

    Not helpful   Helpful but   Very helpful
    Not committed   not committed   Fully committed

Figure 8.3   Feedback questionnaire

provide a perfect panacea for all ailments! Our preferred approach therefore, is to gain acceptance of the fact that there are generally three 'players' who need to be involved in an individual's development: namely the training and development department, the individual's manager and, of course, the individual. Once this principle is accepted, the way is clear to map out an action-oriented personal development plan for that participant.

Figure 8.4 shows the two main routes to development and provides an overview of the various elements that can form the basis of a personal development plan.

To assist with this process, Lee (2000) explains that some organisations have provided what are sometimes referred to as 'development options guides', which provide a series of recommendations as to how a development need for a given criterion might be tackled. Either being paper-based and/or available through the organisation's intranet, these guides can take various forms: they typically offer recommendations on coaching; on-the-job project work; group activities; reading, and other miscellaneous suggestions for each of their designated criteria.

The range of activities that can be undertaken to address different development needs include the following.

TRAINING COURSES

Courses are usually seen as the most obvious option. However, whilst most skill-based training courses have much to offer, the problem is that they are usually designed to meet pre-determined needs which may differ significantly from those highlighted by an assessment centre.

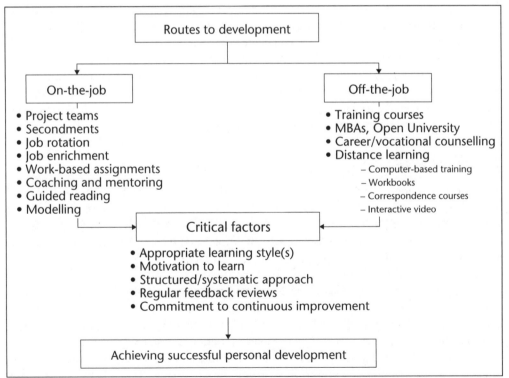

Figure 8.4   The routes to successful personal development

One answer to this problem is to run dedicated workshops for specific criteria. Criteria-based workshops, as we call them, offer the advantage of being highly focused in that the events are normally run for small groups of delegates who naturally are aware of their development need and therefore stand to gain more from the process. The workshops are highly participative and practical in style. We generally use a single criterion, or in some cases a sensible grouping of a few criteria, as the key focus and relate them to the exercise content of the assessment centre.

Our approach, for example, is to start by discussing and exploring the criterion definition so that the delegates become fully conversant with all of the ways in which the criterion might manifest itself. We then encourage the delegates to share their experiences from the assessment/development centre and examine what they did within the different exercises that led to the criterion being defined as a development need. We then explore alternative approaches and strategies and provide fresh opportunities for practice. The duration of these workshops can vary from one to three days, depending upon the number of criteria being tackled at once and the number of delegates.

READING

As most people tend to learn more quickly through practical experience, reading is unlikely to be an effective solution by itself. There is some merit in providing suitable recommended reading lists, particularly for the 'passive' learner, or as Honey and Mumford (1983) would call them, the Reflector-Theorists. Such individuals tend to prefer carefully internalising a concept before seeking to try it for real.

Once again there is scope for providing greater focus to address specific criterion-related development needs, by using dedicated workbooks. We have written a number of criteria-based workbooks for clients targeted at specific criteria. The advantages of such workbooks are that they not only focus on a defined need but they also encourage the individual to work through their own programme of development for that criterion, over a period of time. Such workbooks will typically contain some theory, a number of practical exercises, a series of learning self-review stages and suggestions as to how to seek feedback and measure progress. In essence they constitute a form of distance learning.

EXPERIENTIAL LEARNING

Learning by experience is rightly becoming accepted as an important opportunity in our day-to-day lives, both at work and at home. It is self-evident that there is an abundance of opportunities for exploring and developing those skill areas that have been identified as development needs. The process starts with the individual recognising that they must take responsibility for their own learning. In short, they have to commit to becoming self-developers. Not everyone finds this easy for some are too wrapped up in achieving their tasks without ever giving much consideration to the processes they employ in doing so. They are often blind to 'how they got there'! It may therefore be necessary to gain this understanding and commitment by initially having the individuals attend a self-development workshop. This may have already been tackled on the development centre as explained in Chapter 10.

Once the individual has tuned-in to the concept and is aware of their development need, they are in an immensely powerful position, for as Moshe Feldenkrais, a renowned 'movement re-educator' has said, 'When you know what you are doing, you can do what you want.' It is then a matter of seeking opportunities to learn by observing others, trying new methods and obtaining feedback. Thus it is helpful to seek out role-models who have acknowledged expertise in the appropriate skill area and to discuss with them how they approach such matters and if possible to observe them at first hand. When it comes to trying the new technique for oneself, it is important to arrange to get objective feedback, as well as making the time to review one's own performance.

Another developmental strategy is to discuss with one's manager the possibility of taking on new responsibilities or tasks that will create the opportunity to develop the targeted skills. Once again it is important to arrange for monitoring and feedback to be part of the process. Indeed this is an opportunity where the mentoring concept can be utilised, although as Clutterbuck (1993) explains, this is not something you can introduce overnight and the organisation will need to invest in establishing a mentoring programme if one doesn't already exist.

PROJECT TEAMS

Forming multi-functional project teams is a particularly good way of helping individuals to develop because it offers a highly practical and rich experience which usually necessitates the use of a wide range of skills. Furthermore, if the assessment/development centre has been run as part of a 'fast-track development programme', then the use of project teams for subsequent development can be a useful way of giving those individuals a broader perspective of the organisation. In addition, the participants gain more access and have heightened visibility to senior management who are often asked to act as project champions or sponsors.

FURTHER DEVELOPMENT OPPORTUNITIES

Apart from those development opportunities already discussed, organisations can also consider some of the other items shown on Figure 8.4 such as:

- Job rotation or secondment.
- Job enrichment.
- MBAs and Business School programmes.
- Open University courses.
- External counselling to address career, vocational or personal problems.
- Computer-based training programmes.

Whatever the approach, it is important to remember that the focus should be specifically related to the development needs identified on the assessment/development centre.

As a footnote to this whole issue of post assessment centre development, we would stress that once an organisation decides to go down the assessment/development centre path, they need to be prepared to make the investment at the back-end of the process to continue what has been started – for it is obviously counter-productive to make people aware of their development needs and then to fail to offer any form of support. Fortunately in our experience this rarely, if ever, happens.

9 Validating the Assessment Centre

The validity of assessment centres in general is very good. The same can be said of psychometric tests yet many readers will be aware of the well-publicised difficulties that have surrounded their use by British Rail and London Underground in the UK, and the virtual disappearance of personality questionnaires in occupational assessment in the United States. Much of the criticism has been driven by a concern with questions of bias and, albeit unintended, ethnic and gender discrimination. There is almost certainly more criticism to come as the number of poorly designed but quick to administer tests grows in the marketplace.

As it is with psychometrics, so it is also unfortunately with assessment centres. Just because properly designed and applied centres work well, it does not mean that any process lasting longer than a traditional interview, containing some form of group exercise, is equally good. We have recently encountered a number of examples of poor design, including one centre which had the following features:

- No assessor training was given.
- No evidence existed for a relationship between what was being assessed and what is significant for performance in the target job.
- A group exercise that specifically required people to roleplay.

The Human Resource Manager, not surprisingly, was dismayed at what had turned out to be a disruptive event running contrary to his expectation of providing important insight into the development needs of ten senior managers. In this case, the damage that had been done was so obvious and so extensive that remedial action was taken straight away. This kind of situation is extremely rare but it does underline the need to examine and review two key questions:

- Does your assessment centre do what it is supposed to do?
- Does your assessment centre work as well as it could?

These questions are the underlying themes that are at the heart of any attempt to validate an assessment centre, whether a particular event or the process in general. The latter is the focus of academic research; the former is of more direct relevance to the practitioner. The following sections describe some of the practical measures that can be taken to validate an assessment centre.

Qualitative validation

Qualitative validation is essentially asking for reactions to the process from all the people involved. This will always include participants and assessors. In the case of a development centre or a promotion board the participant's managers would also be canvassed. There are a number of ways of doing this, the most obvious of which is to talk to people directly. This can be rather time-consuming and even if any analysis is done on the data, it is likely to reside in the head of one or two individuals. If there is any possibility that there may have to be some changes to the programme that you might subsequently wish to monitor, this argues for a questionnaire.

Questionnaire design is as much an art form as a science and the key is to keep a balance between an appropriate degree of focus and totally free comment. A good format therefore is to have a number of open questions and a number of questions that have multiple choice responses indicating varying degrees of satisfaction. The issues will vary with the audience, but the point of focus should be the experience of assessing or being assessed.

PARTICIPANT REACTIONS

It is assumed that the survey would take place shortly after initial feedback has been given. The main points to ask participants to consider are:

- The quality and extent of any briefing before attending.
- Overall feelings about the assessment centre.
- Whether they liked or disliked any particular exercises (list).
- Comment as to why they liked or disliked any exercise.
- Extent to which any strengths or weakness identified concurs with their own view of self.
- Importance and relevance of criteria selected to assess current or future role.
- Any perceived difference between the way they behaved at the centre and the way they normally behave at work.
- Identify anything that may have inhibited them from doing better.
- Comment on impact on self-perception and career aspirations.
- If feedback was given, the extent to which information needs were met.
- The extent to which any feedback reflects their view of performance, ability and development needs.
- The sensitivity of the person giving feedback.

ASSESSOR REACTIONS

There are two broad themes to consider in understanding the reactions of assessors: their reaction to the process and any view of potential spin-off benefits. The main points to consider are:

- How well does the centre assess participants' strengths and weaknesses?
- How much help is this to the participant?
- The extent to which promotion decisions should rely on assessment centre observations.
- The accuracy of overall judgements.
- The accuracy and ease of identifying criteria.

- The relevance of criteria and exercises to future roles.
- What effect has assessor training and acting as an assessor had on ability to evaluate people generally, conduct appraisals, select new staff and discipline staff?
- The quality and length of assessor training, as preparation to assess.
- Anything to improve in assessor training?
- Comments on the administration of the centre.
- Were there any surprises?
- Would they serve as an assessor again?

MANAGERS' REACTIONS

Managers may or may not have acted as assessors, but they play an important role in nominating participants and in sponsoring any development action plan. You need to gauge their reactions on the following:

- The quality and depth of guidance for nomination of participants.
- Their understanding of the purpose of an assessment/development centre.
- What they would like to know more about.
- The utility of assessment centre reports and any improvement needs identified within them.
- Degree of confidence in the judgements of strengths and weaknesses, or career potential.
- Were there any surprises?
- Would you nominate anyone again? If not, why not?
- Any observation on the participant's behaviour after the experience.

The issues identified above should enable an organisation to get a good grip on any perceived deficiencies and to consider what, if any, remedial action is required. Although there will always be a range of views, a properly constructed event should meet with a broadly positive response to all of these questions.

Quantitative research

The main method of validating assessment centres is to assess their predictive validity, which cannot be done in the very short term. This will be examined at some length later. Nonetheless, there are ways to examine the structure of an assessment centre which can give an indication of potential weaknesses from the outset. If the data analysis is set up with the first use of the centre, the procedure should become semi-automatic as each subsequent centre proceeds. As statisticians will point out, there is considerable room for error if your first calculations deal with a population as small as ten. With a population of, say, 50 observations you can begin to feel confident that the results are not haphazard. All the statistics should be rerun periodically and concentrate on analysing the relationships among the assessment ratings.

MAKING A START

Start by calculating the mean and standard deviation for each unit in the criteria–exercise matrix (for example, interpersonal sensitivity as it occurs in each one-on-one exercise and each group discussion separately). Comparing the mean scores enables one to see whether higher evaluations are being awarded in one type of exercise over another.

The standard deviation is an indicator of spread of scores, so a wide spread would indicate that assessors are using the range of evaluations whereas a narrow one would indicate assessors giving everyone much the same mark. If that mark is the middle of a range, say 3 in the usual 5-point scale, the chances are that assessors are prone to central tendency. This is usually a sign that assessors are not sure of their judgement and are opting for the 'safe bet' category. A possible implication of this phenomenon, which might be confirmed by checking that criterion in different situations, is that assessors are not able to 'see' the behaviour. If this is only true for one exercise, it is likely that the exercise is not working as intended. If it is true for all exercises there are two possibilities: either the assessors have been poorly trained or, worse, the criterion is ill-defined, possibly meaningless. Among other things, poor assessor training is more likely to be exhibited in a grand mean central tendency. In other words, the average of all the cells in the matrix would have a small standard deviation. If the uniform mark is either high or low, with a small standard deviation, this would indicate an inappropriate level of difficulty on this criterion and within this exercise.

Once a reasonable volume of data is available, one can check that raters are using the full width of the scale by identifying the frequency with which each mark is allocated. On a normal distribution curve one would expect some 40 per cent of ratings to be 3, 25 to 30 per cent to be 4 or 2, and 10 per cent to be either 5 or 1. There are three main possibilities to explain any significant deviation from this:

- Particularly good or weak participants.
- The exercise is badly constructed for the target group.
- Assessors are not well trained.

No one can actually tell from the statistics which of these is the appropriate answer, but combining the quantitative data with the qualitative data should give some useful pointers as to which of these explanations is most likely.

POTENTIAL REDUNDANCY OF CRITERIA

A very high correlation between the overall ratings for two criteria across all the circumstances that they share tends to indicate either that they are the same thing masquerading under two labels or that they are not being differentiated in the minds of assessors. It is often said that if the distinction is meaningful, the solution is likely to be more assessor training. To some degree this is tautological. If the distinction is amenable to definition, this should already have been covered since it is one of the most important practical issues in assessor training. If the distinction is not satisfactorily amenable to definition (see Chapter 3), then no amount of training will enable assessors to see it as a useful distinction.

EXERCISES AND CRITERIA

There are two further calculations that can be made which can provide some pointers to further development. Means and standard deviations can be calculated for each exercise averaged across criteria and for each criterion across all the exercises in which it appears. If an OAR is produced, it may be possible to correlate it with exercise means and criterion means. If there are statistically significant correlations, this might indicate that a particular exercise or particular criterion is influencing overall judgements.

Comparing the means for each exercise will show whether some exercises are performed at an apparently higher standard than others, perhaps because they are easier. The standard deviations will show the extent of differentiation between participants. Similarly, comparing the means for the criteria will indicate whether some criteria tend to get higher scores than others and are more influential in the overall result.

Some caution is needed here because it may be the assessors' view that the criterion *is* more important for successful job functioning than other criteria. As a general result, it has been found that performance within an exercise is assessed with a notable degree of homogeneity across criteria, despite all the exhortation to avoid falling foul of the 'halo' effect. Further, there is repeated evidence from the earliest research (Vernon and Parry, 1949) to the present day that assessors place more emphasis on group discussion exercises than other kinds of exercise, particularly written exercises. This has led some researchers to conclude (Herriot, 1986) that the idea of assessing people's capability against criteria should be revised if we are to develop a better understanding of how assessment centres work. We will return to this issue later on.

Reliability

One of the best established arguments in researching assessment and selection methods as a whole is that reliability is a limiting factor in the computation of validity coefficients. High reliability does not assure good validity coefficients but low reliability assures low ones (Guion, 1987). In common-sense terms, this means that if an organisation does nothing else, it should attempt to ensure that any assessment mechanism it uses works consistently. In reality, this means that an assessment centre should meet the best practice standards which by now should be clear to the reader.

This point was well made in a research study whose aim was to improve the validity of one of the best-established assessment centres, the Admiralty Interview Board. The conclusion was that attempts to provide highly differentiated dimensions (criteria) and elaborate methods for managing the assessor discussion were not important once a basic level of assessment centre technology was available (Jones et al., 1991). The basic level was taken to be:

- Identification of broad area of concern (job analysis).
- Procedures for discussion and review of evidence (consensus meeting).
- Training of assessors in procedures.
- The composition of a procedure to reflect the broad areas of concern (appropriate content).

Using the methods that have been identified in this chapter to conduct research and by ensuring that best practice standards are met, the reader should be able to establish that their assessment or development centre is reliable. We now move on to the vexed question of validity.

Assessment centre validity

As we remarked earlier, people become ardent fans of assessment centres because of the compelling logic of their design. Quite frequently this gets to the point where validation studies are thought to be unnecessary and rather an academic issue. On a practical note, we would argue that any organisation should be interested in assessing whether they have spent their quite large sums of money wisely.

The techniques we have demonstrated up to this point are mainly for proving and improving the reliability of the centre. In principle, the focus of a validity study is to demonstrate that the predictions made at the centre are accurate and useful. The research design for traditional assessment centres is comparatively simple.

Taking the example of AT&T, the prediction element is identified as a job grade or organisational level that the participant is expected to achieve. The validation study consists of comparing the predicted outcome with what actually happens some years later. By comparing the proportion of people who achieve that outcome with the proportion who either fail to do so, or who go on to exceed that expectation, you arrive at a correlation coefficient. The statistical calculation is comparatively straightforward.

As with all statistics, particularly those relating to the social sciences, the concern is with interpreting the data. Whereas other scientists can attempt to control experimental conditions and variables, in psychology it is rarely possible to achieve a situation where something is proved beyond reasonable doubt. In the field of selection and development we do need to understand some of the issues that make it difficult for us to view validity as a precise and absolute measure. We now briefly review some of these issues.

THE LACK OF A CONTROL GROUP

Much of the work concerned with testing the efficacy of drugs, for example, builds in the idea of the control group. You compare and contrast the treatment regime and amelioration of symptoms related to the drug with a group of people who receive some neutral substance. If there is a difference in average rates of recovery in the target group, which is not shown in the control group, one can begin to argue that the drug has an effect. If one were to use a similar methodological approach in assessment, the control group would be people who failed to pass the selection event. The test of validity would be whether people who passed were deemed to be performing well at some future stage and those who failed were, on average, not performing acceptably. It is interesting as a concept but wholly impractical. The problem is that we have no hard evidence of how the people who were not selected would have performed.

LIFE IS NOT STATIC

As argued ardently by Robertson and Smith (1993), the idea of predictive validity assumes a static state of affairs which is simply not borne out by commonplace experience. If the measurement point is, say, five years after an appointment or a promotion, people could mature in their outlook, degenerate into depression, marry, divorce and many other things. In relation to work, both the employer and the employee will be working to help the job match. New incumbents bring with them personal strengths which contribute significantly to the way the role actually evolves. Employers provide training, appraisal and coaching to help the person become effective in the new situation. In many situations, therefore, poor selection decisions are turned into acceptable ones by adjusting either the job or the people, and usually both, until an acceptable degree of fit is attained.

STATISTICAL ARTEFACTS

Any small-scale study is prone to errors of measurement to a very considerable degree. One of the great virtues of meta-analysis, by which all the results of several known studies are combined together, is that it provides much more reliable data than any one study. In the field of selection research, the average number of subjects in any individual study is 68 (Lent et al., 1971).

Proponents of meta-analysis demonstrate that it is possible through sampling errors, inappropriate and unsophisticated measurement techniques and a variety of other factors, including the standard error of the correlation coefficient, to reduce the predictive validity of a particular ability test from 0.75 to 0.20 (Hunter et al., 1982). If this is true for well-validated instruments, it is also likely to be true for other methods of assessment. How can we be certain that any validity coefficient generated by a small population is accurate?

WHO SAYS WHAT GOOD PERFORMANCE IS?

The number of selection studies that contain good measures of performance – that is content valid work sample tests – as a means of measuring how effective a person has become, is negligible. Researchers in the field mainly do what managers do when they want to find out how effective someone is – they ask the person's immediate supervisor. They then plot the supervisor's rating against performance on the original test to demonstrate a correlation. Frequently the rating is assessed on a simple five-point scale, although significant apparent improvements in correlation can be observed by having inter-rater comparisons built in and by having the rating done over a wide range of criteria, rather than one overall score.

On the face of it, these improved correlations tend to support assessment centre techniques as inter-rater comparisons across a range of criteria are central features of their design. Although this 'proof' is seductive, the danger is that one could end up using assessment centre techniques to test whether assessment centres are effective. Whatever the statistics might say, the argument can be construed as a circular one.

THE 'GOOD CHAP' SYNDROME

One of the criticisms of assessment centres is that they are not as objective as their proponents would have us believe. Opponents claim that a high degree of subjectivity creeps in – for example, assessor ratings of performance are based on some intuitive understanding of the type of person who progresses in the organisation. Equally, the people supplying the information for a job analysis share that same understanding of the good sort. Anyone who has the slightest understanding of corporate culture should not be surprised by this.

Different organisations do have clear preferences for particular types of people. What the design process does is to give a clear picture of the performance characteristics of the successful job holder rather than vague notions of fit. The fact that similar types of people continue to be selected does not of itself invalidate the process, provided that judgements are clearly mediated through criteria.

ARE PERFORMANCE OUTCOMES RELATED TO POTENTIAL?

In a world where rigid, multi-layered hierarchies are rapidly giving way to flexible multi-layered relationships and fewer clear promotion opportunities, does it make sense to predict a person's final grade (as is done in AT&T and Shell)? Apart from anything else promotion and salary progression may not necessarily be indicative of performance. There are many who would advocate that the rate of progress is likely to be a fairer measure than current performance, as assessed by immediate supervisors (Dulewicz and Haley, 1989). One only has to examine the pay award schemes in many large organisations to realise that performance and promotion are only notionally linked.

THE SELF-FULFILLING PROPHECY

Many academic researchers point out, quite rightly, that if the results of an assessment centre become known, it is quite likely that this will induce a self-fulfilling prophecy. Particularly in events that are aimed at 'fast-track' identification, the people selected will have a boost to their self-confidence. Equally, those who manage them will have higher expectations of them and will work hard to expose them to increasing responsibility. This combination of behaviours ensures that those selected do indeed progress as quickly as they are capable and probably faster than those who have not been selected.

In much the same way, development centres would be very difficult to validate because their intention is clearly to intervene in a person's development to make sure that the prophecy is fulfilled.

THE PARADOX

To summarise the academic debate, we seem to have a situation where there is reasonably wide agreement that assessment centres work as predictors of future performance, at least as well as any other known method of selection. In certain specific situations, where the objective is to assess overall potential, their validity is extremely high (Gaugler et al., 1987).

The evidence that they work on the basis that they are supposed to does not hold up so well. There is evidence of higher consistency of ratings within an exercise than within criteria, leading some to suggest that the available research consistently demonstrates a lack of evidence for construct validity (Klimoski and Brickner, 1987). We find this less surprising than the researchers do, because the way in which any criterion is expressed is likely to be quite different in different exercises.

The most compelling evidence from any single source remains the work done by AT&T. It is important to note that their studies, which have tracked the career progress of several thousand employees, gave rise to predictions which were never released into the organisation. The fact that they have been able to demonstrate high levels of validity over a 30-year period serves to support the argument in favour of assessment centres.

To return to where we started from, it must be worthwhile for any human resource manager to ask him or herself whether their investment in this approach is justified. If problems are encountered as a result of raising this question, it is probable that the resolution will lead to better human resource practices. If the questions are not raised in any systematic way, there is an equal probability that a poorly designed assessment centre will remain in place – with commensurate results.

10 *Development Centres*

The development centre represents the most significant evolution in the area of assessment centres. With today's organisations facing increased global competition and an environment of accelerating change, the need to adopt new ways of working is greater than ever before. Development centres have steadily 'come of age', as it has been recognised that they can play an important role in helping organisations meet these challenges.

Assessment centres versus development centres

As the comments above suggest, the leaner and flatter organisations of today are continually faced with the need to make their people more effective. Towards the end of the twentieth century, concepts such as empowerment, the learning organisation and total quality management (TQM) meant that people and organisations were encouraged to take a broader and more positive view of the need to develop. These trends have fuelled the growth of the development centre, a powerful diagnostic tool which helps people to undertake focused development. This highlights the main difference between an assessment centre and a development centre, for both use the same technology but with different purposes:

Assessment Centres	Development Centres
Selection:	Development:
• External recruitment	• Identifying 'fast-track' potential
• Internal promotion	• Diagnosing job-related strengths and weaknesses
The *end* of a process.	The *start* of a process.

The concept of using assessment centres for developmental as opposed to selection purposes is not new – AT&T in the US started to do so as early as 1971 and in the UK ICL were using them in the mid-1970s. However, the term 'development centre' is more of a British phenomenon and, as far as we are aware, was first used by Rodger and Mabey (1987) to describe a centre run at British Telecom, as part of a management development strategy. So how might a development centre be described? We use the following definition:

A development centre is the use of assessment centre technology for the identification of individual strengths and weaknesses, in order to diagnose development needs that will facilitate more effective job performance and/or career advancement, which in turn contributes to the attainment of greater organisational success.

Although this definition may seem long-winded, it does embrace the key elements of development centres and allows for the fact that there are even variations within development centres themselves!

Key features of development centres

It is worth elaborating further on what differentiates a development centre from an assessment centre. The term development centre is widely used these days, but as is often reported (Kerr and Davenport,1989; Ferguson,1991), some of them are only different to assessment centres in name. The following points represent some of the distinguishing features of a development centre:

- *It is not a pass/fail event.* Unlike the assessment centre, where some form of unitary decision is reached to hire/not hire or to promote/not promote, the development centre's purpose is to facilitate the development process.
- *Duration and cost.* The development centre is usually longer and therefore more costly than an assessment centre. This is principally for two reasons. Firstly, it is often necessary to gather more data in order to be able to define criterion-related strengths and weaknesses with greater precision. Secondly, the feedback and development processes are part of the event itself, rather than being left until after the event.
- *Ownership of the data.* With assessment centres the organisation will nearly always have ownership of the data. With a development centre the individual will not only have access, but often shares or is viewed as the principal owner of the data. This greater freedom and access to the data serves to empower the individual in a manner that is consistent with the evolving values within many organisations today.
- *Feedback occurs during the event.* Development centres may often entail feedback being given after each exercise, rather than waiting until the very end of the centre. This allows the individual to demonstrate adaptability and experiment as the event progresses. The format for this might go through four stages as described by Hunter (1990); namely Exercise-Feedback-Training input-Similar Exercise. In this way participants are able to learn from both the feedback and the training input, and the assessors are able to observe how the participant is able to absorb and try new behavioural strategies.
- *Development occurs during the event.* This can be tackled in a number of different ways. It can be linked to the feedback on exercise performance, as described in the previous point, or it can be linked to non-assessed activities aimed at providing further self-insights into strengths and weaknesses. A variety of questionnaires and additional exercises might be included.
- *Focus on learning and self-development.* Time needs to be allocated to enable participants to learn during the course of the event, if they are to go away with sufficient commitment to learning and experimenting with new skills. Kerr and Davenport (1989) describe how they came to revise one of the first development centres in British Telecom, so as to allow more time for participants to focus on the latter stages of Kolb's (1975) Learning Cycle. Kolb's model advocates that learning is a four stage process that involves *experiencing* an activity, having time for *reflection*, drawing conclusions and *theorising* what one has learnt, and then planning the future *application* of what has been learnt. Kerr and Davenport found that the percentage of time spent on the original development centre was 75 per cent for experience. This led to a perception amongst participants that the emphasis was more on assessment than development and they consequently adjusted the balance to 40 per cent experience, 20 per cent reflection, 20 per cent theorising and 20 per cent application.

    Ironically the insufficient allocation of time and effort for development is probably the most common failing of most development centres!

- *Greater need for counselling and facilitation skills.* The developmental nature of the event requires that either the centre manager or the assessors and/or additional resources need to take on the role of counsellors and facilitators.
- *Focus on criteria that can be developed.* It is an interesting, but sometimes overlooked point, that while a job analysis may suggest particular criteria for a development centre, there is little value in including those criteria if they cannot be developed. This is because the main purpose of the development centre is to help develop current and future job performance, and certainly isn't to demotivate, so there is little point in assessing non-trainable intellectual aptitudes such as numerical reasoning ability and so on.
- *An opportunity for pre-centre activities.* Unlike the traditional assessment centre, where there is almost an aura of mystique around the event, the development centre requires and gains from a much greater degree of openness. This can include making sure participants are fully aware of the criteria being assessed on the centre. Indeed participants are often asked to rate themselves against the criteria before attending the development centre. This process sometimes involves their direct manager. Some development centres gather data from instruments such as 360° feedback questionnaires aimed at providing the participants with additional views from the workplace.
- *The need for post-centre activities.* Given that the development centre is the start of a process, it is very important that the individual and the organisation are able to enter into what might be termed a 'learning contract'. The individual needs to be prepared to put in the effort to progress their own development, while the organisation needs to provide the necessary resources to support the process. These resources include an appropriate budget and a suitable level of management commitment.
- *The opportunity for self- and peer-assessment.* Because the development centre is not making selection decisions, it is not so critical if the level of accuracy suffers. This means there is an opportunity to involve participants as assessors, either in conjunction with dedicated assessors or instead of them (see the reference to the self-insight assessment centre (SIAC) later in this chapter). The main benefit of this approach is that the participants' greater involvement makes the whole process more acceptable and less threatening. It also usually results in a greater commitment to the personal development plan from the participant, since they helped to define the development needs and appropriate actions.

So, having established the differences between development centres and assessment centres, it is interesting to note that Boehm and Hoyle (1977) go one stage further and refer to two different types of developmental assessment centre (development centre) namely the Identification Strategy and the Diagnostic Strategy.

The Identification Strategy involves the early identification of people with high potential. Such development centres are often referred to as identifying 'fast-track' potential, which by implication means creating an elite band of individuals who will receive special treatment. The Diagnostic Strategy has a very different purpose, in that, while identifying future potential is inevitably part of the output, the primary focus is on the individual's strengths and weaknesses and how to develop job performance. The differences between these two strategies are best summarised in Figure 10.1 which is adapted from Boehm and Hoyle (1977).

Feature	Identification Strategy	Diagnostic Strategy
Purpose	Early identification of people with high potential to enable rapid advancement.	To improve current job performance and employee motivation and morale.
Target population	People who are already identified as having high potential.	Usually open to most if not all at a given job level.
Nomination procedure	By invitation only, based on meeting qualifying criteria.	By volunteering or asking to be put forward.
Nature of the decision/outcome from the centre	More of a pass/fail decision for future advancement (not an immediate promotion as with an assessment centre).	Focusing on relative strengths and weaknesses.
Nature of the feedback report	Highlights the need for high-level developmental activities to aid rapid advancement.	Detailed profile of strengths and weaknesses to enable subsequent discussions and action planning.
Level of organisational control and monitoring	Highly centralised control and monitoring due to very high profile of participants and their perceived value to the organisation.	Local management control, coupled with a reliance on individual motivation for self-development. May also involve mentoring.

Figure 10.1   A comparison of the features of different development centre strategies

The Identification Strategy is more aligned with the traditional assessment centre than the Diagnostic Strategy; it has a more tangible and distinct purpose, it is shorter in duration and therefore less expensive, and it is focused on high potential people thus maximising the return on investment. Not surprisingly, therefore, Boehm (1985) reports that the Identification Strategy has been favoured by most organisations over the Diagnostic Strategy, which has often been seen as less relevant to organisational goals and is therefore harder to sell.

As development centres have begun to establish themselves, we have started to see a shift in emphasis towards the Diagnostic Strategy. This may be because the Identification Strategy has been criticised as being elitist and demotivating for those that fail to be selected or remain with the programme. It may also be because organisational policies of downsizing and decentralising create a need for greater autonomy and empowerment, which necessitates continual development of manpower resources. Whatever the reasons, in our experience organisations often seem to want a hybrid development centre in which they are striving to get the best of both worlds. They want to be able to identify future potential, but they also want to develop people in their current jobs, particularly where future opportunities are not immediately forthcoming.

Woodruffe (2000) argues against this approach, claiming that assessment and development do not go well together and he suggests that the term 'development centre' should be reserved for centres whose purpose is *only* developmental, but we beg to differ. In our view there is no one standard format or approach to development centres, but rather they operate along a continuum as indicated in Figure 10.2.

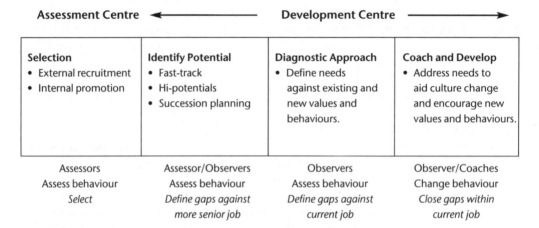

Assessment Centre ⟵————————   **Development Centre** ————————⟶

Selection	**Identify Potential**	**Diagnostic Approach**	**Coach and Develop**
• External recruitment • Internal promotion	• Fast-track • Hi-potentials • Succession planning	• Define needs against existing and new values and behaviours.	• Address needs to aid culture change and encourage new values and behaviours.

Assessors	Assessor/Observers	Observers	Observer/Coaches
Assess behaviour	Assess behaviour	Assess behaviour	Change behaviour
Select	*Define gaps against more senior job*	*Define gaps against current job*	*Close gaps within current job*

Figure 10.2   The assessment–development centre continuum

On the left of the continuum we have the traditional assessment centre, which is staffed by assessors whose role is to assess behaviour with the unequivocal purpose of making a selection decision. The remainder of the continuum shows the versatility of development centres, which can take various forms. These include the identifying potential and diagnostic strategies described by Boehm and Hoyle, along with a development centre whose focus is to coach and develop participants, which we describe later. While we agree you should not call an event, which has no development intention or component, a development centre, we would not go so far as to suggest that development centres should not have an assessment component. Indeed it is difficult for people to develop their skills without having the opportunity to demonstrate the required behaviours in some form of practice session, followed by receiving feedback on their performance. For the feedback to be meaningful and effective it needs to be specific, accurate and objective and this is only possible with some form of assessment, even if it lacks the formality of the 'full-blown' behavioural assessment process described in Chapter 6.

Growth of development centres

Development centres were first evident during the early 1970s, although they hadn't started to catch on until the 1980s. Since then their growth has taken off. A survey in the UK by the Industrial Society (1996) based on responses from 414 organisations revealed that 43 per cent were using development centres, with a further 15 per cent considering their use. Another UK survey by Roffey Park Management Institute (1999) reported similar findings, with the additional observation that respondents predicted a continuing shift from assessment centres to development centres. Indeed as specialist practitioners in the assessment and development centre field, we can confirm that our own activities have recently been much more strongly focused on development centres rather than assessment centres.

So what are the reasons behind this growth in popularity? To answer this question it is helpful to consider the benefits of using a development centre. The 283 respondents in the Industrial Society's survey (1996) who were using or planning to use development centres gave the following main benefits:

- Identifies areas for development   48%
- Provides a more objective evaluation of strengths/weaknesses   37%
- Identifies potential   33%
- Encourages ownership of development priorities   27%
- Can be tailored to business priorities   23%

Rather surprisingly only 8 per cent felt that a development centre would enhance an individual's commitment and motivation, given that Griffiths and Allen (1987) amongst others, cite this as one of the main benefits of development centres, which is a point we would echo.

Another important benefit in our view is that the use of development centres sends a strong message throughout the organisation that it is committed to developing its people and as such plays an important role in its HR strategy. Indeed this is well evidenced in the UK Public Sector, where the *Modernising Government* White Paper espouses the doctrine of 'Bringing on Talent', which has led to numerous Government departments and agencies running development centres.

Evolution of development centres

Griffiths and Goodge (1994) have attempted to map out the growth of development centres, portraying them as evolving through three generations of design as shown in Figure 10.3.

Centre type	First generation	Second generation	Third generation
Participant involvement	Minimal – participants simply tackle exercises.	Feedback to participants at end of centre, sometimes after each exercise.	Joint decision-making on competencies displayed after each exercise.
Exercises and tests	Off-the-shelf exercises and psychological tests.	Mainly off-the-shelf exercises and psychological tests.	Mainly real-life business problems.
Development planning	Little – perhaps part of post-centre feedback.	Some time given on the centre to planning, with monitoring and support afterwards.	More time given on the centre, with significant monitoring and mentoring afterwards.

Figure 10.3   Characteristics of development centre design

They describe 'first generation' designs (1970s and early 1980s) as being little different from assessment centres, typically of 1–1.5 days duration and purely assessment oriented with a focus on selection or identifying potential. The 'second generation' designs (late 1980s and early 1990s) had two major differences, in that they incorporated feedback and some time for development planning during the centre. In this respect they were seen as more 'employee-friendly' (Goodge, 1997), although their focus was still largely to do with identifying potential. The 'third generation' designs (mid–late 1990s) offered three further changes:

- First, real work-related issues/problems were used as the basis of exercises, rather than using off-the-shelf materials.
- Secondly, more time and attention was given to development planning both at the centre and afterwards.
- Thirdly and perhaps most radical of all, participants were 'empowered' by actively involving them in generating their own assessments.

At the time, Griffiths and Goodge reported that 75 per cent of the organisations they surveyed were using first generation designs, 20 per cent second generation designs and only 5 per cent third generation designs. It is therefore of little surprise that they suggested that we would see an increase in the use of third generation designs, which they claim are best suited to diagnosing development needs, as might be required to re-skill people when restructuring, or simply to develop competencies within jobs.

Whilst the simplicity of this evolutionary path has an obvious appeal, we agree with Lee (2000) that these transitions were never clear cut. Indeed, he points out that customised, rather than off-the-shelf exercises, were in use in some first and second generation centres. Also, participant involvement in the assessment process was a feature of some development centres in the 1970s, as described in the reference to the SIAC later in this chapter. So if it looks as if this evolution happened in clearly defined waves that would be a false impression, because there were third generation centres taking place when many organisations were still selecting on the basis of 'school tie'. Nor would it be true that any particular generation has died out or faded into the background. There are many events called 'development centres' today where the participant hardly gets any input into their own development from anybody, experts included. However, despite these blurred edges, Griffiths and Goodge's model does help to convey a gradual progressive trend (rather than a smooth transition), which highlights some useful milestones.

THE DIAGNOSTIC STRATEGY

As already stated, third generation designs clearly belong in the realms of Boehm and Hoyle's Diagnostic Strategy and if they are to grow in popularity, then as Boehm (1985) suggests, we need to address some of the underlying assumptions. Firstly, it is assumed that individuals can improve their skills in the areas measured on the development centre. Unfortunately there is little evidence to prove that this is so, since most research has been focused on the predictive validity of the assessment centre in a selection context. Thornton and Byham (1982), however, echo the popular view that people can change if subjected to a major developmental effort targeted to their particular and specific needs.

Secondly, it is assumed that people will be sufficiently motivated to undertake appropriate development activities and follow through with their development plan. Again little research has been conducted in this area but we are certainly aware of anecdotal evidence that would suggest that this assumption is not always justified.

Thirdly, it is assumed that we know enough to specify which developmental experiences are likely to impact on particular skills. Paradoxically, the dilemma here is the degree of precision which the development centre seems to provide. For example, if it identifies a development need in a criterion such as problem analysis, how confidently can we pinpoint appropriate developmental activities? Some organisations have produced Development Option Guides as mentioned in Chapter 8, however there is little evidence available to show how those options were identified or indeed their validity as activities that can improve skills in a given criterion.

One way of attempting to address the first two of these issues is to seek to involve the participants in the process of the development centre by putting them through a self-development module, while the assessors are involved in the wash-up. The possible format for a three-day development centre is shown in Figure 10.4. Naturally the content of the self-

	Participants	Assessors

Day One	<ul><li>Icebreaker</li><li>Exercises
	  – Group discussion
	  – In-basket
	  – Fact find
	  – Interview simulation
	  – Criteria based interview</li><li>Psychometrics
	  – Personality
	  – Leadership styles, and so on</li></ul>
		<ul><li>Observe</li><li>Record</li><li>Classify</li><li>Evaluate</li></ul>

Day Two	<ul><li>Continue exercises
	  – Analysis exercise
	  – Group discussion
	  – Presentation</li></ul>
		<ul><li>Complete assessments</li></ul>

	<ul><li>Self-development module
	  – Self assessment of:
	    Exercises
	    Workbook
	    Learning styles</li></ul>
		<ul><li>Assessor discussion</li></ul>

Day Three		<ul><li>Assessor discussion and prepare feedback</li></ul>
	<ul><li>Receive feedback</li><li>Develop personal development plan</li></ul>	<ul><li>Give feedback</li><li>Help develop personal development plan</li></ul>

Figure 10.4 Possible format for a three-day development centre

development module will vary from one development centre to another, depending upon the objectives of the centre, the level and background of the participants and the organisation's philosophy and attitude towards learning. In general, participants would experience some or all of the following:

- Exploring the criteria being used on the centre in some detail.
- Analysing any pre-centre work that they completed.
- Receiving any appropriate feedback from other sources such as 360° questionnaires, peer reviews and so on.
- Conducting some form of self-review of their own performance on the centre.
- Completing the Learning Styles Questionnaire and exploring the Learning Cycle, so as to facilitate their own learning at the point when they are constructing their personal development plans.
- Participating in some further exercises to heighten self-awareness and create a sense of fun after the demands of the development centre.
- Developing a receptiveness and willingness to experiment, in readiness for receiving their feedback.
- Starting to complete a workbook aimed at forming the basis of their own learning resource, which can and should be used after the event.
- Observing video recordings of their own performance on some of the exercises (most likely the group exercises) and discussing how they might have performed differently and/or better.

Such activities help to prepare the participant for the feedback process and reduce the likelihood of any unanticipated shocks or surprises. They also help to enhance the participant's level of acceptance and commitment to actioning their resulting development plan.

THE SELF-INSIGHT ASSESSMENT CENTRE

An even more elaborate way of involving the participant in the development centre is to use a 'Self-Insight Assessment Centre' (SIAC) approach, which in reality has many of the features of third generation designs.

The SIAC was originally conceived in the mid- to late 1970s by Mike van Oudtshoorn in conjunction with Roger Pryor and David Henson of ICL. Steel and Howard (1980) explain how ICL were keen to familiarise their personnel practitioners with assessment centre practices, as well as to develop a process which linked assessment centre technology with experiential self-discovery and peer learning. A Self-Insight Assessment Centre, as the name suggests, is an assessment centre requiring a significant involvement from those taking part. The main objectives of the event are:

- Identification of strengths and development needs against predetermined job-related performance criteria in job-related simulations.
- Formulation of a personal development plan to meet identified development needs and build on existing strengths.
- To develop participants' skills in performance evaluation techniques.
- Familiarisation with assessment centre technology and practices.

So the SIAC, like any assessment or development centre, requires the identification of appropriate criteria and job-related simulations, prior to staging the actual event. Once this has been completed, the SIAC (which usually lasts five days) starts with the participants going through an intensive day of exercises and tests.

The first main difference from traditional assessment or development centres is the absence of any assessors, with the data from the interactive sessions being recorded on video or audio tape for later analysis. Day two sees the participants reviewing the behavioural criteria to be used on the event and includes an explanation of how and why those criteria came to be chosen. In this manner the participants start to gain their first insight into the requirements of the target job and begin to see the relevance of the simulations they have just completed. The day continues with an intensive bout of assessor training.

Days three and four then deal with the bulk of the assessments. Each of the participants acts as an assessor and does a full assessment of their own performance (the self-insight process) and that of a different colleague, for each of the exercises. Once each exercise has been fully analysed, the participant acting as the assessor gives feedback to the recipient. These feedback sessions are generally very positive and constructive, partly due to the fact that the recipient of the feedback has already had an opportunity of assessing their own performance, thus facilitating a more objective self-perception. On the fifth day, each participant collates all of their own data collected from the various feedback sessions and integrates it into a structured personal development plan. One of the features of this approach is that the participant is the only person with the complete picture regarding their own performance. In this way, the SIAC is a non-threatening event and acts as an excellent vehicle for self-development.

Another attractive aspect of the SIAC is the fact that it actually takes participants through the four stages of Kolb's Learning Cycle, as mentioned earlier in this chapter. Participating in the exercises represents the experience; analysing one's own performance involves reflection; the feedback discussion provide an opportunity for theorising, and formulating a personal development plan requires consideration of the issues for subsequent application. Povah (1986) explains how ICL took this concept a stage further by linking the SIAC to a subsequent selection assessment centre containing exercises similar in type to those covered on the SIAC. In this way, the SIAC was clearly seen as a development event which enabled participants to receive feedback on their performance, before being 're-tested' at the selection centre, some 6–12 months later. It is interesting to recall how participants would often comment after the SIAC: that they now knew what they needed to do to pass the selection assessment centre, as if they had furtively gained some form of advantage. Our response was usually 'Yes and if you can do it there, you will also be able to do it on the job!'

The principal benefits of the SIAC over other development centres are:

- Participants are much clearer about their development needs; after all they played a major role in identifying them. Furthermore, as feedback occurs after each exercise, their understanding of their overall performance is much more comprehensive than it might be, when the feedback is provided in a summary form at the end of a development centre. This serves to enhance the participant's commitment to the actions contained within their personal development plan.
- The SIAC enhances the assessment, evaluation and feedback skills of the participants thus providing pay-offs in:

- Selection interviewing, as managers can use a structured form of criteria based interview.
- Appraisal interviewing, where the criteria provide an input to the appraisal process.
- Review and feedback skills, where there is a strong underlying emphasis upon providing objective evidence when making evaluations.
- Developing a strong base of trained assessors who can resource on future assessment centres.
- SIACs are cost-effective as they do not require the presence of any management resources acting as assessors. In fact, from the implementation point of view, the SIAC is probably no more expensive than any other five-day training course, except that it requires an accomplished facilitator who can take on the role of centre manager, trainer, coach and counsellor.
- Participants tend to respond very favourably to the SIAC process. For example, Steel and Howard (1980) report the following results from 240 people anonymously surveyed after attending a SIAC:
  - Over 70 per cent referred to the event as informative, challenging, revealing and stimulating, whilst only 4 per cent felt it was threatening, discouraging or embarrassing.
  - 75 per cent reported that the event had been very accurate and the other 25 per cent fairly accurate, in identifying strengths and development needs.
  - 69 per cent reported that the event was much better at identifying development needs than other methods such as performance appraisal.
  - 71 per cent reported that the results from the event were of much help in planning their self-development and 23 per cent reported they were fairly helpful. Only 6 per cent said of little help.

SIACs have been run in quite a number of organisations over the last 20 years or so and generally speaking the concept has been well received, sometimes with interesting developments. One such development was reported by Brown (1989) at the 2nd European Congress on the Assessment Centre Method, where she explained how TSB had linked a SIAC to an outdoors learning experience, as part of an eight-day programme.

The event was targetted at young managers who were deemed to have senior management potential. The objective behind the event was to measure people's ability to cope with significant change, given that the financial services industry faces new competition, new markets and technologies and growing customer sophistication. By using a SIAC as the first part of the event, participants were able to start gaining an appreciation of their ability and inclination to display skills against a range of criteria related to the concept of change. Participants then plan how they will attempt to use different behavioural strategies during the outdoor part of the event. The fact that participants have to transfer skills from a classroom-based setting on the SIAC, to an outdoors setting is itself a measure of their ability to cope with change. Furthermore, the design of the outdoors stage created additional unanticipated demands on their ability to cope with change.

After each exercise participants would run their own feedback sessions using the behavioural language they had acquired on the SIAC and specific learning points would be identified for individuals and the team. At the end of the event itself, participants put together a personal self-development plan for the next 18 to 24 months. This plan was then agreed with a nominated senior management facilitator, acting in a type of 'mentor' role. Brown reported that initial responses to this programme were favourable and further developments were planned.

This example is a further illustration of the opportunities that exist to enhance the developmental aspects of development centres, particularly through establishing the link with experiential or action-based learning. Thus the SIAC presents some interesting possibilities. Most obviously, it can be used as an alternative to the more traditional approach to development centres where line managers act as the assessors. Alternatively, it can be combined with the traditional approach to create a hybrid event, with line managers assessing some exercises and self/peer assessment being used for other exercises, which is something we have successfully run many times over the years.

FOURTH GENERATION DEVELOPMENT CENTRES

Ever since Griffiths and Goodge's attempt to describe the three generations of development centres, people have been speculating as to what would constitute the fourth generation. However, before addressing this question it is important to remember that all development centres should focus on assessing developable criteria, using valid assessment techniques (including simulation exercises), that are assessed by multiple, trained assessors. So using this as our starting point, the question arises as to what other features would define a fourth generation development centre?

Andrew Constable (1999) at Roffey Park Management Institute has suggested that fourth generation centres should be 'peer centres', epitomised by:

- peer feedback and coaching after each exercise
- integration of off-the-shelf tests and exercises, real-life problems and activities to identify personal values
- personal and group planning on the centre, greater emphasis on follow-up, for example, through mentoring and use of learning sets.

Whilst we see these features as generally desirable, they are already to some extent evident in third generation designs, although it is true that they may warrant greater emphasis.

One of the commonly stated concerns about development centres is that post-centre development often fails to materialise (Griffiths and Goodge, 1994) for which there may be many reasons. Among them is the fact highlighted by Griffiths and Goodge (1994) that only 38 per cent of the organisations they surveyed – who were using third generation designs – spent three or more hours on development planning. In our view, the feature that is most significant in distinguishing fourth generation designs from earlier iterations, is therefore, the practice of starting to work on development needs, rather than simply identifying and planning to address them. In this respect fourth generation designs could be regarded as employing a 'Developing Strategy', in order to differentiate them from Boehm and Hoyle's Identification and Diagnostic Strategies, which were described earlier in Figure 10.1. This focus on development does not preclude any form of diagnosis or assessment, as it may still be necessary to define the precise nature of the development need in the context of the exercises which simulate the job circumstances. So even if the development needs are already known, perhaps as a result of attending an assessment centre or from a performance appraisal, it is still useful for the assessor to observe the relevant, dysfunctional behaviours in order to be able to help the participant improve their performance.

We recognise that it is dangerous to be too definitive about the precise nature of so-called fourth generation designs and we therefore suggest that they will probably have a number of the features described below:

Coaching to address development needs

As stated above, this is probably one of the most, if not the most important feature to distinguish fourth generation designs from earlier iterations. The primary goal of these centres is to bring about behavioural change and they are typified by the participant engaging in a number of appropriate simulations and receiving immediate feedback and coaching in how to improve their performance. In this respect it may sound like most training courses, but the key differences are that the observed behaviour is generated from job-related exercise simulations and the performance is analysed by the assessor (usually called an observer or coach in these events), using the standard behavioural assessment process. The nature of these events is purely developmental and it is important that participants are able to feel that it is a 'safe' environment in which their 'mistakes' can be viewed as opportunities for improvement and not as a negative mark on their employment record. The immediacy of the feedback is also an important feature, as it allows the participant to quickly identify the key performance issues and how they can best be tackled, prior to having another chance to demonstrate their handling of this type of situation in a similar but different exercise. Also given the 'safe' environment, it is perfectly reasonable to involve other participants in the process of peer feedback, as this should be beneficial to all, providing that appropriate guidelines are followed and training in feedback skills has been covered. Although the focus is on addressing development needs and closing performance gaps, there is still scope to identify further areas for development, which had previously escaped attention. Whether this is the case or not, there will inevitably be the need to put together an action plan to continue the development process, as it is unrealistic to expect to fully address these needs in a 3–5 day event. We have run a number of development centres of this type, which we regard as being at the right end of the continuum given in Figure 10.2.

Use of job-related simulations

As already mentioned, these centres usually use job-related exercise simulations, based on real scenarios, so that performance improvement can be achieved in a relevant context. Whilst this may also be true of some third generation designs, it is an even more important feature of fourth generation designs. So for example we ran a series of centres for the customer services division of a major IT manufacturer, in which staff had to deal with the issues arising from a customer's central computer system crashing. The scenario was based upon a real situation and the numerous engineers who went through the programme commented that they had previously failed to appreciate some of the finer points of handling customers in such situations, and that they would be better equipped to do so in future. A further extension to this approach has entailed individuals bringing their own challenging real work scenarios with them to the centre and practising these 'real exercises' in front of the observer/coach who provides feedback and guidance on how to improve performance.

Another important factor in the use of job-related exercises in a fourth generation development centre is that the whole atmosphere under which they are run should not portray so much of an 'examination setting', but should be more relaxed and convey the nature of the work environment. Woodruffe (2000) highlights the opportunity to be more flexible – for example, with regard to timings – suggesting that an exercise could be interrupted so that the coach could explain to participants what they are doing/not doing, so they can experiment with different behaviours in order to achieve the desired outcome. Matheson and Evans (2001) describe how their third generation centre went some way towards this by providing participants with their schedule for the centre through electronic diaries and referring to the interactive exercises as business meetings. Even more interesting was the fact that the in-tray was given to the participants at the beginning of the day so they could then decide how they apportioned time to work on it and other activities, such as preparing for some of the forthcoming meetings. This highly flexible approach is equally relevant to third and fourth generation designs in our view, as it could be used for both diagnostic and development purposes.

Seamless transition to workplace development

Given the focus on addressing development needs in fourth generation designs, it follows that every effort needs to be made to ensure that progress in this direction is continued beyond the centre itself. In this respect third and fourth generation designs may be little different, except as already explained, third generation designs are unlikely to have made any start on addressing the development needs, so development planning and subsequent implementation takes on even greater importance.

Ideas for post-centre development are covered in some detail in Chapter 8, but one aspect which we have often incorporated into these fourth generation designs is to set up 'real-time coaching' as a follow-up activity. This entails the observer/coaches agreeing a 'coaching contract' with each participant, which involves them visiting the participant at their workplace to either observe and/or review them handling real work situations. This has proved to be very powerful in helping participants implement their development plans and to see meaningful improvements in their performance. Variations on this theme include running ½–1 day follow-up sessions with small groups of four to six participants at which they get to discuss their attempts to try certain things in the workplace and if appropriate to practice them in this 'safe' environment, before trying them in the real world.

Peer assessment and feedback

Peer assessment and feedback can be integrated into a centre in a number of different ways. For example, a 360° instrument can be used to gather feedback from a number of sources including 'real peers' and this data can be incorporated into the centre, alongside other evidence of performance. Alternatively, 'peers' in the guise of fellow participants can undertake assessments of each other's performance during the centre, as described in the SIAC. Yet another option is for 'peers' to provide less-formal feedback based on their observations of one another in the group discussion exercises, for example. These different methods can of course be employed alongside assessments conducted by assessors in the usual fashion, or indeed in any combination. Lee (2000) highlights that one of the benefits of peer feedback, is that it creates an opportunity to assess certain less-accessible competencies such as maturity, self-awareness, learning from others or developing others, as how the feedback is delivered and/or received itself becomes a legitimate 'exercise' for assessment.

Involving the participants in this way clearly requires that they receive training in assessor and/or feedback skills. Matheson and Evans (2001) described how participants had to attend a 1-day feedback skills workshop prior to the development centre, which emphasised the power of giving and receiving positive feedback and the potential damage of negative feedback. However, an important issue to consider with peer feedback is the need to encourage honesty and candour, as there is the risk that participants might be tempted to disregard development issues in order to avoid any potential conflict. Indeed some participants might see this as an opportunity for 'you scratch my back and I will scratch yours!' Nevertheless, the benefits of peer feedback almost certainly outweigh the disadvantages and its inclusion should be considered.

Self-assessment

This too can take several forms, most notably through participants being trained as assessors to assess their own performance, or through the use of 'raw' self-assessment ratings. In the case of the former, such assessments can be undertaken in conjunction with peer feedback as described in the SIAC, or in addition to assessor feedback, or even in isolation. Given the desire for greater participant involvement, self-assessment has more obvious appeal than peer assessment, particularly if it is a case of having to choose between the two and there is much to be said for incorporating it into the design, where feasible.

In the case of 'raw' self-assessment ratings, which typically entail asking participants to complete questionnaires rating their performance after each exercise, the question arises as to their level of accuracy. Several studies (Clapham, 1998; Franks et al., 1998; Randall et al., 2000) have shown a general trend suggesting that correlations between assessor and self-ratings are low and self-ratings are more lenient and less varied than assessor ratings. However, most of these studies had a selection element associated with them and it is not unreasonable to expect participants to wish to portray themselves favourably, even if they had been assured that these ratings would not be used within the decision-making process.

Halman and Fletcher (2000) were able to overcome this natural inclination to display bias by collecting self-assessment ratings on a series of development centres for 111 customer service staff before and after attending. They found that the level of congruency across the ten criteria, between assessor ratings and self-ratings, rose from two criteria before the centre, to six criteria after the centre. Of course this trend could be predicted, given that the post-centre self-ratings were probably influenced by the feedback received on the centre. However, it at least supports the view that development centres enhance the level of self-awareness and thus have a greater likelihood of gaining the participants' commitment to take action on their development plan. Apart from this benefit, they also found that participants' self-esteem levels rose as a result of attending the development centre. Nevertheless their findings regarding the accuracy of self-assessment ratings were broadly consistent with other studies, which suggest that participants generally rate themselves more favourably.

The conclusion from these studies is that while self-ratings based upon questionnaires may be a valuable way of involving participants in the development centre process, they contribute very little to the process of accurately defining development needs. If self-assessment is seen as desirable, and we think it should be, the better option to improve the accuracy would be to engage the participants in the assessment process in the capacity of an assessor, as described earlier.

Ongoing challenges for development centres

Development centres have made major strides forward in the way they operate and have changed more radically than their assessment centre 'ancestors'. All of the evidence suggests that they will continue this evolution, in order to meet the needs of modern organisations. However, for this to happen, we need to attend to some of the challenges they face. The UK survey by the Industrial Society (1996) revealed that the main concerns of the 283 respondents about development centres were as follows:

- Raises expectations that the organisation may not be able to meet   25%
- Difficult to translate development plans back at work   16%
- Lack of line manager support for the individual   14%
- Financial cost   14%

RAISED EXPECTATIONS

This first concern is an understandable one, which needs careful handling as it is very easy for such events to be seen as the pathway to promotion. Fortunately however, the answer is simple as it lies in providing clear and unequivocal communication about the centre and its purpose. As we explained in Chapter 2, this is well aided by the use of a policy statement. Of course this alone may not suffice, as sometimes people are determined to perceive a 'hidden agenda', even where one does not exist (Miller and Best, 1993). If the centre is therefore going to operate in an environment of suspicion or mistrust, then it is essential that all face-to-face communications reinforce the right message and it may also be beneficial to schedule specific briefings for potential participants and their line managers.

MAKING POST-CENTRE DEVELOPMENT HAPPEN

As previously mentioned this second concern is probably the most important of all and we have already provided some suggestions as to how fourth generation designs could help. However, in order to ensure we do all that we can to tackle this issue, we need to ask the question: what are the key obstacles? Surprisingly little research has been done to answer this question, so we offer below the most common anecdotal responses that we have heard and noticed:

- Not enough time to focus on development when faced with 'real-world' tasks
- Lack of encouragement or support from boss and/or colleagues
- Lack of organisation commitment (time, effort, resources) to helping with personal development
- Disagree with the diagnosis of the development needs
- Lack of motivational incentive (extrinsic or intrinsic)
- Lack of true personal commitment to address development issues
- Lack of knowledge or understanding in how to develop.

Clearly there is no 'magic wand' to deal with all of these and they demand a strategic approach in order to ensure that all such obstacles are overcome. We therefore suggest some potential remedies:

- *Lack of time* – Try to build development actions into the job so that some real-time, on-the-job learning can be undertaken and avoid development being seen as an extra burden on top of other duties. This will go some way to tackling the time-constraint problem that is often cited.

- *Lack of line manager support* – Although also shown as the third main concern in the Industrial Society survey, line manager support is clearly a key aspect of making post-centre development happen and we approach it from this perspective. We believe the answer lies in ensuring that mechanisms are put in place to involve the participants' line managers in the development centre process, an all too common failing, highlighted by Jackson and Yeates (1993). This can be done in several ways including having them attend the centre as assessors (although not when their own staff attend), so they fully understand the process and likely outcomes. Regardless of whether this is the case or not, Ferguson (1991) stresses that line managers should ideally be involved before the centre (through nomination, briefings and/or preparation) and should have some form of ownership of the development plan along with the participant. We have successfully managed to tackle this latter point by scheduling post-centre feedback discussions between the participant, their line manager and the assessor who provided the feedback. We often liken these sessions to 'passing the baton' in the relay race, because the dialogue built up between the participant and the assessor is transferred to the participant and their manager.

  A related concern cited by Francis-Smythe and Smith (1997) was that line managers were more interested in participating in the post-centre development of those who had obtained higher ratings than those who had not. This view was echoed by Arnold (2002) who described the results of a survey, which found that a degree of elitism was perceived to exist for those awarded the highest grades, despite subsequent attempts to move away from the policy of using grades to indicate future potential. Of course this is not to suggest that second generation centres, such as this are inappropriate, but it illustrates the difficulty of trying to successfully achieve the twin objectives of assessing future potential and developing people. Perhaps one way of avoiding accusations of elitism and the observation by Jackson and Yeates (1993) that the 'winners' usually receive the most developmental resource, would have been to ensure that all participants receive a reasonably fair allocation of development support. In this way development could have been given 'equal billing' with assessment, thus justifying the use of the term development centre and protecting its integrity.

- *Lack of organisation commitment* – In our opinion this should never happen, as organisations should recognise that in undertaking a development centre, they are embarking on a process which requires follow-through and commitment to development. We always advise our clients that if they lack this commitment then they shouldn't start down this road. Unfortunately however, we fear quite a few organisations do, as they fail to appreciate what they are starting. Furthermore, we believe that organisations often overlook the subtle importance of demonstrating their commitment to development by failing to have the message reinforced by a senior manager, acting as a 'champion' for the development centre. On the occasions when this has been evident, for example by having a senior figure issue personal invitations to attend the centre, or to make the welcome/closing address, we have noted that it has had high impact, with resulting commitment. There is also undoubted value in having high-profile role models who themselves have been seen to put effort into their own development and have benefited as a result.

- *Disagree with the diagnosis* – This is largely a validity issue, as the participants' willingness will be strongly influenced by their perception of the legitimacy of the feedback. This is aided by having precisely defined and relevant criteria (construct validity), which are easily understood and that can be readily observed in exercises which are recognised as being relevant to the job (face and content validity). The other factor to influence this is how well the assessors perform in making their assessments and providing convincing and constructive feedback.

- *Lack of motivation or personal commitment* – There is no easy answer to these issues as they are classic management challenges, well beyond the scope of this book. However, one obvious point is that any description of the purpose of the centre should emphasise the potential benefits of attending it and undertaking development, both for the individual and the organisation. Beyond this, it is obviously important that everyone involved with the centres and the participants' line managers should all reinforce the need for the participants to give full attention to their development.

- *Lack of knowledge of how to develop* – Again one would hope that this would not happen, as the centre should point the participants towards various means for tackling their development needs. Unfortunately, this isn't always the case, as was evident when we met with a prospective client who told us that they had just run their first development centre with help from an external consultant. However, they now had ten demotivated individuals, who didn't know what to do about their development needs because when they asked the consultant for help, they had been told, 'Sorry, we don't do that, we just run development centres'!

FINANCIAL COST AND RETURN ON INVESTMENT (ROI)

It is undoubtedly true that development centres can be quite expensive, although it also has to be recognised that they vary so much in purpose, format and duration that it is difficult to generalise. However, regardless of the cost it is important to look at the potential benefits, whereupon the key question is 'what return on investment (ROI) can the development centre deliver?' To answer this question we need to consider how development centres are evaluated and the related issue of their validation, which we address in the next section.

Validating development centres

As might be expected, validating a development centre is more problematic than validating an assessment centre because the purpose is not as clear cut. With assessment centres, validation research aims to check that good selection decisions have been made, based upon accurate predictions about future potential. However, with development centres, the validation can either focus on just the centre itself, or the centre and the implementation of the development plan. In the case of the former, the question is to do with how accurately the centre has diagnosed the development needs, while with the latter, the focus relates to the more important question of whether the centre has helped to bring about an improvement in job performance.

With regard to the validation of the centre itself, Carrick and Williams (1999) note that the developmental value of centres is largely untested. Perhaps this is explained by the fact that up until recently most centres have tended to focus on doing little more than defining development plans, and we have only seen relatively few fourth generation designs which actually attempt to address development needs.

Clearly the question of improved job performance is of more value to the organisation as it focuses on tangible outputs, whereas the output from the centre itself is usually little more than an input to the development plan. However, in focusing on this bottom line 'added-value', we face the classic training evaluation challenge, of having to establish causality and show that the improvement in job performance is linked to the implementation of the participants' development plan and not as a result of any other factors. This perhaps explains why again there is little evidence to demonstrate whether or not development centres result in improved job performance. Indeed two studies in 1995 had contrasting results. Engelbrecht and Fischer (1995) found that attendance at a development centre had a positive impact on the development of six of the eight competencies, when compared with a group of people who had not attended the centre. However, Jones and Whitmore (1995) found that the promotion rates of people who had attended a development centre were little different to those who had not.

So what are we to make of these findings? Well one thing is for sure, more research needs to be done to show the true value of development centres, for although there is much anecdotal evidence to support their use, some hard financial data to demonstrate their value would be useful. Lee and Beard (1994) conducted one such evaluation study for a development centre they ran for BT's sales force. Using critical incident interviews with senior sales managers they were able to identify the costs associated with various failures caused by sales staff before and after attending the centre, and were able to demonstrate cost savings in the region of £67 million. Interestingly, this research was part of a wider study at BT conducted by Lee et al. (1993), which looked at the skills uplift provided by a series of separate training courses, based on improvements in line manager ratings. They found that the different courses, which covered topics such as assertiveness, presentation skills, effective meetings, personal effectiveness and project management, achieved rating improvements in the region of 14–28 per cent. However, these results were completely overshadowed by the development centre, which achieved an astonishing rating improvement of 109 per cent. Needless to say development centres have continued to play an important role in BT for many years.

Although this finding is most welcome, it would be good to see more research of this nature, as we are certain that many more boards would be endorsing the use of development centres if they were provided with the hard evidence of their worth.

The role of 360° feedback in development centres

We have seen a significant growth in the use of 360° feedback over the last 10–15 years and it has started to impact on development centres in a number of different ways. Firstly, 360° feedback offers a good opportunity to add further information to the data set, which should help the participant to gain clearer insight to perceived strengths and weaknesses, from work-based colleagues. A number of centres seek to collect 360° data on each participant prior to their attendance, so that the information can be integrated along with the data from the simulations. Alternatively, if participants have access to their 360° data either prior to attending or at the beginning of the centre, then they can consider how they might choose to tackle issues flagged up by the feedback in their handling of the simulations. For example, if a participant's 360° feedback highlights a development need in leadership style, then this is something they could seek to experiment with during the centre. Secondly, 360° feedback is a very useful tool for monitoring the post-centre progress on addressing the identified development needs after a suitable interval of say 6–18 months. Clearly it may also be worth considering measuring such progress at several intervals over such a period.

Generally speaking there is a reasonable level of consistency between the data from the 360° feedback and the data from the exercise simulations. However, on occasions they conflict and this might be explained by the fact that the 360° data are based on past and present evidence as noticed by untrained observers, whereas the simulation data are based upon observations of present evidence which is often referenced against future potential by trained observers. Indeed Goodge (1997) highlights this particular limitation of 360° feedback, by pointing out that it is important to use a development centre to measure the skills and competencies required when the job is subject to change. Another limitation of 360° feedback, is that it also suffers from the same problem as self-assessment, in that it can tend to be generous and, without corroboration from other sources, its accuracy is questionable. In our view, these reasons, amongst others, explain why 360° feedback could never fully replace a development centre.

Future prospects for development centres

In the first edition we wrote of the possible threats to the ongoing use of development centres and referred to concerns around their validation, cost and being replaced by wider initiatives such as 'the learning organisation'. We have addressed the first two concerns earlier in this chapter, and elsewhere within the book, while our response to the third concern remains as before. The concept of the learning organisation likens the organisation to a living organism whose growth and evolution are subject to continual learning. The true learning organisation is one in which high value is placed upon the desire to learn and it is recognised that this is a continuous process, based upon every day experiences. One obvious implication of this is that assessment and development should be driven by the individual, not sporadically, but continually. If this nirvana were ever to be achieved then the need for development centres could come into question, for it would not be necessary to have a focal event to address what should already be a continuous process. However, given that the concept of the learning organisation has been around for over a decade now, it is evident that the development centre is a long way from being extinct. Indeed there is no reason why the two cannot complement one another, as was mentioned earlier in this chapter in relation to the SIAC.

In fact, the relationship between the development centre and the learning organisation can go even further, for Crombie (1981) suggested that such organisations should establish a location which promotes enquiry and learning throughout the organisation. In 1999 the University for Industry (UfI) established 70 locations around the UK which were described by their Chairman, Sir Ron Dearing as, '. . . the beginning of the revolution in learning promised by the UfI.' They called them development centres!

11 *Current Issues and Future Trends*

Assessment centres have come a long way since their early beginnings during the Second World War. Much research has been conducted which has led to an increase in use and an ongoing refinement of the whole technology. This chapter reviews some of the more recent developments as well as looking to the future. We look at the dramatic increase in the use of technology, some relatively new assessment centre ingredients, the ongoing debate around construct validity, the heightened emphasis of equal opportunities and diversity, and the implications of running centres in different cultures.

The use of technology

The use of technology in assessment centres is not just about the universal availability of computers (in advanced economies), but it would be a reasonable place to start this section. We will then go on to look at some of the other technological advances that have been achieved since the first edition. The computer-based applications fall into two groups: administration of the centre and administration of the exercises.

ADMINISTRATION OF THE CENTRE

The market has already seen the launch of at least two software programs from test publishers for the administration of complete centres. To some extent, these programs simply replace the dependence on dedicated secretarial support staff at a centre, for example:

- Instead of the traditional report form, which is hand written and subsequently typed, some assessors go straight to a computer to produce their reports in a pre-recorded format.
- Reports are drawn up very quickly by 'cutting and pasting' relevant remarks to the appropriate file (after agreement about the component parts in the wash-up).
- Entering scores on to the scoring grid electronically, which can still be done so the assessors don't see each other's scores until the wash-up.
- They provide a library of back-up copies of all the documents that you use at any centre, if materials do not arrive for any reason.

In addition to these functions the real pay-off for the centre manager is that once you have a template of all the activities for any particular centre, such as the Assessor–Participant–Exercise matrix in Chapter 7 (see Figure 7.1), the program will allow you to automate all the logistics of allocating assessors to participants, rooms to assessors, timing the events and so on. Personalised timetables, giving all the relevant details, can then be generated at the touch of a button for everyone concerned. Furthermore, so long as you plan the principle in advance, you can work out exactly how the logistics will be affected and advise others very quickly if, for instance, an assessor or a participant doesn't turn up on the day. Finally, if you want to collect scores to form the basis for subsequent statistical evaluations, like the ones suggested in Chapter 9, the software will compile the basic data automatically. This completes current developments in centre administration.

ADMINISTRATION OF THE EXERCISES

So far as exercises are concerned, there have been some clear developments since the first edition, although it remains true that classical one-to-one exercises and group discussions continue to be very popular as directly observed exercises. Not surprisingly, it is the written 'working alone' type of exercises that have seen the biggest changes. Just as many people's workload doesn't come to them in an in-tray or in-basket any more, this type of exercise is being superseded by e-mail equivalents and, as we noted in Chapter 4, such exercises are now commercially available.

Another notable impact of the use of technology is that participants often comment that they hardly ever write things anymore and they are used to typing, so they feel uncomfortable if asked to write reports in longhand. As a consequence it is not unusual to offer them the facility to work on laptops which are either provided or they are invited to bring their own.

OTHER TECHNICAL ADVANCES

In Chapter 4 we identified the kind of exercise that is known as 'a day in the life of'. Rather like the e-mail type of exercise, this delivers to the participant a highly face-valid experience which really does feel more like a day at work; albeit a day that has a lot of stretch points in it, rather than a series of discrete hoops to jump through, which is what a traditional assessment centre feels like. It also has the advantage of completely standardising the administration. All participants get the e-mail that requires rework of the presentation at the same time, notice of a meeting later on at the same time, and so on. As far as we are aware though, there is no significant advantage to the assessors and the evaluation process remains low-tech, based on direct observation through one-way mirrors.

Moving away from strict assessment centres to development centres, a number of centres make use of interactive video and DVD vignettes, but this is much more to do with developing learning and is most successful when building up knowledge of a subject at a fairly elementary level.

On-line assessment

There has been a great deal of activity in the whole area of what is currently referred to as 'on-line assessment' or 'on-line testing' and although to date this has only had a limited impact on assessment centres, its potential cannot be ignored. Most activity with on-line assessment has been in the use of on-line application forms and psychometric testing. The appeal behind the use of such on-line tools is that they provide the following benefits:

• Staff time is saved due to faster sifting mechanisms and the early elimination of clearly unsuitable candidates thus reducing unnecessary screening activity.

- Money is saved in terms of reduced staff costs and reduced candidate travel and subsistence costs.
- Candidate information/data can be easily distributed to hiring managers within different parts of the organisation for consideration.
- Creates the impression of being technologically advanced.
- Allows the inclusion of psychometric tests and other measures at an early stage of the sifting process.
- Ensures a level of computer literacy amongst candidates.
- Allows candidates the opportunity to gain some job-insight early in the recruitment process and to get useful feedback which helps them to deselect if appropriate.

It is not difficult to see that these same benefits would apply to the use of on-line assessment centre simulations, although one is clearly limited to the non-interactive exercises such as in-baskets or analysis exercises. The main difference is that the use of psychometric tests can be entirely automated and the only input required from the HR recruiter is the interpretation of the participants' performance data against the needs of the job and a decision as to whether or not to progress the candidate to the next stage. Assessment centre simulations on the other hand tend to require the involvement of an assessor in making judgements about the candidate's handling of the exercise. However, technological advances with exercises such as electronic in-baskets create opportunities for semi-automated marking processes, which inevitably reduce the level of input required from the assessor, although we are a long way from being able to dispense with it altogether.

As on-line assessment methodologies continue to progress, more thought will need to be given to overcoming the problems and challenges they pose, which can take various forms. For example, candidates have reported a dehumanising effect (Price and Patterson, 2003) with the potential to make them feel that they are not being treated as a personal applicant, and that the process was perceived as unreal. This resulted in potential inaccuracies, due to a carefree attitude and a tendency to respond in a socially desirable way. Other challenges concern the reliability of technology, access to computers and the level of privacy available. However, the biggest challenge of all is for the recruiters who are faced with the concern of establishing the authenticity of the candidate's submission, for example, is it their work or have they had any help? At present the only effective way of establishing this fact is through some form of retest, when the candidate is finally brought in for the face-to-face stage of the recruitment process.

Nevertheless the benefits of on-line assessment do outweigh the challenges and this ensures that further attempts will be made to refine and improve the process.

New ingredients

As with all established technologies, researchers, academics and practitioners are always looking for new ways of doing things in order to try and improve their efficiency and effectiveness. We describe below some of the recent developments that have been spawned in the spirit of continuous improvement.

SITUATIONAL JUDGEMENT TESTS

Joiner (2002) describes a recent trend in the US, which has seen the integration of situational judgement tests (SJTs) into assessment centres. These tests, which are sometimes referred to as written simulation tests or low-fidelity simulations, present participants with a series of short situations usually in writing, although sometimes on video. Participants are then asked to choose the best course of action (and sometimes the worst), usually from a range of four options. Responses are scored by awarding one point for a correct answer, or by providing weighted scores favouring the most appropriate responses. McDaniel et al. (2001) refer to meta-analysis research showing a predictive validity of 0.34, supporting the fact that SJTs are good predictors of job performance. Also in another study, McDaniel and Nguyen (2001) pointed out that whilst SJTs correlated well with cognitive ability tests, they showed less racial adverse impact.

Strictly speaking an SJT is not a typical assessment centre component and it fails to meet the definition of what constitutes an assessment centre simulation, as quoted in the *Guidelines and Ethical Considerations for Assessment Center Operations* (2000), which state:

Assessment procedures that do not require the assessee to demonstrate overt behavioral responses are not behavioral simulations, and thus any assessment program that consists solely of such procedures is not an assessment center as defined herein. Examples of these are computerized in-baskets calling only for multiple choice responses, situation interviews calling only for behavioral intentions, and written competency tests.

It would seem that practitioners have taken heed of this advice, as those that have used SJTs have done so either as a screening device prior to the assessment centre or have incorporated them into the centre as a weighted component, which is acknowledged by the guidelines as acceptable practice:

Procedures not requiring an assessee to demonstrate overt behavioral responses may be used within an assessment center, but must be coupled with at least one simulation requiring the overt display of behaviors.

A variant of the concept of SJTs, which has recently been used in assessment centres, is a multiple situations exercise. This differs from SJTs in that rather than offering multiple choice responses, it requires the participant to construct the response. The exercise entails describing a series of supervisory/management situations to participants through written or oral narrative and inviting them to describe their response. Whilst such exercises clearly cannot compare with real simulations in which participants get involved and take action, as opposed to describing intended hypothetical actions; they do have the merit of allowing 15–20 multiple situations to be assessed in the same timeframe required for one interactive simulation. It is quite possible that we will see more of these types of activities being incorporated into assessment centres as practitioners continue to experiment with new tools.

PORTFOLIO-BASED (SITUATED) ASSESSMENT

Another relatively new addition to the tools that have been included in assessment centres is the use of what has been referred to as portfolio-based assessment (Jacobsen et al. 1997), which entails the individual submitting a portfolio of their work collected over a specified period of time. Jacobsen et al. describe how this approach was used in an educational context, in which trainee teachers were required to provide a collection of work-related (situated) evidence, in order to determine if they could be licensed to teach. They explain that the term 'portfolio' is not meant to depict a container but more a vehicle for assessment and professional development. In the educational context the portfolio could include a range of source material such as videotapes of classroom teaching, instructional artefacts, teaching materials, student work and so on. Once material has been collected it is subject to assessment by trained assessors, who have undergone extensive training in how to evaluate such material. Some of the attractions of this approach are:

- It necessitates giving the participants plenty of advanced notice of what they need to provide and this encourages good preparation and thus aids professional development.
- It naturally requires the active involvement of the participants which usually entails a degree of reflection and self-evaluation.
- It is possible to specify the range of data sources that must be used, thus ensuring a broad view of performance and an accurate understanding of the participants' ability.
- It is well suited to assessing abilities which are best exhibited over a period of time, such as how students respond to the teaching methods employed and how the teacher adapts their approach to meet the needs of their students.

However, portfolio-based assessment also poses some challenges, such as:

- Communications and the logistics of arranging the collection of the portfolios from participants are quite time-consuming and inevitably span a period of time.
- Assessor training is intensive and time-consuming and can last 3–5 days.
- Gathering evidence about participants' thoughts about their students, staff, instructional methods, and so on, primarily relies on written responses, which narrows the data sources.
- Scoring of portfolios requires considerable familiarity and understanding of the situational context and it is time-consuming, as each one can take up to two days to score.
- Ensuring the authenticity of the submitted work and that it is the participant's own work and not largely due to collaboration or help from others.

Another concern, which the authors fail to raise, is the fact that the sample of behaviour that has been submitted may not be truly representative of how the participant usually behaves and could be as a result of numerous previous unsuccessful attempts. Whilst this might suggest learning and improvement has taken place, it might also indicate that the participant can only get it right occasionally, in which case it is unlikely that standards have truly been met.

For these reasons it is difficult to foresee the widespread use of this particular approach without building certain checks and refinements into the process. If it is to catch on, then it is most likely to be used in a development context (for example, as part of a continuous professional development initiative) where distance learning is an acceptable or preferred approach. Furthermore, it would also probably benefit from having tighter assessment guidelines established, so that assessor marking-time can be reduced.

The construct validity debate

The whole of Chapter 9 of this book refers to techniques that you can use to validate that your centre is doing what it is intended to. That type of validation is known as criterion-related validity and it is criterion-related validity that is always cited when we talk of the power of assessment centres to predict whether a person will be successful in the job. Rather more precisely, we are saying that 'typically' those who score high go on to be more highly regarded in the job and those who have lower scores, while they may actually get the job, will tend not to perform so well in the job. This has been the consistent finding in over 50 years of research, although the extent of that predictability is hotly debated.

In the academic literature, there has been a high concentration of research on the vexed question (Woodruffe, 2000) of construct validity. It is not our purpose to produce an academic text, as we said in the first edition, but this issue has had so much recent prominence that it would be worthwhile to consider some of the recent critique, so that the practitioner can be ready to debate the topic.

To start with an attempt at a definition, *construct validity* means that the test or simulation or other form of assessment can be related to some theoretical construct. A theoretical construct is an idea that relates to human behavioural characteristics that are common to many specific activities, examples of which would be general intelligence, and aptitude, for example, for languages or manual dexterity. Manual dexterity, for example, would be quite an important selection criterion for a typist, or certain types of surgery, or playing a musical instrument – but a surgeon doesn't have to know how to type or read musical scores in order to operate an endoscope.

THE ISSUE UNDER DEBATE

The particular construct that has come in for a lot of recent criticism is the idea that behaviour (that is performance on the centre) is mediated through criteria/dimensions/competencies which are identified through job analysis as important for job functioning. As we have said elsewhere, Sacket and Dreher's (1982) seminal work, which has been regularly supported by subsequent research (for example, Russell and Domm, 1995), identified that behaviour at assessment centres was situationally specific. That is, they identified that there was more consistency of scores within an exercise than within a criterion. This has become known among practitioners as 'the exercise effect' (referred to in Chapter 4). Although this might appear to be a somewhat theoretical consideration, the argument is that we need to understand not just that assessment centres work, but how and why they work. This is particularly important for development centres which 'by definition, require a valid and distinct assessment of dimensions' (Lievens, 2001). Hoeft and Schuler (2001) in an excellent review of the main findings point out, among other things, that the earliest research was predicated on the situationally specific nature of the tasks that people were asked to do in an assessment centre and only later did people start talking about dimensions or criteria. They also underline that what we are actually talking about is assessors' ratings of performance, rather than 'actual' performance, which is exactly the point picked up by the study of assessor discrimination (broadly the failure of line managers to do so effectively) by Sagie and Magnezy (1997) in Chapter 6. In the same paper Hoeft and Schuler (2001) say that 'One has to take into consideration that for each exercise only specific facets of general dimensions are recordable' – indeed we say the same in Chapter 4. We would recognise that when assessors comment on leadership in an in–basket exercise, for instance, it is limited to the participant's ability to delegate and not at all like the evidence drawn from a one-on-one interview simulation, where the participant is allowed a significant opportunity to demonstrate both task-oriented and person-oriented skills.

SO SHOULD WE BE CONCERNED?

The broad run of the academic argument is that there are other constructs that might be in play, which we do not yet fully understand. One of the earlier responses to the Sackett and Dreher finding was from Klimoski and Brickner (1987) who confirmed the general finding, but hypothesised that there must be some sort of intervening variable, which they labelled 'managerial intelligence'. Several other psychologists (Lance et al., 2000; Robertson et al., 1987) have suggested that the traits that underlie successful managerial performance are actually general cognitive ability and certain aspects of personality (which are well-established constructs), but that the 'dimensions' are situationally specific expressions of those underlying traits. If this argument were pursued to the limit, we would end up replacing 'planning and organising' and 'oral communication ability' with general intelligence and, probably, extraversion. However, these constructs would still have to be made operational in the context of the exercises so that 'lay' assessors could make reasoned judgements. Later Chan (1996) tried to do this by looking at the question of external construct validity within a study of predictability and concluded that, 'Taken together, there was no evidence that dimensions were more highly correlated with conceptually related constructs than with non-related constructs.'

In other words, the case for assessment centre constructs as approximations for (established) traits, such as intelligence, is not yet made. A recent article by Craik et al. (2002) goes rather further down the route of 'confirmatory factor analysis', as it is now becoming known. They subjected several groups of MBA students to whole batteries of tests, which included some psychometric instruments, typical assessment centre exercises and several other non-conventional tests such as TAT (Thematic Apperception Test) blanks and a life interview. Further factor analysis revealed two clusters of behaviour that they have called Strategic Management Style (SMS) and Interpersonal Management Style (IMS), both of which correlate highly with the overall assessment of managerial potential (MP). Interestingly, performance on the in-basket turned out to be a good indicator of SMS and the leaderless group discussion was a good indicator of IMS. In this paper there were some associations between these generalised style questions (SMS and IMS) and both cognitive and personality profiles via the overall rating (MP), but it must be said that they were fairly modest.

PRACTICAL IMPLICATIONS

To summarise, at present we believe that the debate is interesting and will in due course enable us to have a more refined understanding of why and how assessment centres work. As practitioners, however, we need to find ways of incorporating the findings into best practice. Taken together with the earlier comments on assessor training and using psychological expertise in Chapter 6, we suggest the following to ensure that you get as close as possible to construct validity:

- Design exercises so that they have a maximum of six criteria to measure.
- Design behavioural checklists that are specific to the behaviours in the exercise.
- Train assessors adequately in the skills of spotting criteria, using such enhancing methods as 'frame of reference' (FOR) training.
- Make sure assessors are trained to assess all exercises so they can contribute to the wash-up critique of each other's assessments.

- Focus wash-up discussions about a candidate to one criterion at a time, do not reveal the whole matrix, so that possible influence from other criteria is avoided.
- As the centre manager, try to discourage repeated assessor discussion about how a participant did in an exercise.

Equal opportunities and diversity

THE LEGAL FRAMEWORK

Recent developments within the EU, and by extension in the UK, have led to a resurgence of interest in the provision of equal opportunity and the management of diversity. In the early days, the Race Relations Act, the Sex Discrimination Act and the Equal Pay Act defined the legal scope of discrimination and introduced us to the idea of indirect discrimination in employment matters. More recently, we have had the Disability Discrimination Act, and in 2006 an extension to the Employment Act, which is in line with the European Charter on Human Rights, will make it illegal to discriminate against a person on the grounds of religion or age. In due course it is likely that European legislation will extend to cover discrimination on the grounds of sexual orientation, membership of political parties, membership of trade unions and even language. Unlike the US, however, our legislation has never imposed or supported the idea of positive discrimination, favouring for example ethnic minorities, so the concern in the UK is to create, wherever possible, a level playing field at the point of entry.

TESTS AS INDIRECT DISCRIMINATION

The point about indirect discrimination is that tests, simulations, interviews, handwriting sampling and so on are all potentially capable of disadvantaging any subgroup of the population, because they may appear to demonstrate that one group of applicants, on average, score markedly less well than the average for the general population.

This is quite a complex problem, made worse by the vocabulary. When psychologists talk about the ability of a test to discriminate, they don't mean the ability of a test to disadvantage anyone, they mean that the test can identify the difference between someone who does well and someone who does less well against some pre-established point of comparison. It implies that the difference in the score is meaningful in terms of an outcome, in our case in the world of work, the ability to function well in the job.

A further complication, which has seen the almost complete demise of occupational psychometric testing in the US, is the fact that some well-established instruments give results that show, for example, black Americans scoring significantly worse than whites as overall populations. Similar results have been obtained in the UK by H.J. Eysenck in relation to the Irish as a sub-population of the British. Even so, there is a huge range in both black and white populations, which means that there are millions of black people in the US who score higher than average whites. Therefore, despite the finding of difference between the two populations overall, this does not necessarily mean that the test is intrinsically unfair. It can become potentially unfair when you set the 'criterion score'; the score at which you decide to accept or reject a particular applicant and this is very much a practical matter of doing some job analysis research.

TESTS AND OCCUPATIONAL NEED

If you do not do the research you can end up, as did British Rail, disproportionately turning down ethnic Asian applicants for promotion. The reason this happened was that they set a pass mark on a pencil and paper test (the criterion score) when there was no evidence that scores higher than the pass-mark equated with more ability in the job. Nor was there any evidence that people who scored higher, or for that matter lower, did any better on the training course to convert from one job to another. Had they been able to demonstrate that, for instance, people who scored lower than 50 struggled to complete the training, there would have been a defensible reason for making 50 the cut-off point for acceptance on to the course. The ultimate question in relation to fairness is whether the test criteria are related to occupational need, that is, the needs of the job compared with the capability of the applicant. This is because we mustn't lose sight of the fact that every employer also wants the best candidates that they can get access to. In some respects it is a less passionate debate if we talk about language in circumstances like an English speaker applying for a job in an Afrikaans-speaking bank in South Africa. If he or she were otherwise a suitable applicant and willing to work in the area, it would probably be ethnic discrimination to turn him or her down because the application form is completed in English. On the other hand if the person refused to conduct the interview in Afrikaans, then it would quite likely be held as fair rejection on the grounds that they would need to speak daily to colleagues and customers in that language. In other words, speaking in Afrikaans is a genuine occupational need. In the same way, your simulations and pencil and paper tests, if they are used, should have both content and elicit competencies that are clearly related to the job need and can be demonstrated as such by reference to job analysis.

TOWARDS FAIR ASSESSMENTS

In general, there are two selection methods that are both highly valid and have low adverse impact on potential employees, namely assessment centres and work sample testing. This should be no surprise because assessment centres are in many ways a form of multiple work sampling. Even so, we need to have some regard to the question of fairness in the design and content of assessment centres. There are some general principles that have been elaborated in the guidelines published by the Commission for Racial Equality, which are of limited use in guiding the construction of an assessment centre, and practical advice in this area has been limited to the construction of psychometric tests. Kandola (1996) has identified five potential sources of bias in occupational testing, these are:

- bias due to atmosphere
- bias due to abilities measured
- bias due to irrelevant standards
- bias due to lack of validity
- bias in society.

Bias due to atmosphere

The main issues connected with atmosphere are time constraints and lack of test sophistication. The argument here is that some members of some minority groups are simply not used to examination-like conditions and may become inappropriately disadvantaged because they do not know what to expect. To counter this, every effort should be made to welcome participants with warmth and openness, rather that creating the kind of atmosphere that used to be prevalent where assessors remained aloof from their 'subjects' and everything possible was done to intimidate 'candidates'. Equally, it is good practice to give as much advanced information as possible and even arrange for some of the test materials to be sent in advance so that participants can get a good feel for what they will be confronted by in the event – but you should do that for every candidate.

Bias due to abilities measured

The abilities or competencies that are being assessed may be overly dependent on job analysis techniques that rely on the study of current job incumbents. There have been a number of articles in the literature that have clearly identified that women and men in the same occupational role use different concepts when talking about their job. The need here is to ensure that you have taken account of, for instance, shifting work patterns and therefore not to fall into the trap of seeking to measure irrelevant or even occasionally redundant skills.

Bias due to irrelevant standards

There is a big temptation when confronted with a large population of applicants to look for a much higher level of skill or attainment than is actually required by the demands of the target job. This is quite evident in the policy of a number of organisations that recruit their graduates from a very limited number of universities, despite the probability that there may well be perfectly acceptable candidates in other institutions. Equally, a common problem in all personnel selection is that line managers want fully formed operators at all levels of the organisation and frequently fail to acknowledge that it can take them some years to get up to speed.

Bias due to lack of validity

Within the context of assessment centres, there is a temptation to use an exercise that has been successful in the past in a different context without regard to its validity in selection for the current job role. Bias will be inevitable if the criteria that the exercise elicits are not demonstrably part of the job role that the person is being assessed for.

Bias in society

We cannot overlook the fact that bias exists in society. Despite the best endeavours of designers to try and build in culture fairness so that, for example, simulations do not rely on particular kinds of educational background or cultural assumptions, there is much evidence that the outcomes are no less prejudicial to minority groups than tests which do not attempt to design such bias out. Indeed there is quite a lot of anecdotal evidence from cross cultural studies that even something as apparently innocent as setting a group to work together on problem solving elicits quite different responses in the US when compared with Sweden or Britain.

DESIGNING FAIRNESS IN

We need to be aware of the potential problem of bias at all stages of the construction of an assessment centre and, where possible, develop strategies to ensure that our centres are monitored after they have been implemented to record the impact on minorities, among other things.

To conclude, it should be our aim to design bias out while retaining the ability to correctly discriminate between job relevant effectiveness and ineffectiveness. To do so at all stages of the design process should ensure that fairness is always part of the consideration. We can do this by:

- having a design committee that has a good gender and ethnic balance
- ensuring that, within the constraints of a job analysis sample, there is a representative sample of different gender/age/ethnic background and so on
- in addition to all the normal editorial checking when exercises are being designed, specifically scanning for appropriate language and the avoidance of unfortunate cultural stereotypes
- including some form of cultural awareness/sensitivity training in assessor training.

Cultural issues and international centres

Despite the extensive amount of research into assessment centres over the last 50 years, very little attention has been paid to their international use and related cultural issues. The few studies that have been conducted have tended to focus on the levels of usage of assessment centres within different countries. Levy-Leboyer (1994) summarised a number of studies (dating from 1984 to 1991), which reported moderate use of assessment centres in the UK, Belgium, and the Netherlands, low levels of use in France, Germany, Finland, Norway, Australia and Singapore and no reported use in Italy. However, there are signs that these levels of use are increasing, just as they have in the US and the UK.

Clearly, there are many possible explanations for these varying levels of use, including different laws, regulations and cultural values. For example, there are differing approaches to selection in the US and Europe. In the US, there is strong concern in selection with trying to predict a candidate's future performance. In Europe, the selection process is seen much more as a decision-making negotiation between the employer and the applicant, with costs and benefits for the firm and individual, as well as for society as a whole taken into account (Levy-Leboyer, 1994).

However, it is evident, in the international context, that multinational firms require a type of manager with special skills. These include the ability to link the local subsidiary national culture with the parent company's culture (Hofstede, 1992) and thus be able to function in environments where more than one culture is operative. Littlefield (1995) describes how an assessment centre for Novotel's hotel managers, which had originally been designed in France to encourage better focus on customer service, had to be adapted for use in other countries. The original emphasis on customer service had drifted over the years as the organisation had grown internationally and it had lost sight of one of its core values. The assessment centre aimed to bring this back into focus, but it had to be recognised that different cultural styles prevailed in different countries and these needed to be considered in the design of the centre. This necessitated some changes to the exercise content and recognition that participants from different cultures would often handle the challenges before them in different ways.

Indeed it has been known for some time now that management style and leadership behaviour varies across cultural and national groupings. For example, in collectivist cultures, effectiveness depends on getting the group to perform. Striving for personal excellence can alienate the individual from those around him or her. Schmidt and Yeh (1992) concluded that many specific work-related social skills and attitudes are highly culture-bound. These include leadership behaviour and styles, such as the use of sanctions, methods of reasoning, appeals to higher authority, friendliness, assertiveness, coalition formation, corporate communication patterns and networks, bargaining styles and strategies for conflict resolution. Also, further differences have been noted in terms of decision-making styles and approaches to information processing, with the Japanese preferring to go from the general to the specific, while Westerners like to get details out of the way before talking about larger issues.

ADDRESSING CULTURAL AND INTERNATIONAL REQUIREMENTS

Briscoe (1997) points out that applying a template of approved communication patterns and management behaviours from one culture to individuals from all cultures is clearly problematic. Given the obvious impact that these differences will have on individual performance levels, he suggests ways in which these cultural issues should be taken into account when designing and implementing assessment centres. He relates his recommendations to four different areas as follows:

Design of assessment centres

- *Choosing who will design the centre.* What is their knowledge of, and sensitivity to, cultural issues? Which cultures and countries do they come from? Are representatives from multiple countries and cultures included in the design team?
- *The choice and design of exercises.* Should the exercises tap into a participant's knowledge of, and sensitivity to, cultural issues? If the organisation is a multinational, should the exercises derive from various cultural or national experiences? Which skills and behaviours from various cultures need to be assessed? Does the design of the exercises take account of cultural and national differences in desired management styles? Should the exercises emphasise only individual performance or include recognition of group/team/consensus-based performance?
- *Choice and preparation of assessors.* Should assessors have specific knowledge and sensitivity to national and cultural issues? Should they come from varying national and cultural backgrounds? How should they be prepared and trained for the task of assessing in terms of concerns for national and cultural differences?

Implementation of assessment centres

- *Choice of participants.* Should individuals from different cultural and national backgrounds be assessed together or separately? Will all participants from differing cultural and national backgrounds react to all assessment instruments in the same way? If not, how should this be taken into account? Are all the assessment instruments appropriate to all participants? That is, are they all used in each country and culture and are they equally familiar to all participants?
- *Behaviour of participants.* Since desired behaviour differs from culture to culture and country to country, should all types of behaviour be assessed as equivalent? How will the assessors take into account varying cultural and national backgrounds in evaluating participant behaviour on the various assessment instruments? For example, how should participants that come from cultures in which deference to authority is expected be evaluated in the context of a leaderless group exercise?

Assessment judgements

- *Attention and interpretation by assessors.* Assessors themselves will come from various cultural and national backgrounds, and thus may pay attention to differing factors or interpret factors differently. How will this be taken into account?
- *Problems arising from a multicultural assessment team.* The assessor team itself may have difficulty reaching consensus on their assessments because of language and translation problems and cultural differences in perceptions, values and understanding. Attempts to minimise these forces by homogenising the team of assessors or the group of participants may heighten the problem of finding managers who function effectively in multicultural or multinational environments.

Provision of feedback

- *Participant attitudes to feedback.* The very act of providing individualised feedback, which is the 'normal' practice in assessment centres, is valued differently in different countries and cultures. In some individualistic cultures (such as the US) this is highly valued. In other, more collectivist, cultures (such as Japan) it is very problematic.
- *Participant approaches to receiving feedback.* How will assessors be prepared to take into account varying listening and learning styles, stemming from national and cultural differences when they provide feedback to participants?

However, despite these useful recommendations, Briscoe concludes that given the increasingly diverse, multicultural and multinational nature of today's organisations, there is a need for more comparative research to examine the differences between assessment centres developed for different cultures/ countries.

What next?

Our vision in the crystal ball is probably no clearer than anyone else's. However, there are a few points worth mentioning.

- It seems to us that the prevalence of assessment and development centres in the workplace will lead to demands for absolute standards, so that HR professionals and consultants can check out best practice standards. In time such standards may come to be like the current level A and B certificates in occupational testing. While you will still be able to find and buy examples of poorly validated 'quick and dirty' tests, good employers will be able to access materials through a limited number of reputable design houses.
- The drive will continue to reduce the administrative workload of a typical centre and the cognitive workload on the assessors. As the construct validity debate goes on, it is quite likely that we will come to understand more about the relationship between fundamental psychological traits and assessment centre dimensions. Both of these effects are likely to lead to assessment centres that have much more standardised evaluation regimes.
- The dream of fully automating the scores of in-baskets or e-mail equivalents is likely to continue as a major challenge. We graduated in the 1970s when artificial intelligence was flavour of the month and the visionaries told us then that machines would learn to learn before long. We would do well to remember that it has taken IBM nearly forty years since to develop a computer that can defeat Gary Kasparov at chess, which is a relatively linear

activity with clearly defined rules and nothing like the subtle complexity of interpreting observed behaviour in a much less clearly structured exercise such as an in-basket.

- The ever increasing speed and depth of change in corporate life will put a premium on methods that will allow people to demonstrate 'openness to change' as a key component of successful managerial behaviour. So far exercises designed to do that have not been very successful.

Design, Implementation and Evaluation of Assessment and Development Centres

Best Practice Guidelines

British Psychological Society

Contents

1 Development of the Guidelines

These guidelines were developed by The British Psychological Society Steering Committee on Test Standards and Division of Occupational Psychology.

The following individuals contributed to the content of these guidelines:

Iain Ballantyne, *Assessment and Development Consultants Ltd.*
Sean Boyle, *Pearn Kandola*
Andrew Brooks, *British Telecom*
James Bywater, *SHL Group*
Robert Edenborough, *KPMG Search and Selection*
Amanda Parker, *NFER-Nelson*
Nigel Povah, *Assessment and Development Consultants Ltd.*
Sarah Stear, *SHL Group*
Philip Wilson (Chair), *London Fire Service.*

Additional comments were provided by:

Professor Neil Anderson, *University of Amsterdam*
Helen Baron, *Independent Consultant*
Professor Clive Fletcher, *Personnel Assessment Ltd.*
Richard Kwiatkowski, *Cranfield University*
Charles Woodruffe, *Human Assets.*

These guidelines, which were published on 10 November 2003, may be downloaded
in HTML or pdf format from the BPS website:
http://www.psychtesting.org.uk/public/downloads.asp?sub=true

2 *Overview*

1. Introduction

Assessment/development centres have gained wide recognition as a systematic and rigorous means of identifying behaviour for the purposes of recruitment, selection, promotion and development within the workplace. Good assessment/development centres provide the following benefits:

- Highly relevant/observable and comprehensive information.
- Effective decision-making, including workforce planning.
- Added fairness from multiple judgements (versus single judgements).
- An enhanced image of the organisation among participants.
- An effective preview of the role or job level.
- Developmental pay offs to candidates/participants arising from self-insight obtained.
- Developmental pay offs to assessors/observers arising from involvement in the process.
- A legally defensible selection system.
- A method of assessment that predicts work performance.

2. Aim and intended audience of the guidelines

These guidelines aim to provide up-to-date, best practice guidance to human resource managers, occupational psychologists and other specialists, to help establish the effective design, implementation and evaluation of assessment and development centres. A key reference used to assist in the design of these guidelines was the United States *Guidelines and Ethical Considerations for Assessment Center Operations* (2000).

NOTE ON TERMINOLOGY

The guidelines encompass both **assessment centres** and **development centres**. Whilst the purpose and design of assessment centres will differ from development centres, their constituent features have broad similarity.

The term **assessor** is used alongside the term **observer** in these guidelines – assessor is more commonly used within assessment centres and observer is more commonly used within development centres. Similarly, the term **candidate** is used alongside **participant** – candidate is more commonly used within assessment centres and participant is more commonly used within development centres.

Terms presented in bold within these guidelines are defined in the final section (Glossary).

3 What are Assessment/ Development Centres?

1. Key features of assessment/development centres

Assessment/development centres have a number of key features. They are essentially multiple assessment processes, and there are various ways in which that is so: a group of candidates/participants takes part in a variety of exercises, observed by a team of trained assessors/observers, who evaluate each candidate/participant against a number of predetermined, job-related behaviours. Decisions (for assessment or development) are then made by pooling shared data. These aspects are described below.

MULTIPLE CANDIDATES/PARTICIPANTS

One of the key features of an assessment/development centre is that a number of candidates/participants are brought together for the event (physically or via information technology – see later section on the impact of information technology).

COMBINATION OF METHODS

The focal point of most assessment/development centres is the use of **simulations**. The principle of their design is to replicate, so far as is possible, the key aspects of situations that individuals would encounter in the job for which they are being considered. To gain a full understanding of a person's range of capabilities, it is usually the case that one simulation is insufficient to develop anything like a complete picture.

Some of the various types of simulations and other exercises are shown in Table A.1 below.

Table A.1   Example exercise formats

Exercise	Description
Presentation	Simulation of briefing to a relevant audience group.
Group discussion	Team interaction exercise based around given information.
One-to-one role play	Communication/negotiation exercise within one-to-one interaction.
In-tray/e-basket	Simulation of role-based in-tray/in-box, requiring action and prioritisation.
Written analysis	Written problem analysis exercise against work-based issue.
Interview	Structured interview, gathering information against key criteria.
Psychometric assessment	Standardised assessment of cognitive ability, personality, motivational or interest profiles (normally these would be purchased direct from test publishers, but could also be developed in-house).

TEAM OF ASSESSORS/OBSERVERS

To break out of the difficulties that are associated with the one-on-one interview, used either as a means of selection or in some aspects of performance measurement, it is important to use a team of assessors/observers. Ideally each assessor/observer should be able to observe each participant in at least one of the various situations in which they are asked to perform, to aid objectivity. The team of assessors/observers all need appropriate training in the behavioural assessment process and in its application to the particular exercises that are used. In addition, wherever possible the trained assessor/observer group should be selected to represent as diverse a pool as possible (in terms of ethnicity, gender and age specifically), often supplemented by specialists, such as occupational psychologists.

JOB-RELATED BEHAVIOURS

As with any other method of assessment, the starting point has to be some analysis of the job (or perhaps job level) to determine what are the critical areas that discriminate between the performance of good and poor job incumbents. The number of such areas should not be excessive (normally up to around ten areas), otherwise effective measurement of these areas may become more difficult. There are a wide variety of terms for these job aspects, among them are attributes, dimensions, criteria and, most recently, **competencies**.

Successful performance in any job is likely to be founded on a combination of things, such as: disposition, attitudes, particular skills that have been developed over time, energy levels, ways of thinking or problem-solving and knowledge. One of the objectives of a job analysis is to determine which of these things are most important in the target job – particularly in the future. Other aspects of appropriate job analysis include understanding the context in which behaviour takes place and the level of difficulty of common problems encountered in the job. Such job analysis should be based on a diverse sample of informants where possible.

SHARED DATA

Data about candidates/participants is shared between the assessors/observers at the end of the process. In the case of a selection decision, no final decision is made until all the evidence is gathered from observations of candidates in all the various situations and combined into a final rating by consensus following a discussion among assessors, or by statistical integration of ratings. In the case of a development centre, there may be no final score, as the primary objective of the data sharing is to collect information together to feed back to participants on their comparative strengths and weaknesses. Indeed, in some development centres the data is shared with the participants as the centre progresses.

2. Criteria for defining assessment/development centres

It is difficult to be adamant about exactly what constitutes an assessment centre and even more so when it comes to the variety of different designs that are regarded as a development centre. However, the following criteria (or standards) can be seen to qualify an event as an assessment/development centre.

- There should be job analysis that defines a set of competencies to be measured, clearly demonstrating the link between them and effective performance in the target job.
- To ensure that a competency is measured in a reliable fashion across the centre, it is usual to duplicate measurement of each competency (through different exercises).
- There are usually at least two simulations amongst the material that confronts candidates/participants.
- There should be clear separation of the component parts into discrete exercises.
- There are assessors/observers who are trained in the Observe, Record, Classify and Evaluate (ORCE) process, and its application in the particular simulations that are used.
- Assessors/observers complete their evaluations independently, including any report from before the integration (or wash-up) session.
- There should be a full integration session involving assessors/observers to summarise and evaluate the behavioural evidence obtained.
- Feedback should be offered to candidates/participants to support development.
- There should be a clear written and published statement of the intent of the centre, how data will be stored, by whom and rights of access to that data by any individual.
- There should be a statement of the limits of the relevance of the centre overall and/or the limits for a particular exercise.

3. Related processes

A number of assessment/development events share some characteristics with assessment/development centres. These include events where no simulations are used, only interviews, or there is only a single assessor. These guidelines are likely to contain much that is relevant for these processes but it is important to consider each case individually. The assessment/development centre process is designed to maximise objectivity and accuracy. Processes which deviate from it are often less effective and more prone to error as a result.

4. Distinguishing between assessment and development centres

Whilst many organisations use hybrid models, it is helpful to clarify the factors that distinguish between assessment and development centres.

- Assessment centres are constructed principally for selection, recruitment, fast tracking and promotion. Development centres principally reflect developmental objectives relating to identification of potential and training needs.
- Development centres, unlike most assessment centres, are not pass/fail events.
- Development centres are likely to be longer and with higher costs – especially considering feedback and subsequent developmental activities.
- Ownership of assessment centre data rests principally with the organisation. The development centre participant has more ownership/access.
- Feedback and development always occur during, or at the conclusion of, the development centre. The assessment centre does not include development activities, but the results may be used to initiate them subsequently.

5. When assessment and development centres may not be the correct organisational option

An assessment or development centre may not necessarily offer the organisation the most appropriate response to recruitment, selection, promotion or development issues. Such occasions could potentially (though not always) include:

- when an alternative approach clearly offers a cost-effective and valid process;
- when seeking to select more junior staff or staff on a short-term contract;
- when there is insufficient time to undertake all necessary stages of a centre implementation (see next section);
- when there is little or no managerial commitment to the centre process or outcomes.

4 Implementing an Assessment/ Development Centre

1. Overview of the stages for implementing an assessment/ development centre

There are a number of stages to implementing assessment/development centres, as shown below. These areas are developed further within these guidelines.

Stage 1: Pre-planning

Identify need	Establish an organisational (or departmental/functional) need for implementing the process.
Commitment	Establish a commitment amongst relevant stakeholders (for example, board members, managers, potential participants/assessors) for implementation of the process.
Objectives	Establish clear objectives for the process; for example, assessment, selection, promotion or development.
Establish policy	Initiate an organisational policy for the assessment/ development centres.

Stage 2: Development of Process

Nominate designer	The designer should have appropriate training and competence for this role.
Conduct job analysis	Using rigorous job analysis techniques, formulate a clear set of competencies/behavioural indicators.
Identify simulations	Using the job analysis outcomes, and further investigation, identify and devise appropriate exercises that simulate key elements of the target job/organisational level.
Design process	Construct the centre integrating a number of exercises to measure the range of defined competencies.
Design format	Prepare the format, timetable and logistics for the centre process.
Training	Design and implement the training to be provided to assessors/ observers, facilitators and role players involved in the process.

Stage 3: Implementation

Pilot/refinement	If possible, pilot the centre on a relevant pool of individuals to ensure the components operate effectively, fairly and the process as a whole operates according to the timetable.
Run centres	Run the centre with candidates/participants, including on-going quality checking.

Stage 4: Post-Implementation

Decision making   Make decisions according to the outcomes of the centre.

Provide feedback   Offer feedback to candidates/participants and development plans according to organisational/participant needs. Also, where appropriate, offer organisational-level feedback on common development needs.

Monitoring   Set up procedures to review and monitor outcomes and development of overall centre. This would include validation to review the relevance of the process to actual work performance and comparison of the performance of participants from different subgroups.

5 *Impact of Information Technology*

1. Overview

Technology, the Internet and other advances are challenging the way that assessment/development centres are performed. Key applications of information technology are to manage the administrative burden of designing and running these events, to automate the presentation of items to the candidate/participant and to automate the scoring once the candidate/participant has responded. In using technology in the assessment/development centre process the following points should be considered:

- If computers are used to ease the administrative burden or as a medium for the delivery of exercises, the same quality and ethical criteria must apply to the process and content as for traditional methods.
- In using computers to administer exercises, a better replication of the twenty-first century work environment may be attained and enhance face-validity, but it is important that the system does not place demands on candidates which affect their ability to demonstrate their competence; for example, a requirement for knowledge of the functioning of a specific piece of software.
- Automated scoring mechanisms have advantages in terms of speed and reliability, so far as routine, frequently occurring or mainly predictable responses are concerned. However, it is important to validate the effectiveness of any automated scoring procedures and particularly confirm their ability to deal appropriately with unusual but valid responses.
- Scoring support systems also exist, which leave the assessor to assign scores, but provide assistance such as displaying the appropriate elements of the candidate's response, scoring guidelines, example scores or adding up the behaviour checklist items ticked. These can aid assessors but should not be used in place of training.

The following sections explore the use of technology in more depth.

2. Specific issues on using information technology

JOB ANALYSIS

There are a number of computer-enhanced job analysis, competency-profiling and competency-definition systems available commercially. They have potential advantages over more conventional, interview-based job analysis techniques.

- They can support a balanced view of the job and help avoid omissions by providing a well researched and comprehensive set of behaviours or other elements on which to base the job analysis.

- They may make prioritisation of the competencies more effective. The computer can be instructed to force the respondent to choose which competencies are essential, rather than merely desirable.
- They enable electronic data collection and this reduces the administrative burden of wide-scale sampling to large numbers of respondents.
- They save the data in electronic format, which is easier to store and recover.
- However effective the technology, the quality of the job analysis will depend largely on the respondents' degree of understanding of the job.

SIMULATIONS – COMPUTER ADMINISTRATION

Computers are increasingly used in their multi-media capacity to schedule, present and administer the simulations. A number of exercises lend themselves in the modern era to being administered by computer. It may make them more **face valid** to the candidates and also reduce the administrative burden on behalf of the organisation. As with all such interventions, the psychometric content of the exercises must be maintained irrespective of the medium in which they are presented. They should always be:

- relevant to the content of the jobs
- simple to understand
- fair to all groups
- able to predict future performance.

RECORDING CANDIDATE/PARTICIPANT EVIDENCE

Assessors/observers may benefit from using technology in their own, conventional assessment process. Behavioural checklists and note pads on palmtop computers may save a significant amount of redrafting in the assessment and integration process.

ASSESSMENT OF CANDIDATE/PARTICIPANT RESPONSES

Computers have the capability to be extremely good at some aspects of the assessment process in terms of evaluating candidate/participant responses, as long as:

- the candidate/participant's responses are entered in a way that the computer can easily interpret;
- there are only a certain number of options available to the candidate/participant, all of which can realistically be predetermined in advance. Where judgement is involved the programming load increases dramatically and many of the advantages are lost.

REPORT WRITING

Report writing from assessment/development centres for feedback or decision-making purposes is an extremely time-consuming and resource-hungry activity. Computer-based expert systems, behavioural statement checklists and other labour saving devices are all ways of reducing the task to manageable proportions. As with other aspects of the process, care must be taken to ensure that such short cuts do not miss out on the rich details that make development centres especially work so well. Ideally the reports should be used in combination with one-to-one feedback discussion and should be validated with both typical and unusual score profiles to ensure their output is appropriate.

3. 'Virtual' assessment/development centres

The **virtual assessment/development centre** in which candidates/participants operate remotely through technology is still in its infancy. At its core is the concept that for many of the components of an assessment/development centre, there is no particular requirement for all candidates/participants to be in a single location. All that is really required is for them to have:

- Good technology infrastructure that allows them to communicate with the assessors/ observers and perhaps each other in a seamless manner, in real-time.
- Quiet, standardised environmental conditions.
- Relevant levels of security. (Are the people working alone, and so on?)
- Good logistical organisation and a willingness to be flexible in the hours that the centre runs.

With these components one can interview, conduct most simulations, score and provide feedback to candidates remotely.

4. Potential problems with new technology

Balanced against the benefits described above are potential problems:

- Candidates/participants may prefer more face-to-face interaction.
- The 'social process' of each side assessing the other would be lessened through technology.
- An impersonal image of the organisation could be conveyed.
- Some processes (such as group exercises) do not lend themselves readily to technology.
- The 'psychometric' properties of some elements may need further investigation.

6 *Training Issues in Assessment/ Development Centres*

1. Training focus – roles to be considered

A number of roles need to be considered in terms of training requirements for assessment/ development centres. The key roles are as follows:

- assessors/observers
- facilitators
- role players
- designers.

These are not necessarily distinct in practice, for example an assessor/observer may also function as a role player, but separate training is required for each role undertaken.

ASSESSORS/OBSERVERS

Assessors/observers are those charged with evaluating the behaviour demonstrated in the exercises. Training of assessors/observers needs to take account of the following:

- assessment/development centre principles
- specific materials to be used
- practical work
- skills decay
- feedback
- the organisational context in which the centre is to operate
- equal opportunities issues in assessment
- confidentiality.

Assessors/observers need an understanding of the basic principles that underlie assessment/development centres, as well as the mechanics of centre operations and current policy and standards. A clear focus of their training should be familiarisation with the exercises and materials to be used, and the relevant competencies for the particular assessment/ development centres with which they are to operate. Should they work in a different centre, they will require further training if it contains new exercises or activities not previously addressed. (If the exercises are very similar then briefing in the form of a 'walk through' of the new materials may be sufficient.)

Assessor/observers need to develop skills in the process of observation, recording, classification and evaluation of evidence. They need to understand and have developed skills in contributing to the process of the assessor/observer decision-making stage. These skills will usually be developed via experience of working through the relevant exercise materials and undertaking exercises as if they were themselves candidates/participants in a centre.

Assessors/observers need to be able to accurately rate the behaviour of people from different backgrounds. This is fundamental to the fairness and effectiveness of the centre. Equal opportunities training should include an understanding of the way observation processes are affected by such things as stereotyping or the presence of an individual in the group who is different, and how factors such as language facility will affect performance. In addition it should cover the implications of equality and other relevant legislation.

Assessors/observers need to understand and be skilled in the processes of feedback. This should include the idea that they are feeding back on behalf of the whole group of assessors/observers on the basis of the behaviour produced in the assessment/development centre. They should be prepared to produce examples of behaviour demonstrated by the candidates/participants and be able to explain what alternative behaviours could have led to different evaluations. Acceptance of the feedback by the candidate/participant should be seen as a minimum aim, along with identification and support around developmental needs.

In a development centre it is likely that the feedback will be followed by development planning activities, which may or may not involve the same assessors/observers. The assessors/observers should be aware of at least the broad content and scope of these activities. They should also be able to position feedback so that it can act as a bridge between the assessed exercises and the development planning. For example, they should be able to indicate the general type of activity that would support development for a particular competency. Assessors/observers also need to understand and be able to respond, at least in outline, to questions on organisational implications of participant needs for development; for example, what organisational support can be provided. Finally, they need to understand and be able to respond to queries on the question of where a particular assessment/development centre sits in processes of decision-making about individuals, whether it is for initial selection, reassignment to another role or promotion.

Assessor/observer training will typically last at least two days and be largely interactive. Some of this time may, however, be fulfilled by pre-work, for example, completing an in-tray or analysis exercise in advance. If possible, assessors/observers should carry out their role in an assessment/development centre within two months of their training or else undertake refresher training. Any assessor/observer who has not assessed for a year should also undertake refresher training.

FACILITATORS

Facilitators have the task of managing the centre process operationally, that is, on the day or days when the centre is run. This will involve two main roles (separate people may fulfil these two roles):

- quality control
- timetabling/venue management.

They need to understand questions of standards and be able to establish and maintain these. These standards include the matters of principle and good practice as set out in these guidelines and standards applicable to the particular centre or centres in which they are to be involved. The latter includes matters such as whether the centre is to function as a distinct hurdle for candidates, so that some might be deemed to have failed it, or alternatively if it is to operate as an information source feeding into a final decision-making process.

Facilitators also need to be able to timetable an assessment/development centre to ensure smooth running. Although the timetable may be set by the assessment/development centre designer, there will sometimes be a need to make adjustments on the spot to deal with contingencies. These could arise in the case of late arrivals, no shows, exercise overruns or other unplanned events such as major interruptions through fire alerts. Facilitators also may need to be trained in venue management including room allocation and layout and liaison with permanent venue staff on catering and other arrangements. Facilitator training is likely to require at least one further day in addition to that for assessors/observers. The availability of appropriate facilities to maintain the security and confidentiality of materials would also be the responsibility of the facilitator.

ROLE PLAYERS

Role players are those who interact with participants to generate behaviour to be assessed. This is often done on a one-to-one basis with a separate assessor/observer present. Role players are trained to understand the overall process in general terms and their part in it, in helping to elicit behaviour. They must be familiar with the particular material of the exercise and the role in which they operate. They also need to be trained in how far to adhere to the prepared 'script' and where they are expected to use discretion, for example in following through a novel line of discussion raised by a participant. Their training should include a process of checking for consistency of standards. This should be subject to periodic review to ensure that these standards are maintained. Where debriefing of role players is to be used to generate supplementary evidence, for example, on their version of what had been agreed, they are to be trained to confine themselves to delivering the information requested rather than making generally discursive comments about a participant.

DESIGNERS

Assessment/development centre **designers** are those who put together the working plan for and specify the content of the centre, often this could be an occupational psychologist. Designers' training should include the following:

- approaches to job analysis
- selecting appropriate exercises
- timetabling the assessment centre
- exercise writing.

In practice, for some assessment/development centres, job analysis will have been undertaken as a separate activity which may support other initiatives such as performance management. In some assessment/development centres, too, all exercises will be drawn from external publishers, or commissioned from authors separate from the staff otherwise involved in the centre. In these cases the designers will have a reduced task, but should still be trained to understand the principles of job analysis and exercise writing respectively.

Job analysis training should enable designers to identify a core set of competencies for any role which will be fundamental for effective performance. It should cover a sufficient range of techniques to allow rich and comprehensive information about a job to be elicited. This might include some or all of the following approaches:

- questionnaires
- focus groups
- repertory grid technique
- critical incident technique
- content-analytic methods
- visionary interviews.

Training in a selection of appropriate exercises should focus on matching exercises to job requirements as defined by the job analysis. It should also cover fundamental principles such as the need to cover each competency in more than one exercise and the need for exercise type to reflect activities in the job concerned. It should also address questions of appropriate reflection of content of the role so that material is sufficiently relevant, but not chosen to give unfair advantage to internal candidates.

Timetabling the centre includes planning for the appropriate number of assessors, role players and facilitators. Training here should also include the use of 'who sees who' charts. With regard to the time span of the process itself, the requirement for multiple activities would seem to set a minimum of half a day of candidate/participant contact time. As a rule of thumb, assessors/observers appear to need about as long for their initial independent evaluations as was spent by the candidates/participants in generating the data. Assessor/ observer panel discussions can vary in length quite widely and insufficient time will affect the quality of the conclusions reached. Designers need to be able to incorporate these different factors against resource constraints in developing the centre timetable.

Training in exercise writing should include examination of the use of instructions, timing of exercises and 'standard scenarios'. The latter would include inherent conflicts as in group discussions or diary clashes in in-trays. It would also include the provision of additional information to roleplayers, not given to candidates. It will, in addition, cover the links from job analysis to exercise type and content. It should address the use of sources, for example, sampling real-life case study information in the development of an analysis exercise. Furthermore, it should address the design and use of activities supplementary to the main content of an exercise, for example, participant report forms and in-tray interviews.

2. Use of psychometrics

Where an assessment/development centre uses standardised psychometric instruments those charged with their choice, administration and interpretation should have the recognised British Psychological Society qualifications in their use (Test Administration, Level A and B qualifications), along with any test publisher requirements. In addition, they should understand the principles of the assessment /development centre process and be aware of the status of the particular assessment/development centre in which they are involved in terms of its role in informing decisions about the participant. They should also be trained in interpreting information from psychometrics in accordance with the competency models being used.

3. Adjustments for people with disabilities

At least one member of the assessment centre team should receive training in the issues surrounding the assessment of people with disabilities. This should include general disability awareness, legal requirements and procedures for dealing with special needs of candidates. The trained person should be familiar with sources of support such as suitably qualified consultants, disability organisations and test publishers. It will be their role to provide guidance to the whole assessment/development centre team when a disabled person is being assessed.

7 Decision-Making with Assessment/ Development Centre Information

1. Making decision judgements

The output of the decision-making process depends on the *objectives* of the centre. Where the emphasis is on a decision to fill a vacancy then the output usually boils down to a single rating (either numerical or a descriptive category) and a recommendation about each candidate (employ, promote, reject, and so on). If feedback is to be provided to candidates then this is usually provided in the form of their personal performance on each criterion supported by the behavioural evidence; though an overall rating may be provided. A range of issues arise in terms of best practice decision-making:

ASSESSMENT CENTRES – DECISION-MAKING

- In assessment centres (as opposed to development centres), after all the data are classified and evaluated from all the instruments, a decision then has to be taken as to whether the candidate has been successful. This is usually done at a **wash-up**/decision-making session following the assessment centre, where the assessment centre criteria ratings of each candidate are considered. It is important that assessors do not confer before the wash-up so that their judgements remain independent. The relative weightings of the criteria should be based on the job analysis or career direction and take into account such factors as their importance, frequency and trainability. It is then necessary to use the weightings of the criteria, usually by applying some form of algorithmic or scoring process, to make the decision. This approach can be coupled with the application of minimum acceptable ratings for each criterion, based on the job analysis findings.
- Sometimes an assessment centre may be part of a larger process where different assessors are using the same assessment centre design with independent groups of candidates, or in different locations or at different times. In this situation, it is essential to have very clear definitions of standards to ensure that the process is being applied consistently. One way of helping to maintain these standards is for some assessors to be common from one centre to another, or alternatively to have a team of quality checkers who visit different centres to review standards.
- Where an assessment centre has used a team of assessors with a single cohort of candidates, then the focus will be on these particular individuals, and their performance can be compared directly against one another. Consistency of standards can thus be finely tuned to take into account those specific individuals and their likely later job performance, based on the job analysis profile.
- The facilitator responsible for the assessment centre normally chairs the wash-up session (though chairing responsibility is often dependent on the seniority of the assessors).

Typically, participants are taken in turn and their performance on each criterion is discussed and assessed by all those who have made observations. Using the job analysis data the team should arrive at a consensus decision clearly supported by evidence from the exercises.

- Although wash-up sessions are more commonly structured around the criteria/ competencies being assessed, it is possible to look at performance on an exercise-by-exercise basis. Here, the emphasis is based on the performance in a particular situation rather than each criterion being considered across all the relevant exercises. This approach views the exercise (task) as being a particular set of circumstances that may not apply in a different situation.
- Statistical combinations of individual assessors' ratings are sometimes used instead of consensus decision-making, or even to replace the wash-up session entirely. Research suggests that this is equally as valid an approach; however the wash-up session has additional benefits such as maintaining a more standardised approach among assessors and challenging inappropriate ratings. Statistical decision systems should at least be supported by strong content validation and if possible criterion related validity. If such a system is automated and makes final selection decisions, candidates have the right under the Data Protection Act (1998) to receive an explanation of the rationale behind the system.

DEVELOPMENT CENTRES – DECISION-MAKING

- In development centres, where the output emphasis is on development, the focus is much broader and each participant is provided with data on their performance on each criterion, along with the behavioural evidence to support this. Observers then work with the participant to produce some plan of action to develop key areas that have been agreed as ones the participant would like to improve.
- In some development centres this process of interaction and feedback happens during the centre, giving the participant a chance to improve their performance during the process and after some initial feedback. The behavioural evidence cited in feedback is nearly always presented orally. Sometimes this will be supported by summary notes and sometimes by a more detailed written report.

2. Using other information (from sources other than the centre)

STRATEGIES FOR INTEGRATING OTHER INFORMATION

Decision-making in assessment and development centres is typically based only on evidence collected within the centre. There are clearly good reasons for doing this such as: avoidance of differing standards that may be used in the workplace; over-positive/negative assessments by the candidates/participants' line manager; prejudice and fixed opinions; work design limitations such as not having the opportunity to demonstrate certain behaviours, and so on. However there are occasions when it is appropriate to include external information in the decision-making or rating process. Each case needs to be considered on its merits, bearing in mind the following points:

1 External information can be integrated in reaching final centre ratings if data
   • exists for all participants;
   • can be mapped against the competency dimensions used in the centre;
   • has been collected with care to ensure validity.
2 A clear framework for integrating external data should be established whether this is part of, or separate from, the centre rating process. This will depend on the objectives of the centre. For example, in development centres the main focus of integration is often the construction of action plans for the participant to develop their skills. These action plans need to take into account the current work performance and situation of the participant.
3 If external information is considered outside the assessment centre decision process, this may occur at an entirely separate meeting or may take place immediately following the wash-up/decision-making session for the centre.

8 *Ethical, Professional and Legal Considerations*

1. Ensuring ethical and professional issues are considered

Ethical, professional and legal issues should be identified and addressed in the design, implementation and review of any centre. A range of ethical and professional considerations are discussed below. Relevant legal considerations include equality and data protection legislation for all centres. Different employment acts will be relevant depending on the purpose of the centre (for example, promotion or redundancy) and the type of participants (for example, internal or external).

2. Candidate/participant issues

CANDIDATE/PARTICIPANT INFORMATION – PRE-CENTRE

The information provided to the candidate/participant should place him/her in a position to decide whether or not to attend the assessment/development centre. If participation in the centre is part of their condition of employment, participants have a right to be fully informed of the purpose of the centre and why they are attending. Ideally the communication should take place at least two to three weeks before the centre, including:

- General content of the assessment /development centre – a broad overview of the types of tests or simulations included.
- General information on the assessor/observer staff including composition, the training they have undertaken and their role in the assessment and decision making process.
- Possible outcomes of the assessment/development centre, how the assessment/development centre results will be used and for what period of time the results will be stored.
- When and what kind of feedback will be given to the candidates/participants and by whom?
- Who will have access to the assessment/development centre reports and under what conditions?
- Practice information or sessions relating to aptitude tests – perhaps including relevant internet sites for practice.
- Points of contact for further information and for candidates/participants to discuss any special needs.

FEEDBACK TO CANDIDATE/PARTICIPANT

A number of issues link to best practice in the provision of feedback:

- If the results have been stored, there is a legal requirement through the Data Protection Act (1998) to give candidates/participants meaningful feedback, should they request it.
- All candidates/participants should be offered feedback on their performance at an assessment/development centre and be informed of any recommendations made.
- In development centres feedback would automatically be given as part of the process.
- Ideally feedback should be provided 'face-to-face', particularly for internal candidates; for external candidates, it is likely to be both practical and more convenient to offer telephone feedback and/or a written feedback summary. The involvement of line manager input may be valuable to offer support in the workplace to address identified developmental needs.
- It is recommended that feedback should be provided promptly after an assessment process (ideally within four weeks).
- Feedback should at a minimum cover key themes emerging from the assessment/development centre (ideally structured by competencies), the outcome of the process and reasons why the candidate/participant was not selected (if applicable).

3. Use of materials and data

ACCESS TO MATERIALS

It is important that control is maintained in terms of access to the various assessment/development centre materials (exercises, assessor/observer guidelines, and so on). All materials should be kept secure under lock and key. Access to material should only be open to those authorised/trained to utilise those materials.

LIFE SPAN OF DATA

The life span of data arising from the assessment/development process will be dependent on what if any development takes place, either naturally in the job or through more specific intervention. Assessment data is generally considered to be relevant for a period of 12–24 months (though this could certainly be longer). After this period it may be appropriate to allow candidates/participants resit processes where necessary.

DATA PROTECTION

Consideration should be given to the way the data is stored during and after the centre. Appropriate security arrangements should be in place, and a policy should be set regarding who may access the data and when and how it will be destroyed. Consent should be obtained from the participants for the storage and use of the data. If the organisation decides to use the data for any other purpose than that originally stated, further consent is needed.

9 *Monitoring of Outcomes*

1. Reviewing centre outcomes

Outcomes arising from assessment/development centres should be monitored. The regularity of reviews should be planned mindful of assessment frequency and volume, and review of the process should take place periodically. Planning for monitoring, reviewing and validating the success of an assessment or development centre should form a fundamental stage of the initial phases of such a project. Issues in monitoring include:

- initial review
- adequacy of content coverage
- equality/diversity
- data gathering and statistical evaluation.

INITIAL REVIEW

The initial review of the assessment/development centre should examine whether it appears to be serving its purpose. Questions here include whether the exercises bear any resemblance to work situations, if they conform to organisational standards and if the assessors/observers are familiar with and are operating to the ORCE process. An independent quality control inspection of a centre in operation is recommended.

ADEQUACY OF CONTENT COVERAGE

Adequacy of content coverage should be examined first at the level of the basic design of the centre to see that the intention has been to cover each competency more than once and in different settings. It is then necessary to establish that in practice the centre has been able to fulfil the intention of the design and reveal the competencies as intended. Subsequent inspection of records will reveal competency gaps or otherwise in the exercise design and trends in extreme or 'no evidence' ratings being awarded frequently.

Design considerations also come into play here, such as the centre timings. The time allowed for each individual exercise, for assessors/observers to carry out their evaluations post-exercise, and for the integration discussion, may all need some adjustment to maintain standards. Simulation exercises need to be reviewed to ensure they remain up-to-date.

EQUALITY AND DIVERSITY

Assessment/development centres are predicated on the notion of providing *objective*, that is *accurate*, information. This means that discriminations made in the centre should be on the basis of demonstrated competency rather than on other grounds. Differential performance or scores associated with membership of a particular ethnic, gender or other group should always be investigated further. If this does not reflect real differences in performance potential on the job, it could well lead to illegal indirect discrimination under the law.

Performance at the centre overall and in the different exercises should be tracked against sub-group membership. For large groups of participants and centres that are used over long periods, statistical analysis should be undertaken. Whatever the numbers passing through the centre, immediate qualitative review of procedures should be initiated whenever group differences are suspected. This should review the design and implementation of the centre for potential biasing factors such as:

- Overemphasis of a characteristic found less frequently in one gender or ethnic group. For example, excessive use of competitive exercises such as assigned role discussion groups could discriminate against people from cultures where overt competitiveness is less socially acceptable.
- The mix of characters depicted in exercises should be representative of the diversity of participants in the centre and among the organisation and its customers.
- Conscious or unconscious bias or prejudice among assessors/observers or failure to challenge bias by the centre facilitator or other assessors/observers.
- Poor coverage of equality issues in training.
- Failure to make appropriate adjustments for candidates with disabilities.

If candidates/participants represent a mix of internal and external applicants, consideration needs to be given to any prior relevant experience of the internal applicants and the implications of existing knowledge about the candidates/participants among the assessors/observers.

DATA GATHERING AND STATISTICAL EVALUATION

Effective scientific evaluations of assessment or development centres start from clear articulation of the centre objectives. This will, in turn, aid in the production of empirical evidence for the **validity** of the assessment centre – in other words did the centre measure what it intended to measure.

Those responsible for evaluating and validating assessment and development centres should apply the following minimum standards:

- Procedures should be implemented to ensure the efficient and accurate gathering of data.
- Evaluation should as much as possible be rigorous and scientific in approach, and might include qualitative content analysis, statistical analysis and candidate/assessor attitude surveys. In addition a key emphasis is to undertake empirical validation studies wherever possible (including matching assessment outcomes to performance outcomes).

10 Organisational Policy Statement – Example Design

1. Developing a policy

Integration of assessment and development centres within the organisation's human resource strategy is likely to enhance the overall effectiveness of the centres; this integration can be clarified within an organisational policy. The sections of this policy may reflect the following:

PURPOSE

The reasons why the organisation is using assessment/development centres should be identified. These could include any combination of external or internal selection, placement and promotion, diagnosis of development needs in the current role, identification of potential, succession planning or skills auditing. This could also include a statement of the intended benefits to the organisation and the candidates/participants.

CANDIDATES/PARTICIPANTS

The target population from which candidates/participants are drawn should be specified. The means by which candidates/participants are selected from this population should be described. It should also be made clear whether participation is voluntary or compulsory. Where appropriate, the alternatives to participation, the consequences of not participating and the circumstances in which re-assessment is undertaken should be made clear.

BRIEFING OF CANDIDATES/PARTICIPANTS

The organisation's policy on advance briefing of candidates/participants should be outlined and detail of the contents of such briefing should be specified.

ASSESSORS/OBSERVERS

Minimum standards of eligibility to operate as an assessor/observer should be set down. This should include training and certification requirements, frequency of assignment as an assessor/observer, organisational level vis-à-vis candidates/participants and arrangements for evaluation of performance. Selection of assessor/observer groups should specify the importance of diversity within that pool where possible (in terms of ethnicity, gender, age and disability). Where external consultants are used as assessors/observers, their experience and qualifications to undertake the role should be specified.

ASSESSMENT MATERIALS AND PROCEDURES

Standards for the design, development and validation of the process should be specified.

USE OF INFORMATION

It should be clearly specified what happens to information collected about candidates/ participants. This should include: what records are retained by the organisation; whether they form part of the participant's personnel records or are maintained separately; who has access to the information and for what purpose; whether the records can be used for any purpose other than that specified for the centre, and for how long the records are regarded as valid for organisational decision-making. In the case of internal selection and promotion, it should be specified how information is combined with other data in reaching decisions.

FEEDBACK TO PARTICIPANTS

Arrangements for feedback to participants should be specified. This should include the level of detail (for example, summary of conclusions versus comprehensive feedback on each exercise), the medium (for example, written report, face-to-face or telephone), who delivers the feedback, and the maximum time elapsed from the conclusion of the centre.

QUALITY ASSURANCE

Procedures for ongoing monitoring and validation of assessment practices to ensure adherence to best practice should be specified.

11 *Further Reading*

A range of publications are available on assessment/development centres. Useful overviews include:

Ballantyne, I. and Povah, N. (2004) *Assessment and Development Centres*. 2nd Ed. Aldershot: Gower.

Woodruffe, C. (2000) *Development and Assessment Centres*. London: Chartered Institute of Personnel and Development.

Guidance parallel to this document may be found in the following:

International Task Force on Assessment Center Guidelines (2000) *Guidelines and Ethical Considerations for Assessment Center Operations*. Endorsed by the 28th International Congress on Assessment Center Methods, May 4, 2000, San Francisco, California, USA. http://www.assessmentcenters.org/images/00guidelines.pdf

12 *Glossary*

Assessment centre	Multiple assessment process involving a number of individuals undertaking a variety of exercises, observed by a team of trained assessors who evaluate performance against predetermined job-related behaviours. Likely to be a pass/fail event.
Assessor	An individual trained to evaluate behaviour observed in exercises (especially at an assessment centre, rather than development centre).
Candidate	One of a number of individuals who undertake assessment centre exercises and receive some form of feedback on outcomes.
Competencies	Key behavioural attributes that identify successful performance within a job role (or group of roles).
Development centre	Multiple assessment process involving a number of individuals undertaking a variety of exercises, observed by a team of trained observers who evaluate performance against predetermined job-related behaviours. Unlike an assessment centre, the emphasis is on identifying training/development needs and establishing a development plan, as opposed to a pass/fail event.
Designer	An individual trained to put together a working plan and specify the content of an assessment/development centre.
Face valid	A process or exercise that is constructed to outwardly appear relevant to the context/target job role.
Facilitator	An individual trained to manage an assessment/development centre to ensure standards are maintained and the timetable and venue operate successfully.
Observer	An individual trained to evaluate behaviour observed in exercises (especially at a development centre, rather than an assessment centre).
ORCE	Acronym for the best practice assessment/observation strategy of Observing performance, Recording that performance, Classifying against competencies and Evaluating using a given evaluation system.
Participant	One of a number of individuals who undertake development centre exercises and receive extensive developmental feedback on outcomes.
Role player	An individual trained to interact with candidates/participants to generate behaviour on which assessments can be made.
Simulations	Assessment/development centre exercises designed to replicate the tasks that an individual does within a job role. (Sometimes referred to as work samples.)

Validity	The extent to which the assessment/development centre process (or elements of that process) measures what it is intended to measure. This may include the extent to which the process predicts subsequent job or training performance or whether the process reflects key job behaviours or traits.
Virtual assessment/ development centre	Assessment/development centre in which candidates/ participants operate remotely through technology.
Wash-up session	Process following the assessment/development centre at which candidate/participant's success and development needs are considered.

Bibliography

Adams, Dawn (1987), 'Assessment Centre Exercises – Bespoke or Ready to Wear?' *Guidance and Assessment Review*, **3**, (1), February.

Ahmed, Y., Payne,T. and Whiddett, S. (1997), 'A Process for Assessment Exercise Design: a Model of Best Practice', *International Journal of Selection and Assessment*, **5**, (1), January.

Arnold, John (2002), 'Tensions Between Assessment, Grading and Development in Development Centres: a Case Study', *International Journal of Human Resource Management*, **13**, (6).

Ballantyne, Iain (1996), 'Towards Quality Standards in Assessment Centres', *Proceedings of the First Test User Conference*, British Psychological Society, 1996.

Ballantyne, Iain (2000), 'Fairness in Graduate Assessment Centres', *Proceedings of the Occupational Psychology Conference*, Leicester: British Psychological Society, 2000.

Ballantyne, Iain (2001), 'Assessment Centres', *AGR Briefing Papers*, **4**.

Bartels, Lynn K. and Doverspike, Dennis (1997), 'Assessing the Assessor: The Relationship of Assessor Personality to Leniency in Assessment Center Ratings', *Journal of Social Behaviour and Personality*, **12**, (5).

Bedford, Tol (1987), 'New Developments in Assessment Centre Design', *Guidance and Assessment Review*, **2**, (3), June.

Bedford, Tol (1988), 'Justifying the Cost of Assessment Centres', *Guidance and Assessment Review*, **4**, (3), June.

Boddy, John (2002), 'Making Role-Plays Work?', *Selection and Development Review*, **18**, (3), June.

Boehm, Virginia R. (1985), 'Using Assessment Centres for Management Development – Five Applications', *Journal of Management Development*, **4**, (4).

Boehm, Virginia R. and Hoyle, David F. (1977), 'Assessment and Management Development', in Joseph L. Moses and William C. Byham (eds), *Applying the Assessment Center Method*, New York: Pergamon Press, 203–24.

Boyatzis, R. (1982), *The Competent Manager*, New York: Wiley.

Boyle, S., Fullerton, J. and Wood, R. (1995), 'Do Assessment/Development Centres Use Optimum Evaluation Procedures? A Survey of Practice in UK Organizations', *International Journal of Selection and Assessment*, **3**, (2), April.

Boyle, S., Fullerton, J. and Yapp, M. (1993), 'The Rise of the Assessment Centre: A Survey of AC Usage in the UK', *Selection and Development Review*, **9**, (3), June.

Briscoe, Dennis R. (1997), 'Assessment Centers: Cross-Cultural and Cross-National Issues', *Journal of Social Behavior & Personality*, **12**, (5).

British Psychological Society (2003), 'Design, Implementation and Evaluation of Assessment and Development Centres – Best Practice Guidelines', Leicester: BPS.

Brown, Pat (1989), 'Linking a Self-Insight Workshop to Outdoors Learning', Unpublished paper given at the 2nd European Congress on the Assessment Centre Method.

Bycio, P. and Zoogah, B. (2002), 'Exercise Order and Assessment Centre Performance', *Journal of Occupational and Organizational Psychology*, **75**, (1).

Byham, W.C. (1971), 'The Assessment Center as an Aid in Management Development', *Training and Development Journal*, December.

Carrick, P. and Williams, R. (1999), 'Development Centres – A Review of Assumptions', *Human Resource Management Journal*, **9**, (2).

Cascio, Wayne F. (1982), *Applied Psychology in Personnel Management*, 2nd edn, Reston, Virginia: Reston Publications.

Chan, D. (1996), 'Criterion and Construct Validation of an Assessment Centre.' *Journal of Occupational and Organizational Psychology*, **69**, (2).

Clapham, Maria M. (1998), 'A Comparison of Assessor and Self Dimension Ratings in an Advanced Management Assessment Centre', *Journal of Occupational and Organizational Psychology*, **71**, (3).

Clutterbuck, David (1993), 'What's Happening in Mentoring?', *Mentor Management Digest*, **2**, (6), October.

Cohen, S. L. (1978), 'How well Standardized is your Organization's Assessment Center?', *The Personnel Administrator*, **23**.

Commission for Racial Equality (1993), *Towards Fair Selection*: A survey of test practice and thirteen case studies. ISBN 1 85442 098.

Constable, Andrew (1999), 'Development Centres', *Proceedings of the HRD Conference, London, Roffrey Park Management Institute*.

Craik, K.H., Ware, A.P., Kamp, J., O'Reilly, C., Staw, B. and Zedeck, S., (2002), 'Explorations of Construct Validity in a Combined Managerial and Personality Assessment Programme', *Journal of Occupational and Organizational Psychology*, **75**, (2).

Crawley, Bronach, Pinder, Robert and Herriot, Peter (1990), 'Assessment Centre Dimensions, Personality and Aptitudes', *Journal of Occupational Psychology*, **63**.

Crombie, A. (1981), 'In Search of the Learning Organisation', *Human Futures*, Spring.

Dukes, J. (1996), 'Meta-analyses and the Validity of Assessment Centres', *Selection and Development Review*, **12**, (2), April.

Dulewicz, Victor (1989), 'Assessment Centres as the Route to Competence', *Personnel Management*, **21**, (11), November.

Dulewicz, Victor (1991), 'Improving Assessment Centres', *Personnel Management*, **23**, (6), June.

Dulewicz, V., Fletcher, C. and Wood, P. (1983), 'A Study of the Internal Validity of an Assessment Centre and of Participants' Background Characteristics and Attitudes: a Comparison between British and American Findings', *Journal of Assessment Centre Technology*, **6**.

Dulewicz, V. and Haley, G. (1989), 'A Long Term Assessment Centre Validation Study in a Major UK Company', *Guidance and Assessment Review*, **5**, (5), December.

Engelbrecht, A.S. and Fischer, A.H. (1995), 'The Managerial Performance Implications of a Developmental Assessment Center Process', *Human Relations*, **48**, (4).

Feltham, Rob (1988a), 'Validity of a Police Assessment Centre: A 1–19 Year Follow-up', *Journal of Occupational Psychology*, **61**, (2), June.

Feltham, Rob (1988b), 'Assessment Centre Decision Making: Judgemental vs Mechanical', *Journal of Occupational Psychology*, **61**, (3), Sept.

Ferguson, Julia (1991), 'When is an Assessment Centre a Development Centre?', *Guidance and Assessment Review*, **7**, (6), December.

Fletcher, Clive and Anderson, Neil (1998), 'A Superficial Assessment', *People Management*, **4**, (10), May.

Fletcher, C. and Kerslake, C. (1993), 'Candidate Anxiety Level and Assessment Center Performance', *Journal of Managerial Psychology*, **8**, (5).

Francis-Smythe, J. and Smith, P.M. (1997), 'The Psychological Impact of Assessment in a Development Center', *Human Relations*, **50**, (2).

Franks, D., Ferguson, E., Rolls, S. and Henderson, F. (1998), 'Self-assessments in HRM: An Example from an Assessment Centre', *Personnel Review*, **28**, (1/2).

Gatewood, Robert, Thornton III, George and Hennessy, Harry (1990), 'Reliability of Exercise Ratings in the Leaderless Group Discussion', *Journal of Occupational Psychology*, **63**.

Gaugler, B.B., Rosenthal, D.B., Thornton, G.C. and Bentson, C. (1987), 'Meta-analysis of Assessment Center Validity', *Journal of Applied Psychology*, **72**, (3).

Gaugler, B.B. and Thornton, G.C. (1989), 'Number of Assessment Center Dimensions as a Determinant of Assessor Accuracy', *Journal of Applied Psychology*, **74**, (4), August.

Glaze, Tony (1989), 'Cadbury's Dictionary of Competence', *Personnel Management*, **21**, (7), July.

Goleman, D. (1996), *Emotional Intelligence*, London: Bloomsbury.

Goodge, Peter (1989), 'Giving Feedback: A Guide for Managers', *Training Officer*, June.

Goodge, Peter (1997), 'Assessment and Development Centres: Practical Design Principles', *Selection and Development Review*, **13**, (3), June.

Goodstone, M.S. and Lopez, F.E. (2001), 'The Frame of Reference Approach as a Solution to an Assessment Center Dilemma', *Consulting Psychology Journal: Practice and Research*, **53**, (2).

Griffiths, Peter and Allen, Barry (1987), 'Assessment Centres: Breaking with Tradition', *Journal of Management Development*, **6**, (1).

Griffiths, Peter and Goodge, Peter (1994), 'Development Centres: The Third Generation', *Personnel Management*, **26**, (b), June.

Guion, P.M. (1987), 'Changing Views for Personnel Selection Research', *Personnel Psychology*, **40**.

Halman, F. and Fletcher, C. (2000), 'The Impact of Development Centre Participation and the Role of Individual Differences in Changing Self-assessments', *Journal of Occupational and Organizational Psychology*, **73**, (4).

Henderson, F., Anderson, N. and Rick, S. (1995), 'Future Competency Profiling: Validating and Redesigning the ICL Graduate Assessment Centre', *Personnel Review*, **24**, (3).

Hennessy, Jo, Mabey, Bill and Warr, Peter (1998), 'Assessment Centre Observation Procedures: An Experimental Comparison of Traditional, Checklist and Coding Methods', *International Journal of Selection and Assessment*, **6**, (4), October.

Hermelin, E. and Robertson, I. (2001), 'A Critique and Standardization of Meta-analytic Validity Coefficients in Personnel Selection', *Journal of Occupational and Organizational Psychology*, **74**, (3).

Herriott, Peter (1986), 'Assessment Centres Revisited', *Guidance and Assessment Review*, **2**, (3), June.

Higgs, Malcolm (1996), 'The Value of Assessment Centres', *Selection and Development Review*, **12**, (5), October.

Hoeft, S. and Schuler, H. (2001) 'The Conceptual Basis of Assessment Centre Ratings', *International Journal of Selection and Assessment*, **9**, (1/2), March.

Hofstede, G. (1992), 'Cultural Dimensions in People Management: The Socialization Perspective.' In V. Pucik, N.M. Tichy and C.K. Barnett (eds), *Globalizing management: Creating and leading the competitive organization,* New York: Wiley.

Honey, P. (1986), *If Looks Could Kill: The Power of Behaviour,* London: Video Arts.

Honey, Peter and Mumford, Alan (1983), *Using Your Learning Styles,* Maidenhead: Peter Honey.

Hough, L.M. (1998), 'Effects of Intentional Distortion in Personality Measurement and Evaluation of Suggested Palliatives', *Human Performance,* **11**.

Hough, L.M. and Oswald, F.L. (2000), 'Personnel Selection: Looking Toward the Future – Remembering the Past', *Annual Review of Psychology,* **51**, February.

Hunter, J.E. and Hunter, R. (1984), 'Validity and Utility of Alternative Predictors of Job Performance', *Journal of Applied Psychology,* **96**, 72–98.

Hunter, J.E., Schmidt, F.L. and Jackson, G.B. (1982), *Meta-Analysis,* Beverley Hills, CA: Sage.

Hunter, Richard (1990), 'Adding developmental value to assessment centres', *The Occupational Psychologist,* (12), December.

Incomes Data Services (1998), 'Assessment Centres', *IDS Studies,* **646**, April.

Industrial Society (1996), 'Assessment and Development Centres', *Managing Best Practice,* **29**, November.

International Taskforce on Assessment Center Guidelines (2000), 'Guidelines and Ethical Considerations for Assessment Center Operations', *Public Personnel Management,* **29**, (3).

Jackson, C. and Yeates, J. (1993), 'Development Centres: Assessing or Developing People?', *Institute of Manpower Studies,* IMS Report, **261**.

Jacobsen, L.S., Lyman, K.M. and Pecheone, R.L. (1997), 'Situated (Portfolio-Based) Assessment: A New Assessment Center Tool?' *Presented to the 25th International Congress on Assessment Center Methods,* London, UK.

Johnston, N. and Smye, M. (1986), 'The interpersonal effectiveness simulation: An application of video based assessment technology to the Assessment Centre method (mimeo)', *Presented to the 14th International Congress on the Assessment Centre Method,* Dearbon, Michigan, USA.

Joiner, Dennis (2002), 'Assessment Centers: What's new?', *Public Personnel Management,* **31**, (2).

Jones, Alan (1988), 'Recruitment and Selection – Recent Developments in the Royal Navy', *Guidance and Assessment Review,* **4**, (1), February.

Jones, A., Herriott, P., Long, B. and Drakeley, R. (1991), 'Attempting to Improve the Validity of a Well Established Assessment Centre', *Journal of Occupational Psychology,* **64**, (1), March.

Jones, R.G. and Whitmore, M.D. (1995), 'Evaluating developmental assessment centers as interventions', *Personnel Psychology,* **48**.

Kandola, R.G. (1996) 'Bias in Testing', *Proceedings of the First Test User Conference,* Leicester: British Psychological Society.

Kane, J.S., Bernardin, H.J., Villanova, P. and Peyrefitte, I. (1995) 'Stability of Rater Leniency: Three Studies', *Academy of Management Journal,* **38**, (4).

Kanter, Rosabeth Moss (1989), 'The New Managerial Work', *Harvard Business Review,* **89**, (6), November.

Kauffman, J., Jex, S., Love, K. and Libkuman, T. (1993), 'The Construct Validity of Assessment Centre Performance Dimensions', *International Journal of Selection and Assessment,* **1**, (4), October.

Kerr, Scott and Davenport, Hugh (1989), 'AC or DC : A Wolf in Sheep's Clothing?', *Guidance and Assessment Review,* **5**, (5), October.

Kleinmann, M., Kuptsch, C. and Koller, O. (1996), 'Transparency: A Necessary Requirement for the Construct Validity of Assessment Centres'. *Applied Psychology: An International Review*, **45**, (1).

Klimoski, R. and Brickner, M. (1987), 'Why do Assessment Centres Work? The Puzzle of Assessment Centre Validity', *Personnel Psychology*, **40**.

Kolb, D. and Fry, R. (1975), 'Towards an Applied Theory of Experiential Learning', in C.L. Cooper (ed.), *Theories of Group Processes*, Chichester: John Wiley and Sons.

Lance, Charles E., Newbolt, William H., Gatewood, Robert D., Foster, Mark R., Nita, R., Smith, David E. (2000), 'Assessment Center Exercise Factors represent Cross-situational Specificity, not Method Bias', *Human Performance*, **13**, (4).

Lee, Geoff (2003), 'Same old Development Centres?' *Selection and Development Review*, **19**, (5), October.

Lee, Geoff (2000), 'The State of the Art in Development Centres', *Selection and Development Review*, **16**, (1), February.

Lee, G. and Beard, D. (1994), *Development Centres: Realizing the Potential of your Employees through Assessment and Development*, London: McGraw Hill.

Lee, G., Coaley, K. and Beard, D. (1993), 'Management Training: Cost or Investment?', *Financial Services Training Journal*, **1**, (3).

Lent, R.H., Aurbach, H.A. and Levin, L.S. (1971), 'Research Design and Validity Assessment', *Personnel Psychology*, **24**.

Levy-Leboyer, C. (1994), 'Selection and Assessment in Europe'. In H.C. Triandis, M.D. Dunnette and L.M. Hough (eds), *Handbook of Industrial and Organizational Psychology* (2nd ed.), Palo Alto, CA: Consulting Psychologists Press.

Lievens, Filip (1998), 'Factors which Improve the Construct Validity of Assessment Centers: A Review', *International Journal of Selection and Assessment*, **6**, (3), July.

Lievens, Filip (2001), 'Assessor Training Strategies and their Effects on Accuracy, Interrater Reliability, and Discriminant Validity', *Journal of Applied Psychology*, **86**, (2).

Lievens, F. and Goemaere, H. (1999), 'A Different Look at Assessment Centers: Views of Assessment Center Users', *International Journal of Selection and Assessment*, **7**, (4), December.

Lievens, F. and Klimoski, R.J. (2001), 'Understanding the Assessment Center Process: Where are we now?' In C.L. Cooper and I.T. Robertson (eds), *International Review of Industrial and Organizational Psychology*, Volume 16, Chichester: Wiley.

Lievens, F. and Van Keer, E. (2001), 'The Construct Validity of a Belgian Assessment Centre: A Comparison of Different Models', *Journal of Occupational and Organizational Psychology*, **74**, (3).

Littlefield, D. (1995), 'Menu for Change at Novotel', *People Management*, **26**, January.

Lorenzo, R.V. (1984), 'The Effects of Assessorship on Managers' Proficiency in Acquiring, Evaluating and Communicating Information about People', *Personnel Psychology*, **37**, (4).

Lowry, P.E. (1993), 'The Assessment Center: An Examination of the Effects of Assessor Characteristics on Assessor Scores', *Public Personnel Management*, **22**, (3).

McCrimmon, Mitch (1993), 'Missing Elements in Assessment Centres', *Selection and Development Review*, **9**, (5), October.

McDaniel, M.A., Morgeson, F.P., Finnegan, E.B., Campion, M.A. and Braverman, E.P. (2001), 'Use of Situational Judgement Tests to Predict Job Performance: A Clarification of the Literature', *Journal of Applied Psychology*, **86**.

McDaniel, M.A. and Nguyen, N.T. (2001), 'Situational Judgements Tests: A Review of Practice and Constructs Assessed', *International Journal of Selection and Assessment*, **9**, (1/2), March.

Mabey, W. (1989), 'The Majority of Large Companies use Occupational Tests', *Guidance and Assessment Review*, **5**, (3), June.

Matheson, I. and Evans, M. (2001) 'Management Development in Action: A Development Centre Approach', *Selection and Development Review*, **17**, (2), April.

Miller, Tony and Best, Bill (1993), 'Is there Life after Development Centres?', *Selection and Development Review*, **9**, (1), February.

Mintzberg, H. (1973), *The Nature of Managerial Work*, New York: Harper & Row.

Moses, Joseph L. and Byham, William C. (1977), *Applying the Assessment Center Method*, Pergamon Press.

Owen, Lynette (1988), 'Assessment Centre Exercises: The Question of Copyright', *Guidance and Assessment Review*, **4**, (2), April.

Pearn, M. and Kandola, R. (1988), *Job Analysis, a Practical Guide for Managers*, London: Institute of Personnel Management.

Povah, Nigel (1986), 'Using Assessment Centres as a means for Self-Development', *Industrial and Commercial Training*, **18**, (2), March/April.

Price, Ruth and Patterson, Fiona (2003), 'On-line Application Forms: Psychological Impact on Applicants and Implications for Recruiters', *Selection and Development Review*, **19**, (2), April.

Randall, R., Ferguson, E. and Patterson, F. (2000), 'Self-assessment Accuracy and Assessment Centre Decisions', *Journal of Occupational and Organizational Psychology*, **73**, (4).

Reddy, Michael (1987), *The Manager's Guide to Counselling at Work*, Leicester: British Psychological Society.

Robertson, Ivan, Gratton, Lynda and Sharpley, David (1987), 'The Psychometric Properties and Design of Managerial Assessment Centres: Dimensions into Exercises Won't Go', *Journal of Occupational Psychology*, **60**, (3), September.

Robertson, I.T. and Smith, M. (1993), 'Personnel Selection Methods'. In M. Smith and I.T. Robertson (eds) *Advances in Selection and Assessment*, Chichester: John Wiley and Sons, 89–112.

Robertson, I.T. and Smith, M. (2001), 'Personnel Selection', *Journal of Occupational and Organizational Psychology*, **74**, (4).

Rodger, David and Mabey, Christopher (1987), 'BT's Leap Forward from Assessment Centres', *Personnel Management*, **19**, (7), July.

Russell, C.J. (1985), 'Individual Decision Processes in an Assessment Center', *Journal of Applied Psychology*, **70**.

Russell, C.J. and Domm, D.R. (1995), 'Two Field Tests of an Explanation of Assessment Centre Validity', *Journal of Occupational and Organizational Psychology*, **68**, (1).

Sackett, Paul R. and Dreher, George F. (1982), 'Constructs and Assessment Center Dimensions : Some Troubling Empirical Findings', *Journal of Applied Psychology*, **67**, (4).

Sackett, Paul R. and Wilson, M.A. (1982), 'Factors Affecting Consensus Judgement Processes in Managerial Assessment Centres', *Journal of Applied Psychology*, **67**, (1).

Sagie, A. and Magnezy, R. (1997), 'Assessor Type, Number of Distinguishable Dimension Categories, and Assessment Centre Construct Validity', *Journal of Occupational and Organizational Psychology*, **70**, (1).

Salgado, J.F. (1999), 'Personnel Selection Methods'. In C.L. Cooper and I.T. Robertson (eds) *International Review of Industrial and Organizational Psychology*, Volume 16, New York: Wiley.

Salgado, J.F., Viswesvaran, C. and Ones, D. (2001), 'Predictors Used for Personnel Selection: An Overview of Constructs, Methods and Techniques', *Handbook of Industrial, Work and Organizational Psychology,* Volume 1.

Sandberg, J. (2000), 'Understanding Human Competence at Work: An Interpretative Approach', *Academy of Management Journal,* **43**.

Schleicher, Deidra J., Day, David V., Mayes, Bronston T., Riggio, Ronald E. (2002), 'A New Frame for Frame-of-Reference Training: Enhancing the Construct Validity of Assessment Centers', *Journal of Applied Psychology,* **87**, (4).

Schmidt, Frank L. and Hunter, John E. (1983), 'Individual Differences in Productivity: An Empirical Test of Estimates Derived from Studies of Selection Procedure Utility', *Journal of Applied Psychology,* **68**, (3).

Schmidt, F.L. and Hunter, J.E. (1998), 'The Validity and Utility of Selection Methods in Personnel Psychology: Practical and Theoretical Implications of 85 Years of Research Findings', *Psychological Bulletin,* **124**, (2).

Schmidt, S.M. and Yeh, R.S. (1992), 'The Structure of Leader Influence: A Cross-national Comparison', *Journal of Cross-Cultural Psychology,* **23**.

Schmitt, Neal et al. (1984), 'Metaanalyses of Validity Studies Published Between 1964 and 1982 and the Investigation of Study Characteristics', *Personnel Psychology,* **37**.

Schneider, J.R. and Schmitt, N. (1992), 'An Exercise Design Approach to Understanding Assessment Center Dimension and Exercise Constructs', *Journal of Applied Psychology,* **77**, (1).

Shevels, Terry (1998), 'Competencies, Competence and Confusion', *Selection and Development Review,* **14**, (5), October.

Smith, Mike (1988), 'Calculating the Sterling Value of Selection', *Guidance and Assessment Review,* **4**, (1), February.

Spencer, Judith (1989), 'Job analysis: a practitioner's view', *Guidance and Assessment Review,* **5**, (3), June.

Spychalski, A.C., Quinones, M.A., Gaugler, B.B. and Pohley, K. (1997), 'A Survey of Assessment Center Practices in Organizations in the United States', *Personnel Psychology,* **50**.

Steel, Vic and Howard, Brian (1980), 'Self-Insight Assessment Centre', *Industrial and Commercial Training,* **12**, (9), September.

Sternberg, R.I. and Wagner, R.K. (eds) (1986), *Practical Intelligence: Nature and Origins of Competence in the Everyday World*, Cambridge: Cambridge University Press.

Stewart, Andrew and Stewart, Valerie (1976), *Tomorrow's Managers Today*, London: Institute of Personnel Management.

Thornton III, George C. and Byham, W.C. (1982), *Assessment Centers and Managerial Performance*, New York: Academic Press.

Tillema, Harm H. (1998), 'Assessment of Potential from Assessment Centers to Development Centers', *International Journal of Selection and Assessment,* **6**, (3), July.

Vernon, P.E. and Parry, J.B. (1949), *Personnel Selection in the British Forces*, London: University of London Press.

Wigfield, David (1997), 'Making Good Selection Decisions with Assessment Centre Data', *Selection and Development Review,* **13**, (5), October.

Woehr, D.J. and Huffcutt, A.I. (1994), 'Rater Training for Performance Appraisal: A quantitative review', *Journal of Occupational and Organizational Psychology,* **67**, (3), September.

Wood, Bob and Scott, Andrew (1989), 'The Gentle Art of Feedback', *Personnel Management*, **21**, (4).

Woodruffe, Charles (2000), *Development and Assessment Centres*, 3rd edn, London: Chartered Institute of Personnel and Development.

Index

A&DC
Assessment & Development
Consultants Ltd

As a consultancy, Assessment & Development Consultants can provide a wide range of services to human resource managers. In relation to assessment and development centres, we can help you with the whole project, or any of the following specific aspects of design and development:

- *Job Analysis and Competency Design*
  In addition to job analysis aimed at identifying criteria for assessment centres, similar techniques can be used to identify training needs to support salary and reward structures.
- *Centre Design and Implementation*
  We have significant experience of designing assessment and development centres for numerous clients. We can also provide consultants to act as assessors and/or centre managers to support you during the implementation of your centres.
- *Training*
  We regularly run 2–3 day training programmes to qualify people to act as assessors or to facilitate the design and implementation of assessment centres within their own organisation.
- *'Off-the-Shelf' Exercises*
  We have the largest selection of 'off-the-shelf' assessment and development centre exercises in the UK and probably the world, which reflect a wide variety of job situations targeted at different job levels.
- *Validation Studies*
  We can conduct validation studies to help reassure you that your competency model is still appropriate, your assessors are operating consistently and that your exercises work well.

In addition to our expertise in assessment and development centre design we can provide:

- Psychometric Assessments including on-line and off-line solutions
- Criteria-Based Interviewing
- Competency-Based Appraisal Systems
- Expert Systems Software
- A wide range of training and development programmes.

For further details please contact:

3 Lammas Gate, Meadrow, Godalming, Surrey, GU7 3HT.
Tel. +44(0)1483 860898
Fax. +44(0)1483 860885
E-mail info@ADCltd.co.uk
www.ADCltd.co.uk

DOCTORUS

Doctorus™ is Iain Ballantyne's company. Set up in 2002, Doctorus™ works with individuals and groups to help them understand and reach their full potential in work-related aspects of life. This typically includes working with the client and with their sponsors in a joint problem-solving approach to improve their satisfaction with work life through:

- An assessment of the people's capability and personality.
- Developing understanding of the likely demands in a job.
- Identifying how the person and the job match
  - where there is a good match working out how to exploit potential opportunities,
  - where there is a mismatch looking at ways to select a more productive way forward, including appropriate retraining.
- Providing on-going support to experiment with new behaviour.

Doctorus ™ works with a number of different sponsoring organisations. About half of the work is within the public and not-for-profit sectors, which includes academic, charitable and professional bodies. Private sector clients are mainly in motorcar retailing.

©Iain Ballantyne
38 Kingsway,
Selsey,
Chichester,
PO20 0SY
(01243) 606450
e-mail doctor.us@virgin.net

If you have found this book useful you may be interested in other titles from Gower

Simulations for Assessment, Training and Development
Julie Hay
0 566 08501 1 (A4 Loose leaf and CD Rom)

Legendary Away Days
The Complete Guide to Running Successful Team Events
Karen Cooley and Kirsty McEwan
0 566 08549 6

How to Set Up and Manage a Corporate Learning Centre
Samuel A. Malone
0 566 08532 1

The Handbook of Work Based Learning
Ian Cunningham, Graham Dawes and Ben Bennett
0 566 08541 0

The HR Guide to Workplace Fraud and Criminal Behaviour
Recognition, Prevention and Management
Michael J. Comer and Timothy E. Stephens
0 566 08555 0

The HR Guide to European Mergers and Acquisitions
James F. Klein with Robert-Charles Kahn
0 566 08564 X

Data Protection for the HR Manager
Mandy Webster
0 566 08596 8

GOWER

Using the PC to Boost Executive Performance
Monica Seeley
0 566 08110 5

The 'How To' Guide for Managers
John Payne and Shirley Payne
0 566 07726 4

Managerial Consulting Skills
A Practical Guide 2ed
Charles J. Margerison
0 566 08292 6

Individual Preferences in e-Learning
Howard Hills
0 566 08456 2

e-HR
Using Intranets to Improve the Effectiveness of Your
People
Bryan Hopkins and James Markham
0 566 08539 9

The People Measurement Manual
Measuring Attitudes, Behaviours and Beliefs in Your
Organization
David Wealleans
0 566 08380 9

For further information on these and all our titles visit
our website – **www.gowerpub.com**
All online orders receive a discount

GOWER

Join our email newsletter

Gower is widely recognised as one of the world's leading publishers on management and business practice. Its programmes range from 1000-page handbooks through practical manuals to popular paperbacks. These cover all the main functions of management: human resource development, sales and marketing, project management, finance, etc. Gower also produces training videos and activities manuals on a wide range of management skills.

As our list is constantly developing you may find it difficult to keep abreast of new titles. With this in mind we offer a free email news service, approximately once every two months, which provides a brief overview of the most recent titles and links into our catalogue, should you wish to read more or see sample pages.

To sign up to this service, send your request via email to **info@gowerpub.com**. Please put your email address in the body of the email as confirmation of your agreement to receive information in this way.

GOWER